Effective Literacy Assessment in the Montessori Classroom

Effective Literacy Assessment in the Montessori Classroom

Using Data to Inform Instruction

Natasha Feinberg and Susan Zoll
With Laura Saylor

Foreword by Maryanne Wolf

TEACHERS COLLEGE PRESS
TEACHERS COLLEGE | COLUMBIA UNIVERSITY
NEW YORK AND LONDON

Published by Teachers College Press,® 1234 Amsterdam Avenue, New York, NY 10027

Front cover image by sanjeri / iStock by Getty Images.

Library of Congress Cataloging-in-Publication Data

Names: Feinberg, Natasha, author. | Zoll, Susan, author. | Saylor, Laura, other.
Title: Effective literacy assessment in the Montessori classroom : using data to inform instruction / Natasha Feinberg and Susan Zoll ; Foreword by Maryanne Wolf.
Description: New York, NY : Teachers College Press, [2025] | Includes bibliographical references and index. | Summary: "Through concrete examples of structured literacy instruction, this book describes how reading research and Montessori's scientific pedagogy and language curriculum play out in diverse classrooms"—Provided by publisher.
Identifiers: LCCN 2024058823 (print) | LCCN 2024058824 (ebook) | ISBN 9780807786703 (paperback) | ISBN 9780807786710 (hardcover) | ISBN 9780807782880 (ebook)
Subjects: LCSH: Montessori method of education. | Reading (Preschool) | Reading (Elementary) | Curriculum evaluation.
Classification: LCC LB1029.M75 F47 2025 (print) | LCC LB1029.M75 (ebook) | DDC 371.39/2—dc23/eng/20250116
LC record available at https://lccn.loc.gov/2024058823
LC ebook record available at https://lccn.loc.gov/2024058824

ISBN 978-0-8077–8670-3 (paper)
ISBN 978-0-8077-8671-0 (hardcover)
ISBN 978-0-8077-8288-0 (ebook)

Printed on acid-free paper
Manufactured in the United States of America

Contents

Foreword by Maryanne Wolf ix

Acknowledgments xi

1. Introduction 1

2. A Contemporaneous and Historical Overview of Structured Literacy and Montessori Education 10

Structured Literacy 10

Defining Terms 11

History of Montessori and Assessment 23

Dr. Montessori's Assessment Practices 25

Understanding Literacy Instruction in Montessori Classrooms Today 28

PART I—STARTING THE SCHOOL YEAR: SETTING THE STAGE SO READING IMPROVES FOR EVERY STUDENT

3. Lesson Application 39

Rituals and Routines 39

Student Interactions 39

Parent Interactions 40

Lesson Implementation 41

The Lesson Plan Format 42

4. Assessment **46**

Assessments and Comprehensive Assessment Systems in Education 47

Screening Assessments—Early Childhood 50

The PALS Pre-K Assessment in Montessori Classrooms 52

Screening Assessments—Elementary 55

Diagnostic Assessments 58

Using Formal Assessment in the Montessori Setting 62

Conclusion 63

5. Schedule/Logistics **65**

Montessori Schedules 65

Work Plans 65

Traditional Schedules 66

Melding a Montessori Classroom With Outside Scheduling Requirements 67

ELA Instruction in Public Schools 68

Montessori Classrooms Melding Commercial ELA Curriculum 70

Case Study Discussion and Analysis With Answer Key (BOY) **73**

Case Study—Early Childhood 73

Case Study—Elementary 82

PART II—ALL SCHOOL YEAR LONG: INTEGRATING DATA, PROGRESS MONITORING, AND INSTRUCTION TO MAXIMIZE READING SUCCESS FOR ALL STUDENTS

6. Lesson Application **89**

The Role of Encoding in Lessons 95

Curriculum Evaluation Guidelines 99

7. Assessment **105**

Determining Where to Start—Analyzing Data Results 106

The Montessori Three-Period Lesson Decision Tree 106

Progress Monitoring 109
Further Individualizing Tier 1 (Core Instruction) and Tiered Interventions 113
Utilizing Observational Data 116
The Importance of Language Instruction and Its Application in Montessori Classrooms 120
Peabody Picture Vocabulary Test 125
The PPVT in Montessori Classrooms 125

8. Schedule/Logistics 127
Melding a Montessori Classroom With Outside Scheduling Requirements 127
History of RtI and MTSS 127
Layering Intervention Instruction Into the Montessori Classroom 130
Explicit Instruction and Eliciting Responses 130
Montessori Three-Period Lesson Aligned to Explicit Instruction 133

Case Study Discussion and Analysis (MOY) 135
Case Study—Early Childhood 135
Case Study—Elementary 140

9. Lesson Application 146
End of School Year Considerations for Lessons 146

PART III: WRAPPING UP THE SCHOOL YEAR: PRIORITIZING, KEEPING ON, AND DEFINING NEXT STEPS

10. Assessment 157
End-of-Year Screeners 157
High-Stakes Testing 157
The CLASS Observation Tool 159
The CLASS in Montessori Classrooms 160

11. Schedule/Logistics **162**

Melding a Montessori Classroom With Outside Scheduling Requirements 162

Case Study Discussion and Analysis (EOY) **166**

Case Study—Early Childhood 166

Case Study—Elementary 168

12. Closing **172**

Working With Families, the Community, and School Personnel to Support Literacy 172

School Personnel to Support Literacy: Instructional and Literacy Coaches 176

Conclusion 178

References **181**

Glossary **189**

Index **193**

About the Authors **201**

Foreword

The 17th-century French philosopher Blaise Pascal once wrote that there are no new ideas on this earth. He did not mean this literally; rather, he was underscoring how each generation can find new and important connections with previous knowledge. The great educators of the past—from the 18th-century innovations by Swiss educator Pestalozzi to the 20th-century contributions of Marie Clay, Lev Vygotsky, and Jean Piaget—have all contributed to the ability of present educators to propel the education of our young. None has contributed more than Maria Montessori, whose work exemplifies how much we can learn from insights into children's learning formed a century ago.

This book and the previous volume, *Powerful Literacy in the Montessori Classroom,* are a testimony to the timeless nature of Montessori's comprehensive understanding of how children learn best. At the same time, together these two volumes offer a highly contemporary rendering of Montessori's knowledge for the educators of the 21st-century classroom. The emphases on language and reading development in the present volume are particularly useful for meeting the unique challenges of Montessori-trained teachers today, many of whom must balance mandates by their states with an ever-expanding knowledge base about the development of literacy.

As a cognitive neuroscientist, I have spent my professional life studying words and their habitat in the convoluted recesses of the human brain. It is from this perspective that the authors invited me to offer a few reflections on the book you are about to read. Underlying each of these reflections lies my appreciation of how the authors used aspects of the "science of reading" to ground their approach to multiple areas, in particular assessment, principles of instruction, and individualized intervention. It is within this context that I wish to offer several complementary recommendations in this expanding science that can extend their use of this knowledge.

First, it is important that our understanding of both the science of reading and foundational skills is reconceptualized in broader terms than the often-narrow characterization of them as consisting largely of phoneme awareness and phonics. Although the authors' well-chosen use of Scarborough's Rope and the Simple View of Reading go well beyond phonics and phoneme awareness, neither of these views provides sufficient emphases on fluency and the range of oral language processes that contribute to both fluency and a more delineated set of comprehension processes, what I call "deep reading" processes.

Specifically, more emphases should be placed on the contribution of morphological and syntactic processes, as well as on a far broader understanding of semantic development than the term *vocabulary* conveys. Research on semantic development involves not only an emphasis on the meaning of words, but also on the *multiple meanings* of words: that is, the *polysemous* nature of many words, particularly the primer words in early literacy development. Furthermore, there needs to be more explicit attention paid to the connected nature of our words; their numerous associations to other words based on similar meaning, sound, and function (think syntax); and their contextual relationships to other words. Vocabulary is too small a concept for the rich relationships that words occupy in our language.

What I find most encouraging in this book's elaboration of language development practices is that a Montessori approach is already intrinsically involved in the enterprise of language's elaboration over development. I only wish here to recommend more intentional emphases in the Montessori classroom on how our language works with multiple meanings, syntactic functions, and the seemingly humble role of the morpheme (i.e., the smallest unit of meaning in our words). For example, the simple intentional introduction of four morphemes (e.g., /ed/, /ing/, / s or es/, and /er/) in 1st grade can help young students learn how words work to make plurals, past and present tense, and to make long words read more fluently.

Equally encouraging to me in this book is its emphasis on the role of assessment and ongoing evaluation of each student over time. The use of developmental data to inform more individualized, differential instruction while still using Montessori-based principles is a critical approach to meeting the individual needs of various students. A great deal of my past and present intervention research involves working to unleash the potential of struggling readers. Just as I have found in my own RAVE-O intervention for readers with dyslexia, the approach espoused in this book—that is, of using data to shape instructional emphases—helps every teacher in the Montessori classroom help every student.

In summary, this book provides a powerful example of what Pascal intended when he said there are no new ideas on this earth. This book illustrates how the careful use of Montessori's prescient, past insights, when informed by our expanding science of reading and language, can help educators today meet the ever-changing needs of more students than ever before. Godspeed to you all.

—Maryanne Wolf
Professor, University of California, Los Angeles
Author of *Reader, Come Home: The Reading Brain in a Digital World*

Acknowledgments

The authors wish to thank our editor, Emily Spangler, for her guidance throughout all stages of writing this book. Emily's responsive feedback and encouragement always went above and beyond anything for which we could ask! We consider ourselves so fortunate to work with such an insightful and talented person. We are grateful to Teachers College Press for their support; you have all made the writing and publication process smooth for us.

We are exceptionally grateful to Maryanne Wolf for her foreword to this book. Maryanne's books have inspired each of the authors throughout their careers. To have her become a part of our book could not make us happier.

Many thanks to Chris Willemsen, Heutink International, Nienhuis Montessori, Julia Volkman, Maitri Learning, Aki Margaritis, ETC Montessori, the Rhode Island Department of Education, and BRIDGE-RI for the use of many images included in this book.

We wish to acknowledge the leadership of the American Montessori Society (AMS), Munir Shivji, executive director; the National Center for Montessori in the Public Sector (NCMPS), specifically Katie Brown, director of research and professional learning, and David Ayer, director of communications; and Annie Frazier and her teacher colleagues, Montessori Partnerships for Georgia, for their insights, collegiality, and dedication to advocacy on behalf of the Montessori administrators and educators who are working to meet state Science of Reading legislation.

Thank you to all who provide us inspiration: the mentors, teachers, and students that we have been so lucky to work and learn.

Susan and Laura would like to express our deep gratitude to Natasha for her leadership and vision for this book. We are grateful for her dedication to melding best practices crafted from conventional education with those used in Montessori classrooms—always with an eye toward maintaining Montessori principles and pedagogy.

And finally, a huge thank you to all of our families and friends who have supported our research and writing endeavors, those who have listened to us talk about this book for over a year, who willingly give us space when we need to work, and who also drag us away from our computers for much-needed breaks.

Our lives are made richer by all of you.

CHAPTER 1

Introduction

There are more than 3,500 Montessori schools in the United States currently identified by the Montessori Census. Of these, just over 600 are publicly funded and recognized as charter, magnet, and public Montessori schools offering access to approximately 200,000 students in 42 states across the country (National Center for Montessori in the Public Sector, n.d.). Montessori education, a child-centered, teacher-guided approach to learning, remains the fastest-growing model of education (Debs, 2019) in the United States.

The methodology was developed by Dr. Maria Montessori, an Italian scientist and educational theorist, more than 100 years ago. Her philosophical and pedagogical vision remains grounded in a fundamental understanding of the development of the child and educational practices that are evidence-based. Classroom instruction is planned, purposeful, explicit, multisensory, and individualized to each student.

As early as 1912–1913, a few publicly funded Montessori schools were located in New York, Philadelphia, and Providence, Rhode Island (Debs, 2019; Zoll, 2017). Historically, Montessori education has primarily been available through a network of independent schools, as the pedagogy's curriculum and instructional practices did not align with the teaching and learning parameters typically offered through the public education system. However, in 1991, the country's first two publicly funded charter schools were established in Minnesota. Bluffview Montessori School was the first to be approved and City Academy High School was the first to open in Minnesota (Schroeder, 2004). The inception of the charter school movement was intended to create opportunities for the development of innovative practices in education, while adhering to close regulation and accountability. Unlike conventional public schools, accountability in charter schools can warrant closure if performance goals are not met or in the case of fiscal mismanagement. Since their inception, charter and other publicly funded Montessori schools have created an equitable pathway for more children to access tuition-free Montessori classrooms. Across the country, students as young as 3 years old can begin their Montessori experience, continue through elementary school, and, in some states, complete middle and high school (NCMPS, n.d.).

The authors hold deep respect for the teachers and administrators who work diligently to offer all children Dr. Montessori's approach to learning and development while also meeting the many mandates and requirements put in place at the school, district, state, and national levels of education. As an example, though the Montessori curriculum offers a comprehensive scope and sequence of educational content covering math, science, geography, art, and reading instruction, publicly funded Montessori schools are often required to also meet a host of reading curriculum, instruction, and assessment mandates issued by state legislation and regulated by state departments of education. It is these educators, those who are balancing reading legislation and implementation of the Montessori pedagogy with fidelity, who are in the forefront of our minds as we write.

As of spring 2024, a total of 40 states and the District of Columbia have passed legislation that influences reading instruction in public schools across the United States (Reading League Compass, n.d.; Schwartz, 2024). Though some variation exists in the scope of mandates schools are required to meet, legislation typically falls within the following six categories:

- Teacher preparation, higher education
- Teacher certification and license renewal
- Professional development and coaching
- The selection of English Language Arts (ELA) curriculum
- Literacy and language assessments
- The instructional approaches and interventions used in classrooms

Table 1.1 provides an overview of how these mandates are distributed across the United States.

Of these six types of reading legislative mandates, this book closely examines three—ELA curriculum, assessments, and instructional interventions—and explores their impact on Montessori schools. We hope this book will provide guidance to public Montessori schools that are developing plans to best meet what may be perceived as competing objectives of addressing reading mandates while also remaining aligned to the Montessori philosophy of education.

As with our first publication, *Powerful Literacy in the Montessori Classroom: Aligning Reading Research and Practice* (Zoll et al., 2023), the authors are committed to identifying "what works" in Montessori settings. This book illustrates how Montessori Language instruction and Structured Literacy, promoted in reading research, can live in the same classroom. Current educational research and instructional practices are reviewed, along with integrated insight from more than 670 survey participants who shared their professional experiences in Montessori classrooms. Though Montessori educators working across school settings may adapt practices from this book to be used in their own classroom, it is the many teachers

Table 1.1. Reading Legislation/Mandates Required by State (Schwartz, 2024)

State	Teacher prep	Teacher cert or license renewal	PD and coaching	Assessment	Materials	Instructional approaches and interventions
AL	✔	✔	✔	✔	✔	✔
GA	✔	✔	✔	✔	✔	✔
KY	✔	✔	✔	✔	✔	✔
MD	✔	✔	✔	✔	✔	✔
MS	✔	✔	✔	✔	✔	✔
NC	✔	✔	✔	✔	✔	✔
TN	✔	✔	✔	✔	✔	✔
VA	✔	✔	✔	✔	✔	✔
WV	✔	✔	✔	✔	✔	✔
WI	✔	✔	✔	✔	✔	✔
AK		✔	✔	✔	✔	✔
AR	✔	✔	✔		✔	✔
CO		✔	✔	✔	✔	✔
FL		✔	✔	✔	✔	✔
IL		✔	✔	✔	✔	✔
MO	✔		✔	✔	✔	✔
OH	✔		✔	✔	✔	✔
UT	✔		✔	✔	✔	✔
AZ			✔	✔	✔	✔
CA	✔	✔	✔	✔		
CT			✔	✔	✔	✔
DC			✔	✔	✔	✔
IN	✔	✔	✔		✔	
KS			✔	✔	✔	✔
MN			✔	✔	✔	✔
NM			✔	✔	✔	✔
OK	✔		✔	✔		✔
OR			✔	✔	✔	✔
TX		✔	✔		✔	✔

and administrators working in publicly funded schools who serve as the book's primary audience. If you are a Montessori educator or administrator whose school is not publicly funded, many of the concepts in this book may be new to you. Though you may not yet be required to meet reading legislation mandates, there will likely be instructional or assessment practices you may want to consider, especially for students in your school who are struggling to become successful readers. Since many states now have reading legislation impacting teacher certification and license renewal, faculty from Montessori teacher preparation programs situated in higher education institutions and professional development organizations will also find this book useful in aligning their early childhood (3–6) and elementary (6–12) Montessori Language coursework with state licensure requirements.

To be clear, this book will not ask you to adopt instructional practices outside of the Montessori curriculum. Rather, this book is about systems development and the protocols and procedures needed to organize school practices to improve classroom instruction and, ultimately, learner outcomes. It is also about using our classroom time wisely. This is especially true for educators who are working with children who have had less opportunity to be engaged in experiences that nurture literacy development and language growth. These evidence-based protocols help mitigate opportunity gaps in children's early learning and serve as a road map to best meet the individual needs of all students. When children are strong readers, they are more likely to successfully navigate their academic careers and ultimately serve as active constituents in their communities.

> The Founding Fathers maintained that the success of the fragile American democracy would depend on the competency of its citizens. They believed strongly that preserving democracy would require an educated population that could understand political and social issues and would participate in civic life, vote wisely, protect their rights and freedoms, and resist tyrants and demagogues. (Kober & Stark Rentner, 2020, p. 2)

Literacy, the ability to read with comprehension, to discern meaning, and to make connections to what is already known, is a human right.

We anticipate that some Montessorians may oppose the use of assessments, defined learning expectations, or certain instructional strategies described in this book. To be clear, the authors advocate for children to have agency in learning and an abundance of opportunities to develop into strong readers. But we reveal our privilege when we hold onto beliefs that all children will come into their own and be successful readers when solely offered time and opportunity. For some children, we will need to provide a more structured instructional approach so as to ensure their success. We encourage teachers, especially those working in Montessori classrooms, to use this book as a professional development tool and to reflect collaboratively with colleagues to determine how the suggested instructional and assessment practices drawn from current research and outlined in this book will best serve your students—especially those who demonstrate needing additional support to be successful readers.

A strong foundation in literacy can be enriched through high-quality early childhood education experiences. When children between the ages of 3 and 6 are enrolled in Montessori classrooms, there are approximately 540 days (180-day school year times 3 years) to provide children with all that the Montessori curriculum offers. As school administrators or teachers, we must ask ourselves whether we are using these precious days well. When they leave your classroom, are students prepared to successfully take part in the elementary curriculum? We can ask similar questions on behalf of those children who are fortunate to also have a publicly funded age 6–9 or 6–12 Montessori school nearby. What assessment tools are we using? Do we utilize the data to identify which students need the most support in developing their reading skills—and in what areas, specifically? To help answer these questions in the affirmative, we must address two broad categories: assessment systems and instructional systems, both critical to designing equitable literacy learning. The authors have crafted multiple strategies to facilitate the use of these systems in your school. First, this book provides a road map of instructional and assessment activities that occur over the course of one academic year, with chapters dedicated to those practices that take place in the beginning of the school year (BOY), at the middle of the year (MOY) and iteratively throughout the year, and those activities that happen near the end of the academic year (EOY). Each section begins with a decision tree, a flow chart that serves as a map to help determine next steps in supporting all students' literacy learning. The chapters dive deeper into the components of each decision tree, offering recommended assessment and instructional practices. You'll note that these systems will require dedicated time to focus on activities that primarily occur outside the classroom (data collection schedules, team-level data analysis, instructional planning) to better inform what happens inside the classroom. There is a strong focus on coordinating information across the academic year to understand what it is our students know and are able to do through a comprehensive system that includes authentic and efficient assessments. This book has been designed with tools and protocols to support your efforts when implementing these practices throughout the school year. Any recommended changes within the classroom are concerned with *which* Montessori lessons and *with what frequency* will best meet the child's language and literacy development. Data analysis may illuminate the need to augment or add to a teacher's instruction so the needs of students can best be met. This book also includes analysis of data that will transform what we understand about children's reading skills into effective classroom practices to meet the needs of all students. Fortified with this information, teachers will of course continue their Montessori instruction, but will now have additional information to guide their instructional decisions.

Finally, each section of the book includes strategies to support reflective practice; case studies and work pages with guiding questions are included throughout the book. The guiding questions work pages have been added to help readers identify gaps or areas of need that are specific to their schools (i.e., selection of screeners, assessment tools, and use of data to inform response to intervention [RtI] and multi-tiered systems of support [MTSSs] requirements). Case studies are teacher stories reflecting what happens in a Montessori classroom as a way to further explore content learned in the text. Each case study will present a classroom situation followed by specific assessment results. Readers are then presented with a resolution that can be applied in their schools. For example, case studies will examine assessment and diagnostic practices, as well as instructional approaches, to ensure that students improve literacy learning so as to become competent readers. Each case study will be followed by questions for the reader to review, preferably as a community of learners working through topics and questions collaboratively to determine next steps in their own settings. We encourage you to explore these case studies with your colleagues, bringing multiple perspectives and situations into the discussion. A matrix outlining key topics for each case study is provided in Table 1.2.

Finally, the authors recognize there may be tension regarding terminology that is not yet familiar and hesitation when considering the use of assessments or frequency of lessons. To build teachers' efficacy in these areas, the book explores assessment tools specific to language and literacy development (see Table 1.2), offering readers insight into practices intentionally implemented across the academic year in many public Montessori schools. It is important to note that the use of these tools and instructional protocols in no way replaces practices expected in Montessori classrooms. By this, the authors mean that teachers' observations, the Montessori work period, and the use of Montessori materials remain paramount to maintaining fidelity to the Montessori pedagogy. Rather, what is described in this book are activities that often occur outside the classroom, managed by curriculum coaches, reading specialists, or other school personnel working in tandem with teachers and families. The classroom data that are collected, including observations conducted by teachers, are just one piece of the assessment puzzle. There also need to be systems in place to analyze all data. These data provide evidence of children's mastery of learning—as well as inform teachers' individualized instruction in an effort to yield positive student outcomes. Part I examines assessment protocols to quickly identify children's literacy learning through baseline data collected at the start of the school year. These data reveal what students have retained over the summer months, as well as areas of literacy that warrant additional attention. Part II considers progress monitoring protocols that highlight what students have learned in the early

Table 1.2. Matrix of Case Studies

	Case Study	Level (by age)	Case Focus	Primary Educational Topic	Assessment Tools
1	BOY Screening	3–6 Primary	Classroom	Letter recognition, letter sounds, baseline data	Phonological Awareness Literacy Screening (PALS Pre-K) PALS will now be recognized as the Pre-K language and literacy screener.
2	BOY Screening	6–9 Lower elementary	Student	Phonological awareness, phonics, fluency, comprehension	PAST diagnostic assessment, the Quick Phonics Screener (QPS), Acadience Nonsense Word Fluency (NWF) and Oral Reading Fluency (ORF), McLeod Comprehension, Words Their Way (WTW) Spelling Inventory
3	MOY Progress Monitoring	3–6 Primary	Classroom	Receptive language development, dual-language learners (DLLs), early literacy, progress monitoring	Peabody Picture Vocabulary Test (PPVT-IV), PALS Pre-K
4	MOY Progress Monitoring	6–12	Student	Reading comprehension, reading fluency, progress monitoring	Acadience ORF

(*continued*)

Table 1.2. (*continued*)

	Case Study	Level (by age)	Case Focus	Primary Educational Topic	Assessment Tools
5	EOY	3–6	Classroom	Name writing, letter recognition, letter sounds	PALS Pre-K
6	EOY	6–12	Classroom		Acadience Reading K–6

Reference links:

PALS Pre-K

https://vkrponline.org/pre-k-language-and-literacy-screener/#:~:text=The%20Pre%2DK%20Language%20%26%20Literacy,knowledge%20of%20early%20literacy%20development

WTW Spelling Inventory

https://mtevansboces.wordpress.com/wp-content/uploads/2014/06/words-their-way-elementary-spelling-inventory-root-cause.pdf

McLeod Comprehension

www.newtunings.com/57/data/Grade.Level.Tools/HS.English/McLeod.Read.Comp.pdf

LETRS QPS

https://learn71.ca/wp-content/uploads/2021/03/LETRS-Phonics-and-Word-Reading-Survey.pdf

PAST

https://thepasttest.com

Peabody Picture Vocabulary Test (PPVT-IV)

www.pearsonassessments.com/store/usassessments/en/Store/Professional-Assessments/Academic-Learning/Peabody-Picture-Vocabulary-Test-%7C-Fourth-Edition/p/100000501.html

Acadience ORF and Reading K–6

https://acadiencelearning.org/acadience-reading/k-grade6

weeks of the school year and where instruction can be further individualized to meet all students' language and literacy development. Part III looks at students' learning across the school year and uses data to recognize growth and learning—and to plan forward into the following school year.

Depending on your state requirements and the range of school faculty and staff who can support these efforts, some practices may be more easily implemented in your school than others. Each teacher and school administrator will have to weigh the practices described in this book with identified needs in one's own particular context. The authors recognize the diversity that exists across the delivery system of Montessori education and through this book wish to build on the commonalities we share, regardless of educational setting. Ultimately, our shared vision is that all children will grow as capable readers who explore books both for pleasure and for learning.

CHAPTER 2

A Contemporaneous and Historical Overview of Structured Literacy and Montessori Education

STRUCTURED LITERACY

The Simple View of Reading and Scarborough's Reading Rope are two theoretical frameworks we continue to rely on in our discussion of reading research. The Science of Reading, the collection of decades of research around how the brain works to learn how to read, carries powerful information that informs best literacy practices in the classroom. The Simple View of Reading (Gough & Tunmer, 1986) summarizes what this research unveils regarding literacy learning in broad strokes with the math equation in Figure 2.1.

Farrell et al. (2020) identify some key takeaways from the Simple View of Reading. First, decoding and language comprehension skills must both be strong in order to successfully comprehend what one reads. Purposefully written as a multiplication equation, lack of skill in either the ability to decode or comprehend language will negatively affect the desired outcome of strong reading comprehension. Literacy instruction must build both of these areas throughout all grade levels. Instruction and interventions for readers must address students' individual areas of need, whether that is in decoding, in language comprehension, or in both areas, so that the individual can ultimately improve reading comprehension. The Science of Reading asserts that classroom instruction must be systematic and explicit, and that interventions are targeted to specific skills. Therefore, any reading assessments that are used must identify students' area(s) of need as decoding or language comprehension with certainty and provide enough information that specific skills within these two areas can be taught.

Hollis Scarborough (2001) provides us with a more detailed model of reading comprehension in her "Reading Rope." Our companion book (Zoll et al., 2023), *Powerful Literacy in the Montessori Classroom*, provides a deep dive into each strand of Scarborough's Rope and how this framework translates into the Montessori classroom. In brief, the Reading Rope

Figure 2.1. Simple View of Reading (Gough & Tunmer, 1986)

breaks reading comprehension into two main strands, Word Recognition and Language Comprehension. It identifies eight substrands: Phonological Awareness, Decoding, Sight Words, Background Knowledge, Vocabulary, Language Structures, Verbal Reasoning, and Literacy Knowledge. As delineated in our first book, Structured Literacy requires that all eight areas must be instructed. Within the Montessori curriculum are didactic materials and exercises that align to each of these strands. While Montessori teachers may recognize the Science of Reading reflected in their instruction, it is important to be able to clarify how Montessori instruction addresses each area. In our previous book, we provided a link to a matrix correlating Montessori literacy activities with the strands of the Reading Rope. We are including this chart here for ease of access (see Table 2.1). You will need to modify this matrix to fit the materials you have available, the age or grade level of your classroom, and so forth.

Through ELA standards and research that identifies key areas of reading instruction, we know "what" we need to teach. It is the use of assessment data that defines the depth, dosage, and duration of instruction each student requires to become a competent reader.

> Nearly all students are capable of learning to read; while specific numbers vary, estimates indicate that approximately 95% of students are capable of learning to read (Fletcher & Vaughn, 2009). Rigorous, systematic, and explicit instruction that addresses the essential components of literacy including phonemic awareness, phonics, fluency, vocabulary and comprehension (NICHHD, 2000), is key to allowing all children to reach their full potential. (Malcolm, 2022)

DEFINING TERMS

The following five terms will be used throughout our discussion: formative assessment, summative assessment, comprehensive assessment system, standards, and tiered instruction. This section defines these terms and describes how we will be using them throughout the subsequent chapters.

Formative Assessment is any data collection that guides future instruction. It includes all the informal check-ins that a teacher does throughout their day. Formative assessment may include (a) questions that the teacher asks a student to gauge depth of understanding, (b) observations made of

Table 2.1. Montessori Materials and Science of Reading Matrix

	WORD RECOGNITION			LANGUAGE COMPREHENSION				
	Phonological Awareness	Decoding	Sight Recognition	Background Knowledge	Vocabulary	Language Structures	Verbal Reasoning	Literacy Knowledge
Sound Cylinders	X (pre-lesson)							
Montessori Bells	X (pre-lesson)							
I Spy Game	X							
Read-Alouds Read by teacher	X			X	X	X	X	X
Reading/Reciting Poetry	X			X	X	X	X	X
Beginning Sound Sort - with Objects - with Pictures	X							
Ending Sound Sort with Pictures	X							
Medial Sound Sort (vowels, CVC) with Pictures	X							
Sandpaper Letters		x						
Metal Insets		X (pre-lesson)						
Movable Alphabet		X						
Small Movable Alphabet		x				x		x
Phonetic Object Box 1, Box 2, and Box 3		X	X					

CVC word cards organized by medial (vowel) sound	X	X					
Puzzle Words	x	x					
Labeling the Environment	x	x	x	x			
Decodable Books Read by Student	X	X			X		X
Phonograms - Consonant Blends - Consonant & Vowel - Digraphs - Trigraphs - Diphthongs - Long Vowel & Silent "e" - R-Control	X	X					
Nomenclature Cards Three-Part Cards Language, Botany, Zoology, Sensorial Geography	X	X	X	X			
Who Am I? Cards	X	X	X	X		X	
Animals and Their Homes - Young - Sounds - Groups	X	X	X	X			

(continued)

Table 2.1. (*continued*)

	WORD RECOGNITION			LANGUAGE COMPREHENSION				
	Phonological Awareness	Decoding	Sight Recognition	Background Knowledge	Vocabulary	Language Structures	Verbal Reasoning	Literacy Knowledge
Command Cards		X	X					
Labeling the Farm		X	X	X	X			
Grammar: - Nouns - Verbs		X	X		X	X		
- Article Game - Logical Adjective Game - Detective Adjective Game - Verb Game - Adverb Game - Conjunction Game - Preposition Game		X	X		X	X	X	
Grammar Boxes: Noun, Article, Adjective, Verb, Preposition, Adverb, Pronoun, Conjunction and Interjection		X	X		X	X		
Timeline of Life Fundamental Needs of Humans		X	X	X	X	X	X	X

Sentence Analysis Charts		X	X			X	X	X
Compound Words		X	X		X	X		
Prefixes, Suffixes, and Root Words		X	X		X	X		
Syllabication		X	X			X		
Homophones, Homonyms, & Homographs		X	X		X	X	X	
Idioms		X	X	X	X	X	X	
Analogies Similes Metaphors		X	X	X	X	X	X	
Alliteration	X	X	X				X	
Matching Object-to-Object (Naming Objects) Object-to-Picture Picture-to-Picture				X	X			
Matching Parts-to-a-Whole				X	X		X	
Sequencing a Story				X	X		X	X
Sorting Objects Sorting Pictures				X	X			

(continued)

Table 2.1. (*continued*)

	WORD RECOGNITION			LANGUAGE COMPREHENSION				
	Phonological Awareness	Decoding	Sight Recognition	Background Knowledge	Vocabulary	Language Structures	Verbal Reasoning	Literacy Knowledge
Trade Books Fluent Student Readers				X	X	X	X	X
Great Stories				X	X	X	X	X

The matrix is a tool developed to support Montessori educators and teacher preparation faculty to visualize the alignment between Montessori Language materials and reading research. It is organized by the skills noted in Scarborough's Reading Rope (2001).

Citation: Zoll et al. (2023). Appendix: Montessori materials and Science of Reading Matrix in *Powerful Literacy in the Montessori Classroom*. Teachers College Press.

For additional information,

visit our website: www.dr-susan-zoll.com

Or send us an email: MontessoriReadingScience@gmail.com

a student performing a task or demonstrating new knowledge, (c) an exit ticket that demonstrates a student's understanding of a new concept, or (d) a simple "turn and talk" when a child explains their thought process. The purpose of formative assessment is for the teacher to ascertain their students' mastery of skills or knowledge to make instructional decisions. Does the student require more practice and additional instruction, or is the student ready to move on in their learning?

Formative assessment is a means of providing teachers and programs with information *during* the instructional process while learning is taking place (Bennett, 2011; Black & William, 1998; Harlen & James, 1997). Formative assessment guides future instruction and instructional decisions. This type of assessment is often used to provide teachers and programs with information on how to improve teaching and learning. Formative assessment can also be used to provide feedback to students about their learning. In conventional classrooms, teachers may require students to complete homework to informally assess the learning of topics covered in class. In-class formative assessment may include *think-pair-share* or Visual Thinking Strategies (Yenawine, 2013); each approach provides students with guiding questions to engage with in small-group and whole-classroom discussions based on a topic of study. In the Montessori early childhood classroom, observations remain a viable assessment of student learning, as most lessons are presented to individuals or small groups. Observations then provide teachers with evidence of children's mastery of skills and guidance about when to move on to new content (Herman & Saylor, 2024; Pickering, 2021). In elementary and middle school classrooms, students may create written reflection journals or electronic portfolios to organize their completed work and have agency in not only determining which learning experiences to engage in, but also in assessing their own learning.

Summative Assessments are formal assessments that usually follow a period of direct instruction. These assessments quantify learning using a more formal grading system. Generally, the summative assessments include some type of comparison of learning. This could be standards-based; did the student meet a predetermined level of skill or knowledge as demonstrated in a specific manner? The student's success is compared to a mastery standard. For example, a student could demonstrate that they know 80% of the material. A summative assessment might also be a comparison against a norm. With a nationally normed assessment, the assessment is given to thousands of students and a typical level of achievement for the students' age and grade is determined.

When an assessment is summative in nature, it often takes place at the *end* of a lesson, semester, or school year. Summative assessment provides teachers and programs with information and feedback summarizing the teaching and learning process and helps identify whether learning objectives were met (Bennett, 2011; Black & William, 1998; Harlen & James, 1997).

High-stakes and teacher-created tests are often integrated into conventional K–12 educational programs. In Montessori classrooms, summative assessments generally include capstone projects and student-led presentations of learning, which are used to assess mastery of a subject, along with end-of-year teacher reports of student learning.

A ***comprehensive assessment system*** coordinates assessment tools and schedules across the academic year to produce "actionable data, evaluate the effectiveness of programs, and ensure that all students are making progress toward achieving learning goals" by providing the instructional supports needed to ensure reading success (Rhode Island Department of Education [RIDE], n.d., p. 3). Analysis of student assessment results provides school administrators with key information that can be used to evaluate the effectiveness of the literacy curriculum and instructional practices. The comprehensive assessment system also allows for data-informed decisions regarding the allocation of professional development budgets and the distribution of human resources such as literacy coaches and volunteer personnel. Together, these tools provide teachers and school administrators with a map that charts a coordinated course toward equitable literacy outcomes.

Standards are the reading expectations that are determined by the state. In 2010, the Common Core State Standards (CCSS) were rolled out in many public schools. The Common Core State Standards listed skills in which students needed proficiency by the end of each grade with the ultimate goal of being college- and career-ready upon high school graduation. Many states have now revised the CCSS to reflect feedback from teachers and/or specific state curriculum. Even with these modifications, the standards that are adopted represent the learning that is expected to be taught in a unified scope and sequence, with skills that build on one another over a child's educational experience. When delving into assessment practices in public schools, standards are often the reference point for whether or not a student is performing at grade level.

There is an extensive history of assessment standards in education at large. Several research reports and national organizations provide guidance on best practices in the use and implementation of assessment with young children. For example, the position statement of the National Association for the Education of Young Children (NAEYC) recommends that assessment tools measure children's strengths and capture areas of identified need, as well as document children's progress over time by using methods that are developmentally, culturally, and linguistically appropriate (NAEYC & National Association of Early Childhood Specialists in State Department of Education (NAECS/SDE, 2003). In an era of ever-growing accountability, the National Research Council (2008) devoted an entire study to guiding the field in the development of purposeful assessment systems inclusive of "medical, educational, and family support services that promote optimal development for all children" (p. 2). More recently, in 2015 the National

Research Council (NCR), in collaboration with the Institute of Medicine (IOM), released a seminal report recommending shared core knowledge and competencies for educators regardless of "commonly cited differences in philosophies, policies, and approaches between early childhood (birth to age 5) and elementary education communities" (IOM & NRC, 2015, p. 331). The purpose of the IOM/NCR report was to make recommendations that would unify the early childhood profession. While Montessori education has long valued the importance of early childhood, traditional formalized education has historically begun in kindergarten. This has led to a fragmented approach to early childhood education in public education. It is only in more recent history that the extreme importance of early childhood education has been recognized. Assessment, especially in early childhood education, is a challenging issue requiring special consideration, and the IOM/NCR report acknowledged this. One recommendation included improved consistency in assessment competencies for educators reflecting "recent research on how children learn and develop, and the role of educators in the process" (2015, p. 339).

Tiered Instruction is the scaffolded framework where a teacher provides core knowledge to all students, and then those students who need additional support are given supplemental instruction in specific areas. Tiered instruction in all classrooms is informed by a host of inputs, including the teacher, the selected curriculum, state and national content standards, students' interests, and assessment results. Of these inputs, assessment results and their use is an area the field continues to improve through schoolwide assessment systems. Two frameworks that help schools organize and translate these data into meaningful tiered instruction are response to intervention (RtI) and multi-tiered systems of support (MTSSs). RtI, described by the Florida Center for Reading Research, is the "fluid, multi-step approach to providing interventions to students who struggle with learning, delivered in increasing levels of intensity" (n.d.). The framework "derived from prevention science wherein tiered models of support across an entire population differentiate treatment to individuals" (Carta & Greenwood, 2023, p. 348). MTSS, a more contemporaneous approach, shares "the goal of identifying and addressing children's learning needs at the earliest possible time" (2023, p. 348).

> Fundamental to both approaches is a data-based decision-making process that guides individualization or differentiation based on a child's demonstrated need. Both are evidence-based practices using performance data in making intervention decisions. While RtI focuses primarily on ways to identify and provide support that is differentiated for struggling learners in academic areas (e.g., reading, math), MTSS expands that concept by creating a continuum of systemwide strategies and structures for addressing barriers to student learning in both academic and behavioral areas (e.g., early literacy and

> social-emotional). The focus on MTSS is on systemwide support for instruction that will benefit all students, with alignment occurring for all practices, programs, and policies at the classroom, school, and district levels. This often means that teachers, administrators, and instructional support personnel change the way they work together as they shift into a more collaborative culture needed to provide individualized supports as early as indicated. (Carta & Greenwood, 2023, p. 348)

Both RtI and MTSS provide a tiered approach to instruction. Some may argue that tiered instruction is already a feature of Montessori instruction. In some ways this is true, since the Montessori curriculum is not a "one-size-fits-all" but an individualized approach to meeting children where they are in their learning across all domains. However, these instructional decisions are at the classroom level and often do not mirror the systems-wide holistic approach to providing support to meet the behavioral, cognitive, and social-emotional needs of all students. For schools with a mission to ensure all students are successful readers who have equitable access to high-quality education, with a goal of decreasing the overidentification of students of color into special education (Carta & Greenwood, 2023; Greenwood et al., 2011), a plan must be developed, first at the state and district levels to organize human, fiscal, and material resources based on a collective review of evidence. The plan can then be further developed at the school level. Principals working with district leadership then align resources to allocate school personnel—teachers, paraprofessionals, speech pathologists, reading specialists, social workers, occupational therapists, special education teachers, and so forth—to inform the "multi-tiered" design of meeting the needs of all children.

Here is one way to consider how RtI and MTSS protocols are applied in schools. After initial literacy data are collected at the beginning of the school year, scores are reviewed at the classroom level. Using predetermined benchmarks, students are assigned to instructional tiers.

Tier 1—All students receive Tier 1 instruction, the core ELA curriculum delivered in their classrooms each day that covers all strands of literacy development (see Scarborough's Reading Rope, 2001). Instruction is led by the classroom teacher and is provided in both whole-group and small-group learning opportunities within a particular schedule of the day (for additional information about teaching schedules in conventional schools, see Chapter 5). Tier 2—Some students, approximately 15% of the class, who do not yet meet expected benchmarks will receive the classroom ELA curriculum (Tier 1), as well as small-group lessons focused on identified areas of need such as decoding or fluency. The depth, dosage, and duration of this small-group work will be based on students' progress, or response, to these supports.

Figure 2.2. Five Core Components of MTSS

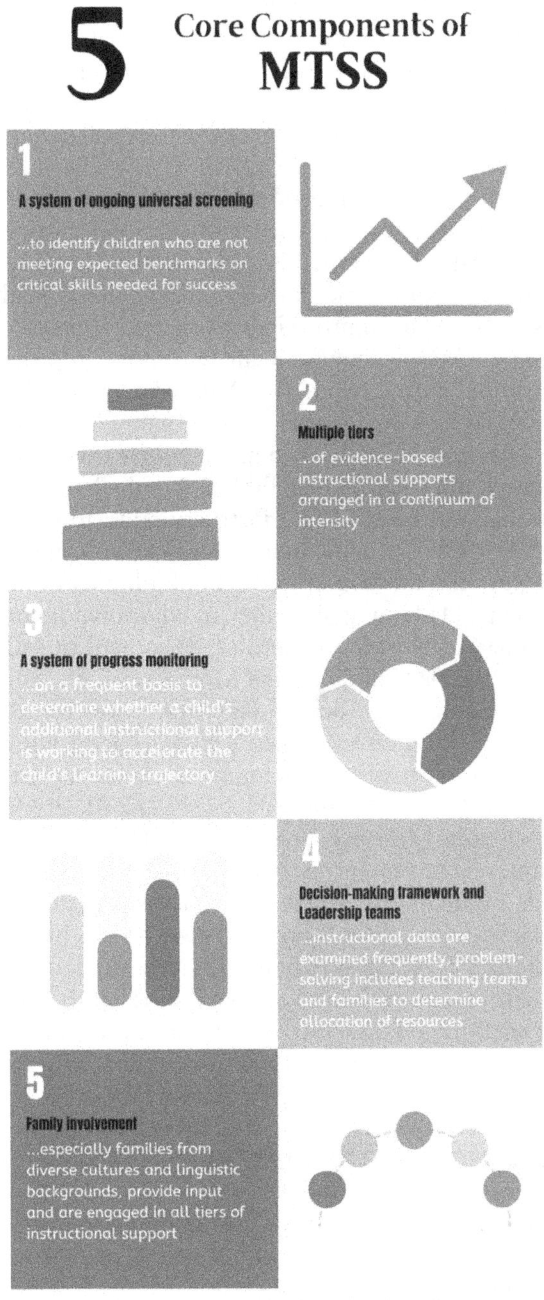

Adapted from Carta & Greenwood, 2023, p. 348

Tier 3 instruction is provided for the smallest subset of students (less than 5%) who demonstrate the greatest need in learning. They will receive the most intensive instructional interventions. As described earlier, these students receive the classroom core ELA instruction (Tier 1) and small-group (Tier 2) instruction, and they also receive more individualized interventions with greater frequency in small groups or as an individual, often with a specialist.

With this information in mind, MTSS helps to determine who will provide the needed support and with what frequency and duration. These protocols make your data not just usable, but invaluable. It is differentiated instruction at its best, but it is not a one-and-done event. Rather, it is an iterative process. As students improve in a given area of literacy development and meet learning goals, their placement will move in a direction requiring less intervention, shifting from Tier 2 supports to a Tier 1 whole-class instruction. Progress monitoring, the weekly or biweekly assessments that check progress, is required for children moving forward toward reading success. For additional information, see Table 2.2 and Chapter 8.

One additional note about Tier 1 instruction in Montessori classrooms must be added. For schools mandated by legislation to implement a state-approved ELA curriculum, district and school administrators will need to consider two points: (1) How will adding an additional literacy curriculum impact the Montessori work cycle, and (2) How will the addition impact teachers' ability to implement either the Montessori curriculum or the secondary ELA curriculum with fidelity? The Montessori work cycle, according to the American Montessori Society's (n.d.-a) accreditation standards, requires "a minimum of two to three hours of uninterrupted work per day for four days a week at the elementary level. The ideal schedule is three hours of uninterrupted work five days a week." Though a question regarding the exact amount of time proposed by Dr. Montessori has been raised by Jana Morgan Herman (2023), there is consensus that a dedicated work period is fundamental to the Montessori pedagogy. Philosophically, this protected morning classroom schedule provides ample time for children "to work through various tasks and responsibilities at their own pace. This uninterrupted work period is vitally important . . . (to) the building of coordination, concentration, independence and order, and the assimilation of information are able to occur" (American Montessori Society, n.d.-a). Careful thought must be given to any external curriculum brought into the Montessori classroom. What is often thought of as additive to the program and in the best interest of students' learning may instead have unintended consequences, especially if the external curriculum diminishes the time and opportunity students have to engage in individualized lessons and interactions with the Montessori materials.

Commercial curriculum will often define specific time blocks within the school day that teachers must adhere to, so as to successfully implement the

ELA program in their setting. This is called *fidelity of implementation*—teachers are faithful to the design and delivery of the curriculum as defined by the publisher. Some ELA curricula are supplemental, requiring 30–60 minutes a day of instructional time over several days each week. These materials are sometimes used in Montessori schools as interventions to further support specific literacy skills (i.e., phonological awareness) or as instructional material for an afternoon work period. Other curricula, however, require a greater investment of time, with dedicated instructional blocks of 60, 90, and even 120 minutes of ELA instruction each day. For programs that wish to meet Montessori accreditation standards, it may be difficult to follow multiple curriculum mandates with fidelity, as well as have time remaining in the school day to cover other learning domains (math, science, art, etc.). For additional information related to reading instruction in Montessori classrooms, see the section "Understanding Literacy Instruction in Montessori Classrooms Today" later in this chapter.

Future research conducted in Montessori classrooms may want to examine the unintended consequences of policies that might usurp innovative practices. State ELA results would be strengthened if information at the district level included defined time designated to the Montessori work cycle, as well as identifying any additional curriculum implemented and the schedule for this implementation during the school day.

HISTORY OF MONTESSORI AND ASSESSMENT

Montessori educators and administrators also have guidance provided by the American Montessori Society (AMS), which addresses child assessment procedures and comprehensive assessment systems to inform teaching practices and improve program quality through Standards 3 and 4 of the 2023 AMS School Accreditation Standards (AMS, 2023). Standard 3 focuses on Teaching and Learning, stating that a

> quality Montessori school implements a Montessori curriculum based on clear and measurable AMS learner outcomes: academic preparation, autonomy and independence, confidence and competence, global citizenship, intrinsic motivation, social responsibility, and spiritual awareness/cosmic education. Students actively engage in the learning process, exhibit joy in learning, and apply their knowledge and skills to real-world situations.(American Montessori Society, 2023, p. 2)

These standards require that the teacher:

3.25 Observes daily the individual students as well as the overall classroom environment and records observations.

3.26 Maintains clear and impartial objectively written records of individual, small group, and large group lessons and activities using a comprehensive record-keeping system that accurately reflects each student's development.
3.29 Implements equity-assessed, bias-free accommodations and interventions to help students meet expectations for student learning in consultation with school administrators and parents/guardians. (American Montessori Society, 2023, p. 4)

Standard 4 focuses on Documenting and Using Results, stating that "the quality Montessori school enacts an ongoing assessment system that monitors and documents learner outcomes that are based in equitable practices and uses these results to improve educational effectiveness" (AMS, 2023). Criteria for a quality Montessori school includes that there is collaboration among the administrative leaders, faculty, and staff to:

4.1 Determine written benchmarks across all program levels that indicate progress toward the AMS Learner Outcomes.
4.2 Create, publish, and implement a data-driven system that provides inclusive qualitative (rubric-based) and quantitative measures (as appropriate to the age level) to assess each student's progress toward the established learner outcomes.
4.3 Analyze recorded data, action research, and classroom observations to examine each student's physical, social-emotional, and cognitive development.
4.4 Use the analysis of this data to make curricular and instructional decisions for individual students.
4.5 Evaluate school-wide effectiveness in meeting established benchmarks using compiled student data.
4.6 Use the results of a systematic analysis of instructional effectiveness to drive continuous improvement of teaching and learning processes. (American Montessori Society, 2023, pp. 4–5)

Although there is overlap in assessment practices documented by NAEYC, NRC, IOM, and the AMS, variability in approaches to assessing children's strengths and areas of need is often made more complex by program accountability dependent on funding requirements. For example, state-funded pre-K classrooms or federally funded Head Start programs may require an integrated assessment approach involving observation, standardized assessment, and screening tools (Halle et al., 2011; Snow, 2011), whereas programs implementing a Reggio Emilia approach focus on documentation to analyze children's development (Wien et al., 2011). Yet, foundational to Montessori practice, and to varying degrees across all early childhood settings, classroom observation remains the standard approach to understanding what it is children know and are able to do (AMS, 2023; Epstein, 2012; O'Shaughnessy, 2016). It should be noted, as the Montessori field continues to diversify its delivery model, that Montessori educators will also experience variability in assessment requirements. In particular, publicly funded programs are likely to experience the greatest tension as teachers implement standards-based assessments delivered individually to each child in the classroom, either via technology or by using paper and pencil, while also adhering to observational practices developed by Dr. Maria Montessori. Also of note, additional research examining student outcomes from state-mandated assessment tools has shown positive results specific to students' literacy learning in charter schools in Arizona (Brown et al., 2024; Woodford, 2024), in Montessori pre-K programs in Miami-Dade, Florida (Ansari & Winsler, 2020), for students enrolled in publicly funded Montessori schools in South Carolina (Culclasure et al., 2018), and for reading outcomes of 4th- and 5th-graders in a large urban school district in Texas (Mallett & Schroeder, 2015).

DR. MONTESSORI'S ASSESSMENT PRACTICES

As early as Dr. Maria Montessori's first international training course in 1913, she clearly stated that the work of the teacher is to observe children. "When you are in a casa dei bambini to observe the children, you are working . . . labouring to learn something which I do not give, which the assistant does not give, and which no one else gives" (Montessori, 1913/2013, p. 20). Dr. Montessori's notes from these sessions also provide key insight into the value she placed on teacher observation and the need for Montessori educators to improve their observational skills as a means of meeting the needs of their students.

> If you do not possess this capacity (to observe), especially this sensitiveness which allows you to learn the intimate facts which the children reveal without warning anyone as to which is an important thing or which is worthy of claiming attention, then this sensitiveness, this capacity for observation is the labour you must accomplish in yourselves. (Montessori, 1913/2013, p. 20)

In her writing, Dr. Montessori raises the important question of who will train the teacher to observe and responds by saying it is solely the work of the teacher to develop this important skill. "You alone can prepare yourselves to observe, as the children must develop themselves by their own exercises" (Montessori, 1913/2013, p. 22). At the same time, however, Dr. Montessori recognized how observational data of children's development and growth could easily be influenced by the observer's own biases. Because of this, Dr. Montessori believed there should be a methodology to observation that would promote objectivity, including the use of assessment tools to avoid error and bias. Objective observation in gathering these data should be carried out with the greatest precision possible, and indeed measurements taken with special instruments are necessary in order to avoid any errors. So we must learn to handle certain instruments, and learn how to measure (Montessori, 1913/2013, p. 46). Whether collecting assessment data through classroom observations or through the use of formative and summative tools, keep in mind that each will take practice, reflection, and an understanding of how to integrate these data into your classroom teaching.

Dr. Montessori's approach to assessing and understanding children is exemplified in two of the assessment tools she provided her participants: the Biographical Chart and the Anthropological Measurements document. The Biographical Chart is a recordkeeping document that provides a framework for teachers' observations of children. Aware of constraints on teachers' time and a need for practical applications for observation data, Dr. Montessori simplified the Biographical Chart by making it less theoretical and more aligned with understanding young children (see Table 2.2). Questions on the form pertained to children's learning, physical development and health, and family demographics, similar to intake forms that may be used when a student enrolls in a new school. In contrast, the Anthropological Measurements document focused on children's physical development, helping teachers assess height, weight, and other quantifiable indicators of children's well-being that were norm-referenced with the larger population at the time (Montessori, 1913/2013).

During the 1913 training, this guide provided new teachers with a tool for the study and observation of their students. The recordkeeping chart provided ample space to note a child's biography according to a specific method so that teachers' pedagogical choices would be evidence based. To understand the context of the family, the following guiding questions were suggested: the age, profession, and background of the child's parents; the family's economic status; the number of adults and children living in the home; and the number of rooms and the condition of the home (Montessori, 1913/1923, p. 52).

Chart 1 in Table 2.2 guided the teacher's observation of the child within the classroom. When does the child begin to show attention to work? What kinds of work does the child do? How long does the child remain with the work? Which work does the child choose and with what consistency? Chart 2 guided teachers' observations specific to children's perseverance and their interactions with others: Does the child respond to invitations to various kinds of work? There were questions about the child's "obedience," perhaps referencing the child's appropriate behavior with the materials and with others, as well as if there are any notable changes in behavior (Montessori, 1913/2023, p. 52).

Table 2.2. Dr. Montessori's Biographical and Observation Charts (Montessori, 2013/1913, p. 52)

Dr. Montessori's Biographical and Observation Charts	
Family History	
Father	Age, profession, background
Mother	Age, profession, background
Economic status of family	
Size of family	How many children, adults live in the home?
How many family members earn a living?	
Number of rooms inhabited by the family	Condition of the home
Chart 1	**Chart 2**
1. When does the child begin to show attention in work?	1. Does the child respond to invitations to various kinds of work?
2a. What kind of work does the child do?	2. Has the child achieved different levels of obedience?
2b. How long does the child stay with the work?	3. Does the level of obedience correspond to the development of work?
3a. To what work does the child apply him/herself?	4. Or to the changes in conduct or character?
3b. With what degree of constancy?	

Dr. Montessori clearly shared her scientific approach to observing and assessing children not just once or twice a year, but consistently over time: ". . . I lay stress on *collecting data* which I believe fundamental: such as weight and height . . . I offer a special schedule, which may help the teacher in the methodical and repeated collection of these measures" (Montessori, 1913/2023, p. 43, emphasis added). It is apparent through Dr. Montessori's writing that she conducted herself as a researcher in her work with children, employing scientific data collection to understand children's learning and development. She envisioned that her assessment data, when organized and interpreted, would inform educators' work with children in their classrooms. Dr. Montessori was not against standardized tests. In fact, she had her students participate in Italy's state examinations. Remarkably, the students who had learning disabilities matched their typically developing peers on these assessments—after receiving instruction via her instructional methods (Timeline of Maria Montessori's Life., n.d.).

UNDERSTANDING LITERACY INSTRUCTION IN MONTESSORI CLASSROOMS TODAY

In spring 2024, the authors submitted a survey to members of the American Montessori Society's Teacher Research Panel, which consists of AMS-credentialed educators and school administrators who voluntarily elect to take part in Montessori-related research. The survey was conducted to better understand current literacy and reading instruction in Montessori classrooms and to bring to life realities of mandates on classroom instruction and pedagogical approaches. Of the 649 anonymous responses received through Qualtrics, 619 participants agreed to take part in the survey. Table 2.3 provides an overview of the respondents' roles in schools.

Qualitative responses from those who selected "other" as their school role fell into three categories: educators who held multiple school roles (e.g., classroom teacher and head of school), those who were support staff (reading interventionist, classroom coach, curriculum or behavior specialist), and those who trained Montessori teachers (college faculty/adjuncts, field consultants, and directors of teacher training programs).

There are two notable trends in these data. The first is the prevalence of teachers who are also managing an additional full-time position within the school, such as a Montessori 3–6 teacher who also serves as the school's assistant director or school principal. The other is the scant number of reading coaches (12) who were identified through this survey. Future research may consider the impact on teaching when teachers also serve as school administrators, as well as exploring the impact on classroom instruction when there are few literacy support staff, such as an on-site reading coach to augment classroom literacy instruction with a specific focus on children who would benefit from additional support.

Table 2.4 breaks down the teacher's role by the age group of their classroom enrollment. A small group of respondents (7%) reported working with children between birth and two-and-a-half years of age. Slightly more than 40% of the teachers worked with children in 3–6-year-old classrooms. And a quarter of the respondents worked in elementary classrooms with children

Table 2.3. Role of Survey Participants

School Role	Percentage
Teacher	62%
School Leader/Principal/Head of School	17%
Assistant Teacher/Paraeducator	3%
Reading Coach	2%
Other	17%

Table 2.4. Teachers by Classroom Age Group

Montessori Classroom Age Group	Percentage
Infant-Toddler: Birth–2.5 years old	7%
Children's House: 2.5–6 years old	43%
Elementary I & II: 6–12 years old	27%
Other	23%

from 6–12 years of age. Interestingly, just as there were multiple roles when teachers selected "other" when describing their role in the school, those who selected "other" to represent the age group they worked with provided qualitative responses that spoke to teachers working across greater age spans, in varying combinations from birth through age 18, rather than the typical 3-year age group recognized in Montessori education.

Almost all of the respondents (90%) agreed that they were able to maintain a 2-to-3-hour dedicated work period where children were offered one-on-one and small-group Montessori lessons daily. Most teachers (88%) agreed that their students worked primarily with Montessori materials rather than supplementary curriculum and activities. When provided with a list of literacy-related Montessori materials, many teachers reported using a wide range of activities from the curriculum. Table 2.5 highlights the three most frequently selected materials used with infants and toddlers in 0–3 classrooms, which included Classification and Three-Part Language Cards, as well as Sandpaper Letters. Montessori Classification and Three-Part Language Cards support children's vocabulary and background knowledge, whereas Sandpaper Letters build alphabet recognition (when letter names are also introduced), phonological awareness, and early phonics skills.

Table 2.6 highlights the most frequently selected Montessori materials used with children between 3 and 6 years of age, including Sandpaper Letters, Three-Part Language Cards, the Large Movable Alphabet, Initial Sound Boxes, Puzzle or Sight Words, and Classification Cards.

Just as with infants and toddlers, the Montessori Classification and Three-Part Language Cards support children's vocabulary and background knowledge. Sandpaper Letters, the Large Movable Alphabet, Initial Sound Boxes, and Puzzle or Sight Words support young children's alphabet recognition, phonological awareness, encoding, decoding, and word recognition skills.

Table 2.7 highlights the greatest range of literacy-related Montessori materials that were used in elementary classrooms across the 6-to-12-year-old age span. The materials most often offered or used in these classrooms include lessons focused on Word Study (suffix, prefix), Grammar Symbols/Sentence Analysis, The Great Lessons or Stories, Classification Cards, and Articles. Montessori Great Stories and Classification Cards support children's vocabulary and background knowledge. Work with the Articles, Grammar

Table 2.5. Montessori Literacy Materials Most Frequently Selected as Used in 0–3 Classrooms

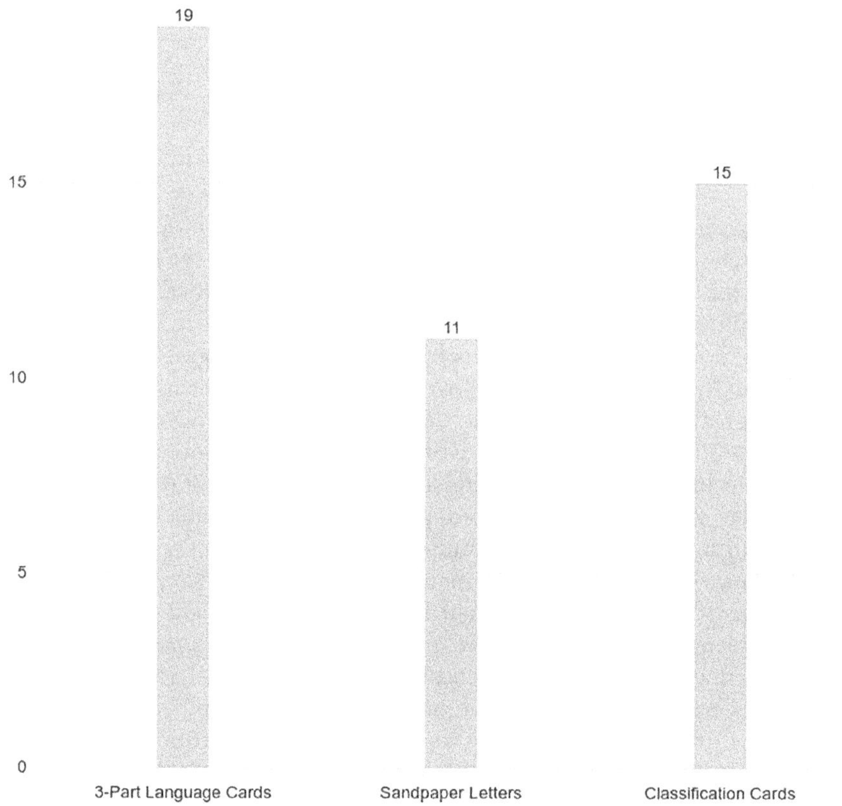

Figure 2.3. Sandpaper Letters

Photo courtesy of Nienhuis Montessori

Table 2.6. Montessori Literacy Materials Most Frequently Selected by Teachers as Implemented in 3–6 Classrooms

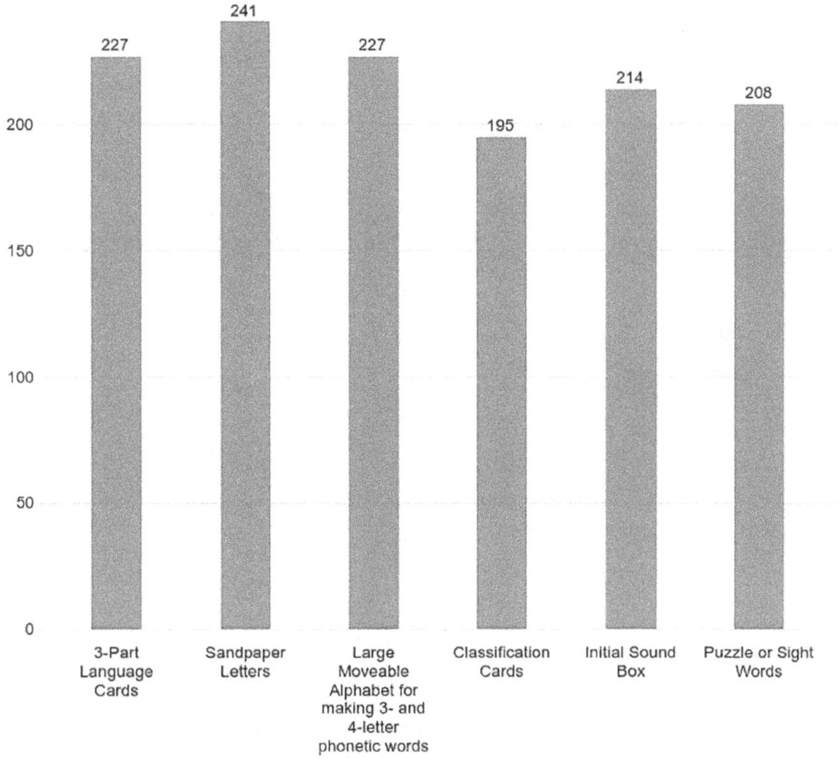

Figure 2.4. Grammar Symbols

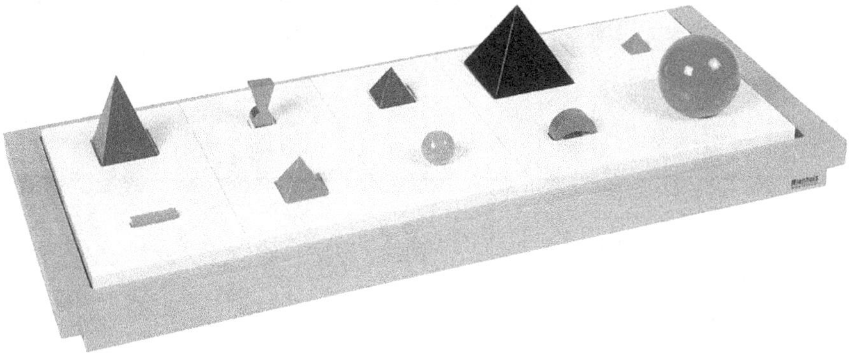

Photo courtesy of Nienhuis Montessori

Figure 2.5. Three-Part Cards Land Formations

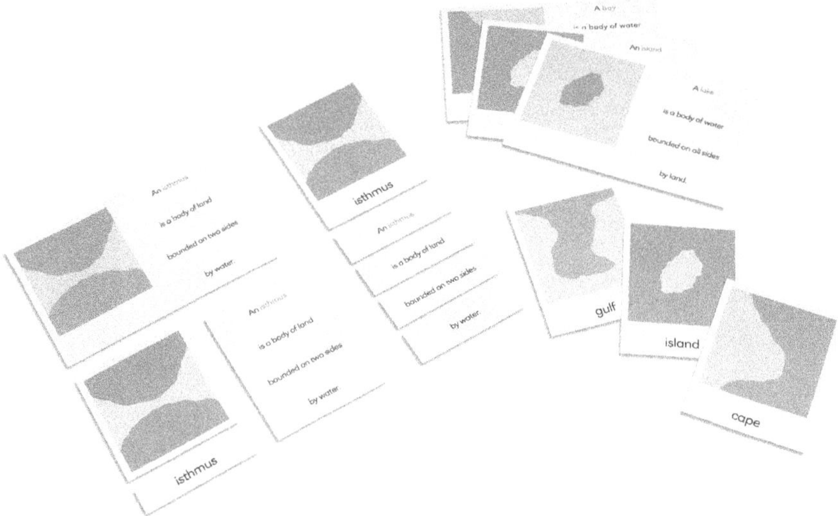

Photo courtesy of Nienhuis Montessori

Table 2.7. Montessori Literacy Materials Most Frequently Selected as Used in 6-12 Classrooms

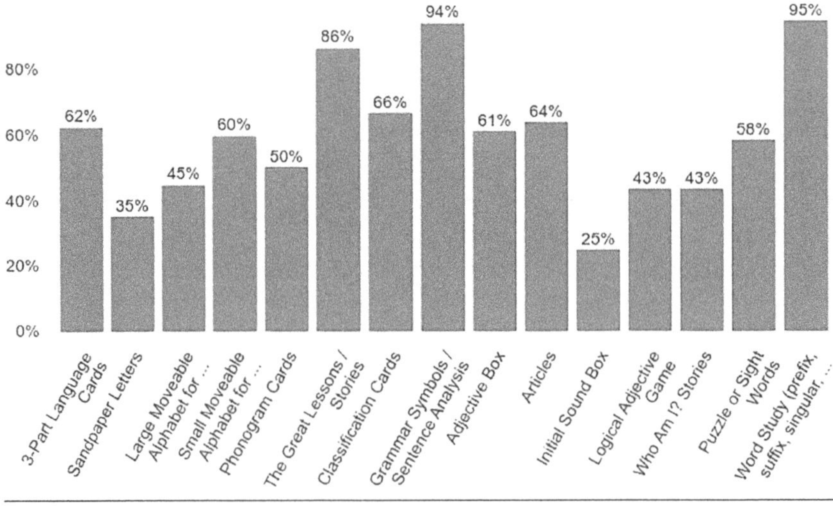

Symbols and Sentence Analysis, and Word Study all support students' language structures, verbal reasoning, and decoding skills.

There is a growing number of publicly funded Montessori schools experiencing the impact of recent state reading legislation. As discussed earlier, this legislation mandates a range of changes from teacher preparation programs, to state licensure regulations, to the use of specific assessment tools, instructional approaches, and ELA curricula that schools must select from a preestablished list from their state's department of education. One way these mandates have impacted public Montessori schools is the requirement that teachers implement a commercial literacy curriculum in addition to the Montessori curriculum. This is a particularly daunting task when these curricula can require up to 2 hours of classroom literacy instruction. Usually, this is 90 minutes of reading instruction and 30 minutes of writing instruction. This would be in addition to the 2-to-3-hour morning work period when the Montessori Language curriculum would be implemented, so as to maintain fidelity to both programs while adhering to Montessori standards (AMS, 2023). There literally are just not enough hours in the school day.

To better understand how these mandates were impacting teachers, a survey question addressed the use of ELA curriculum outside of the Montessori curriculum. Of the 527 educators and school administrators who responded to this survey question, 28% stated that they were required to teach using two English Language Arts curricula (Montessori and a commercial ELA program). Those respondents then provided a list of 60 supplemental curricula used during the 2023–2024 academic year (see Table 2.8).

It should be noted that some responses referred to reading series, such as FlyLeaf Publishing (which also offers phonics materials in addition to decodable books) and the Junior Great Books series. Others shared writing programs, such as Writing Without Tears, or professional development training, such as LETRS. Many additional curricula focused on meeting requirements related to a single strand or two of the Reading Rope (Scarborough, 2001), such as decoding or language comprehension. The Montessori curriculum is inclusive of all learning domains (science, math, geometry, history, etc.) and aligned to key areas of literacy development. Qualitative survey responses highlighted five frequently cited ELA programs respondents used as supplemental to the Montessori curriculum, including Heggerty Phonemic Awareness Curriculum (18), Orton-Gillingham Structured Literacy approach (17), the University of Florida Literacy Institute (UFLI) materials (11), Amplify CKLA (Core Knowledge Language Arts; 11), and Fundations (7). It was encouraging to see that at least some of these supplemental curricula did not take significant time away from Montessori instruction. Heggerty is typically completed in 10–15 minutes a day. Fundations and UFLI are usually taught in a 30-minute time frame. Orton-Gillingham is only used for selected students. However, CKLA is a robust ELA curriculum and requires

Table 2.8. Frequency of Supplemental ELA Curriculum Used in Montessori Classrooms

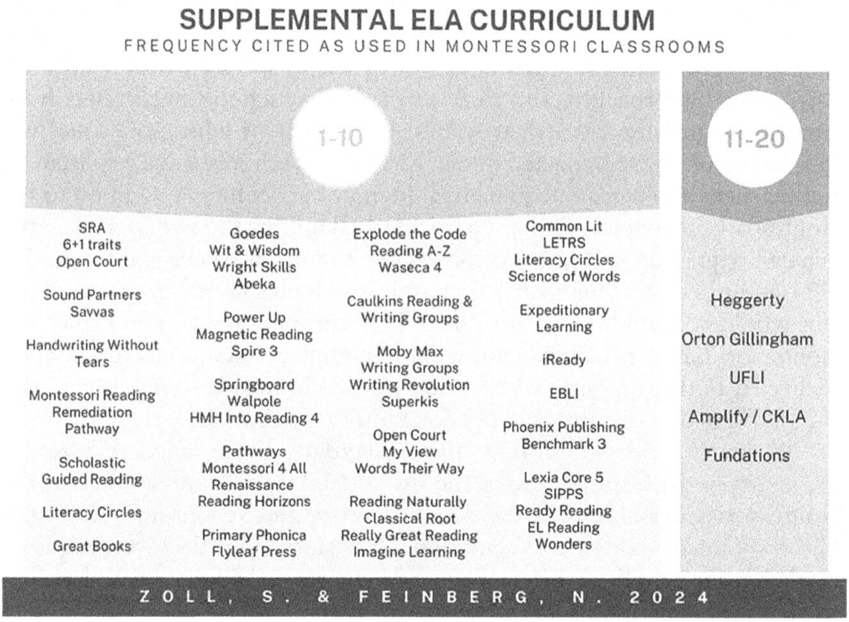

a minimum of 90 minutes per day. (See additional discussion on this topic in Chapter 5.)

Some states have successfully lobbied to have the Montessori curriculum recognized as a high-quality ELA curriculum option. One such notable effort was led by Nirvair Khalsa and Leslie Woodford of Khalsa Montessori School, in collaboration with Kelly Powell from the Arizona Charter School Association, Dr. Katie Brown from the National Center for Montessori in the Public Sector (NCMPS), and the Montessori Public Policy Initiative (MPPI), among others. In collaboration with the Arizona Department of Education (ADE), a study was conducted to review state ELA data "to compare the reading performance of students in Arizona's public Montessori schools, the majority of which are charter schools, to that of the state as a whole" (Brown et al., 2024, p. 2). With a sample size of 4,781 K–8 students representing 26 different Arizona schools between 2016 and 2019, results demonstrated that "year after year, Arizona's public Montessori schools perform well on the AzMERIT (Arizona's state ELA exam), and a few are among the highest performers in the state. Across all grade levels, the median ELA pass rate in Montessori schools was 77 percent compared to 46 percent in all non-treatment schools" (Brown et al., 2024, p. 2). These results served as evidence of the positive influence of the Montessori curriculum on students reading performance, allowing it to be added to Arizona's core program vetted list (www.azed.gov/sites/default/files/2024/07/Montessori%20Rubric.pdf). With this recognition, publicly funded Montessori schools in Arizona may now solely implement the Montessori curriculum without the burden of meeting the objectives and scheduling requirements of a second ELA curriculum during their school day. Future research related to Montessori ELA outcomes could replicate the Arizona exemplar study to determine if similar outcomes might be realized to meet other state ELA requirements through the review of their own state-level summative data.

In this chapter we have developed a common vocabulary that will be used in the upcoming discussion. We have shown how Montessori educators have addressed assessment and used data to guide instruction in the past. We have made a case for the timeliness of this book, as many public Montessori classrooms are integrating public school requirements into their daily instruction. We now highlight the common systems that public Montessori educators are adopting, determine how the Montessori teachers can use these tools to prove the effectiveness of their instructional methods, and discuss ways the Montessori educator can potentially strengthen their language instruction and raise student achievement by incorporating the best of all methods.

Part I

STARTING THE SCHOOL YEAR

Setting the Stage So Reading Improves for Every Student

Figure I.1. Beginning of Year (BOY) Assessment Flowchart

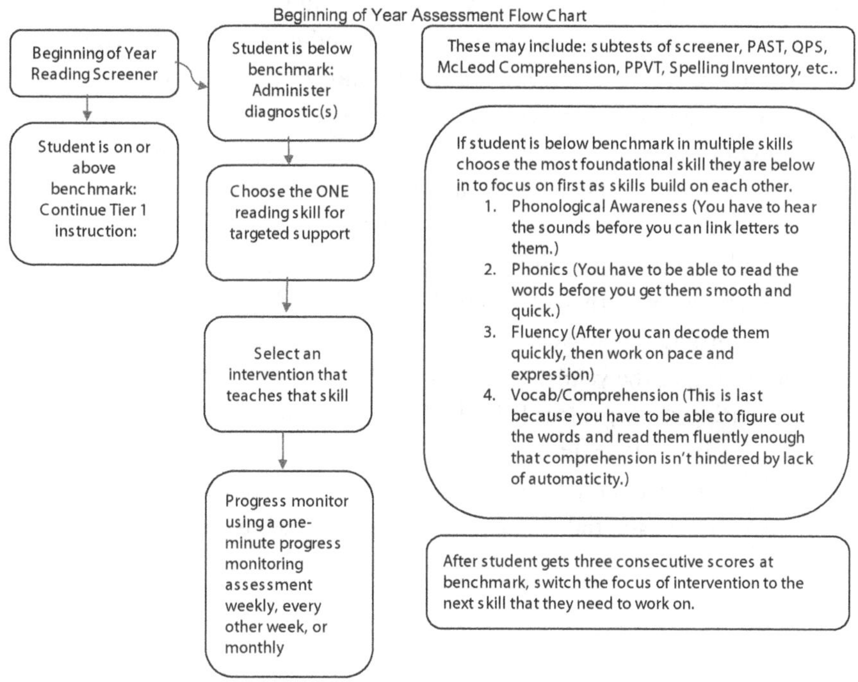

SETTING THE STAGE

You're readying your school for the start of a new academic year! Students are enrolled in their respective classrooms, family partnership opportunities are scheduled, the teaching faculty have carefully prepared their learning environments. Recently, your state has passed reading legislation mandating that the design and use of a comprehensive assessment system is now required to ensure that all students are successful readers. Part I of this book provides an overview of the many curricular decisions you'll address at this time of year, including assessments. Using sourced materials from public Montessori and traditional schools, we will offer recommendations for classroom practice, assessment tools, and schedules to prepare your approach.

So many decisions regarding student enrollment, curriculum, assessment schedules, human resource allocations, family engagement, professional development, and student services (among others!) are all addressed well before children arrive for their first day of school. Collectively, time invested in these decisions can influence the degree to which we can create equitable, effective, and welcoming learning environments. Part I addresses the rituals and routines, student interactions, and family interactions from the perspective of beginning a new school year. It also provides a brief overview of Montessori lessons (Chapter 3). Then, elements of a comprehensive assessment system are discussed, along with suggested screening and diagnostic tools implemented in the first weeks of school to provide teachers with a baseline snapshot of their students' language and literacy development. Figure I.i provides a flowchart that guides assessment decisions at the beginning of the year. This is followed by recommendations for incorporating these protocols in the Montessori setting (Chapter 4). Finally, decisions that inform the development of an assessment system are balanced with maintaining the integrity of an interrupted work period (Chapter 5), an essential element of high-fidelity Montessori schools.

CHAPTER 3

Lesson Application

RITUALS AND ROUTINES

Establishing expectations the moment students enter the door is paramount to how the classroom will operate throughout the coming year. We suggest planning to address rituals and routines in three main areas: student interactions (student-teacher, student-student, and student-classroom), parent interactions (how will you communicate with caregivers, and how will they communicate with you?), and lesson implementation (schedules, lesson structure). While at first this may not seem related to the Science of Reading, rituals and routines lay the foundation for the smooth implementation of any curriculum, increase learning time and time-on-task for students, and ultimately allow for comfort and security in the classroom as students know what to expect. At the beginning of the year, we set the stage for what is expected and what is acceptable in the classroom. This includes which materials to use, how to use them, and when to use them. For some students, this will be a review. For students new to your room, or possibly to Montessori instruction in general, this will be new information that needs explicit instruction.

STUDENT INTERACTIONS

Students need guidelines in how to interact with their peers, their teachers, and the Montessori materials with which they will be working. Keep in mind that any task mastered to a level of automaticity reduces the cognitive load for a child, enabling more brain power to go into new learning. Cognitive load theory (Sweller, 2011) asserts that the human brain has a certain amount of working memory that is utilized when learning. That finite amount of working memory is used when processing information (e.g., learning new material). Therefore, only a certain amount of information can be processed at a time. If a student is comfortable knowing when and where to get materials, has mastered conversing about the materials with a friend, and confidently can ask the teacher questions when needed, they do not waste mental energy on these tasks. Instead, these interactions come more naturally and don't take up space in their working memory (Willingham, 2021).

Just as with content-area learning, operative knowledge of the classroom and the people in it comes with guided modeling and practice. The teacher models positive school interactions and gives students ample time to practice the accepted social conventions and classroom protocols, then releases them to manage these interactions independently. While the teacher may remind students of expectations throughout the year, it is in the first month of school that the tone of the environment is established.

PARENT INTERACTIONS

When developing a comprehensive approach to reaching all learners in your school, an often underresourced yet powerful opportunity can be found in the authentic and effective family engagement opportunities offered at your school. Moving beyond parent-teacher conferences, your school's Family Engagement plan should be collaboratively developed, implemented, and evaluated throughout the school year. Just as there is diversity in the children and families we serve, there should be an array of opportunities for families to engage with their child's school that will encourage roles as co-creators, supporters, encouragers, monitors, advocates, and models for their children (Colorado Department of Education, 2023; Mapp & Kuttner, 2013).

As in any productive relationship, initial connections between families and teachers that foster respect, reciprocal understanding, and a sense of belonging in the school will help to build trusting partnerships. When effective family, school, and community partnerships are leveraged as an additional student learning support, it "has been proven to increase school readiness, improve language, literacy, mathematics, and social-emotional skills, as well as increase the likelihood of high school graduation" (National Association for Family, School and Community Engagement, 2022, p. 4). Results from a meta-analysis conducted by the Flamboyan Foundation (2021) also revealed a significant and large association between family engagement and the academic achievement of urban elementary and middle school students. Of particular note, in a study of Title 1 schools, "growth in reading test scores [was] 50% higher for students whose teachers and schools reported high levels of parental outreach versus those who reported low levels" (Flamboyan Foundation, 2021, p. 1). Just as you plan for beginning-of-year professional development sessions to prepare yourself or your teaching staff, careful attention should be given to evidence-based family engagement practices that can enhance student learning.

Not all family engagement opportunities are created equal. Along a continuum of family engagement strategies, there is a range of events that may have high or low impacts on student success. Each holds value based on desired outcomes. For example, low-impact strategies are "often school-led, not learning focused, and require the family to come to school" (Colorado Department of Education, 2023). At the start of the school year, you may schedule a potluck dinner, create a parent resource room, or host an opening day school celebration to welcome families. To create an inclusive and positive community, these low-impact events are well-suited as beginning of the year activities, as they are primarily focused on building trust and communication with families. Your planning will also need to consider high-impact strategies that from the very first day of school engage families and build partnerships through home visits and positive phone calls home to further strengthen relationships with families. After careful analysis of your beginning of year screening assessment results (described in Chapter 4), you'll be prepared to develop data-informed high-impact family engagement strategies that encourage academic partnering, such as sharing individual student assessment results, goal-setting talks, and modeling learning support activities that can be replicated at home (Flamboyan Foundation, 2022).

LESSON IMPLEMENTATION

The first lessons of the school year build student automaticity with classroom routines. What activities are there to choose from? Where are materials located? Sharing and cooperative learning are fostered through guided practice and positive reinforcement. This is the time to provide plenty of high-probability requests of students (Vanderbilt University, 2024a).

In conventional classrooms, high-probability, or high-p, requests are directions given by the teacher that are easy for the student and therefore more likely to be successfully completed. By establishing the normality of being able to complete the task requested by the teacher (e.g., "Please pass out the paper"), students build a feeling of self-confidence that they will be able to do what is asked of them in the classroom. These high-probability requests are effective for social and academic goals (Common et al., 2019). Many times, students who balk at a teacher's request have not had the positive experience of being able to successfully complete these requested tasks. High-probability requests give students confidence in their ability to receive a favorable response from the teacher. After making many high-probability requests, the teacher can then offer a low-probability request (one that is not as easy and/or favorable) and the student will likely continue on with the positive "behavioral momentum" (Vanderbilt University, 2024a) that they have begun. The benefit of high-probability requests is that the student's success sets them up to approach future complex tasks from a positive and productive mindset.

Montessori classrooms also work toward "normalization" through intentional routines that are established in the first days of the new school year. The early lessons offered by teachers focus on building students' sense of agency and ownership in the classroom.

THE LESSON PLAN FORMAT

Montessori lesson plans follow a particular structure, though there may be some variability based on teacher training experience. Table 3.1 outlines the lesson plan format and provides a brief explanation of each section.

Structured Literacy Plan Using Explicit Instruction

Much of the current reading legislation focuses on teachers implementing curriculum that reflects the Science of Reading. When the Science of Reading becomes actual classroom practice, it is referred to as "Structured Literacy." Structured Literacy is systematic (it has a scope and sequence that builds skills on foundational knowledge) and explicit.

Best practices are made evident in classrooms that follow Structured Literacy, the systematic and explicit instruction of reading skills. At first, Montessori educators may balk at the term "explicit instruction." Yet, as we delve into what really defines this term, there are numerous correlations between Montessori instruction and explicit instruction.

Explicit instruction is perhaps best described by Anita Archer and Charles Hughes in the book *Explicit Instruction* (2011). With explicit instruction, new learning is presented in small steps, with clear language that avoids digressions. Montessori instruction likewise focuses on simplicity and concision. In explicit instruction, the teacher models the new skill, students are given time to practice with the teacher's supervision and immediate feedback, and finally students practice independently. Some refer to this as the *I Do, We Do, You Do* model or the Gradual Release of Responsibility (Archer & Hughes, 2011). In the Montessori classroom, students work with didactic materials that focus on one particular skill. The teacher introduces a new material to the student, showing them how it is used. The materials are made with error control. Error control gives immediate feedback to students so that they realize their mistake as soon as they make it and can self-correct the error. Montessori materials provide repetitive practice opportunities for students, and students work with the materials until they achieve mastery. Similarly, explicit instruction requires practice until the child can demonstrate fluency and automaticity with the skill.

A Montessori lesson plan aligns with the 16 elements of explicit instruction listed in Table 3.2 (Archer & Hughes, 2011) by ensuring clear organization and focus throughout the lesson. The plan begins by identifying the critical content and specifying the materials needed, which aligns

Table 3.1. Montessori Lesson Plan Format

Name of Activity	This is the name of the Montessori material or activity the student will be introduced to or will be revisiting for additional practice.
Area	The lesson plan specifies which part of the Montessori curriculum this lesson falls under (Language, Math, Geography, etc.).
Materials	The lesson includes a list of all the materials, trays, and items specific to the lesson that are needed to complete the activity.
Aims	There are often "direct" aims—the learning or skill that is the purpose of the lesson—as well as "indirect" aims, which are additional skills that students will benefit from mastering during this activity.
Preparation	All lessons describe what skills or previous lessons a student should have experienced before being introduced to this activity.
Age	Lesson plans offer a possible age range to identify when a child may have a particular aptitude for any given lesson. However, Montessori lessons are not age-restricted, and children are offered lessons as they are ready. In a multiyear classroom, a 3-year-old may be introduced to learning activities identified for a 5-year-old student. Age does not drive instruction; readiness does.
Presentation	A detailed description of the lesson from the introduction, to the delivery, and finally to the cumulative review of the initial lesson are outlined for each lesson. This is especially helpful for new teachers as they learn to integrate the Montessori curriculum along with the language and approach of its delivery.
Points of Consciousness	These are the concepts or "aha" moments when a student makes connections between their learning and the lesson. "When the child completes a Montessori exercise, they have gained knowledge both consciously and unconsciously. Montessori's aim was to provide direct preparation, as well as indirect preparation for higher learning in all of her didactic materials. The moment a child can pull information acquired unconsciously and consciously apply that knowledge to a new situation is what Montessori referred to as a point of consciousness" (Reimer, n.d.).
Points of Interest	"Montessori realized that if children spent too long a time on a complex task or failed to master the necessary details, the exercise would cease to interest them. Therefore, she suggested that points of interest be interspersed throughout each activity. These points guide the child toward his or her goal and stimulate repetition and interest by offering immediate feedback, or what Montessori called control of error. The child's performance becomes refined through trial and error, the points of interest acting as signposts along the path to success" (Association Montessori Internationale, n.d.)

(*continued*)

Table 3.1. (*continued*)

Control of Error	Many of the Montessori materials are designed with an embedded assessment feature that allows the child to self-assess their progress, what Dr. Montessori referred to as self-correcting materials.
Variations	After the initial lesson, variations are provided with ways to enhance the delivery of the lesson using the same materials.
Extensions	While extensions also allow for additional use of the same activity, extensions or additional materials may be used to supplement the lesson, often bringing the child to a more advanced level.

with designing organized lessons and focusing on essential skills. It also reviews prior knowledge, preparing students for new concepts, and breaks down complex tasks into smaller, more manageable units. Additionally, the lesson presentation involves step-by-step demonstrations and clear language, ensuring that students can follow along easily. Guided practice, immediate feedback through self-correcting materials, and cumulative review through extensions or variations all ensure that students continually refine their knowledge (see Table 3.2).

Establishing and consistently implementing well-defined rituals and routines from the very first day of school lays a solid foundation for highly effective instruction and a positive learning environment. Through intentional classroom interactions, meaningful engagement with families, and a clear approach to lesson implementation, educators create an atmosphere of security and predictability for students. This structure not only builds trust, but also allows students to flourish by reducing cognitive load and freeing up mental resources for new learning.

This early investment in classroom management pays dividends throughout the year, resulting in smoother transitions, more focused learning, and an overall sense of community and belonging. Whether fostering peer interactions, collaborating with parents as educational partners, or guiding students through structured literacy lessons, the teacher's role in creating a supportive and predictable environment cannot be understated. As we move forward to explore specific instructional strategies and assessments, remember that the foundational work of establishing rituals and routines is what makes deeper, more meaningful learning possible.

Table 3.2. 16 Elements of Explicit Instruction (Archer & Hughes, 2011) Aligned With Elements of the Montessori Lesson Plan Format

Explicit Instruction	Alignment to Montessori Lesson Plan
1. Focus instruction on critical content.	Aims
2. Sequence skills logically.	Presentation
3. Break down complex skills and strategies into smaller instructional units.	Presentation
4. Design organized and focused lessons.	Name of Activity Area Materials Preparation Age of Student
5. Begin lessons with a clear statement of the lesson's goals and your expectations.	Aims Presentation
6. Review prior skills and knowledge before beginning instruction.	Preparation Presentation
7. Provide step-by-step demonstrations.	Presentation
8. Use clear and concise language.	Presentation
9. Provide an adequate range of examples and non-examples.	Presentation
10. Provide guided and supported practice.	Points of Consciousness Points of Interests
11. Require frequent responses.	Control of Error
12. Monitor student performance closely.	Control of Error
13. Provide immediate affirmative and corrective feedback	Control of Error
14. Deliver the lesson at a brisk pace.	Presentation
15. Help students organize knowledge.	Presentation
16. Provide distributed and cumulative practice.	Points of Consciousness Points of Interest Variations Extensions

CHAPTER 4

Assessment

This book began with information, answering questions about the purpose of assessments, differences between "screening" and "diagnostic" assessments, and using assessment results to plan tiered instruction and interventions. If these are new protocols for your school, or if you're looking to refine practices, remember that providing high-quality instruction aligned to the Montessori pedagogy remains the priority, with the addition of gathering pertinent data to best meet the needs of all students. Meaningful change is a process that begins with small adjustments to current practices, identified (and celebrated!) noticeable gains for students, and intentional discussions to further improve and sustain change (McDowell, 2024). Figure 4.1 provides an overview of an iterative assessment cycle that looks at collection and analysis of data in the classroom.

Most Montessori schools collect data. Some use observation notes or apps (Montessori Compass, Transparent Classroom, Brightwheel). Others use formal assessment tools to track students' learning and offer evidence to families in the form of observation notes, images, and videos. These pieces of documentation serve to demonstrate that children are meeting or exceeding developmental expectations and state learning standards. Publicly funded Montessori schools following protocols required of their local district or state department of education are most likely collecting both observation and formal assessment data. What is less clear is how results from these assessments are used or if data are organized in a systematic fashion to improve student outcomes. This is important because a focus on student growth and learning is imperative if teachers want to close learning gaps and ensure that all students meet academic benchmarks. It is important for teachers to know that students are learning and progressing in their academic skills. There is little doubt that understanding each student's strengths and needs helps teachers tailor their instruction to best fit the individuals in their classroom.

In this chapter, we discuss the place and purpose of assessments and elements of a comprehensive assessment system, with a particular look at those practices that take place at the ***beginning of the school year (BOY)***. When

Figure 4.1. Classroom Data Assessment Cycle

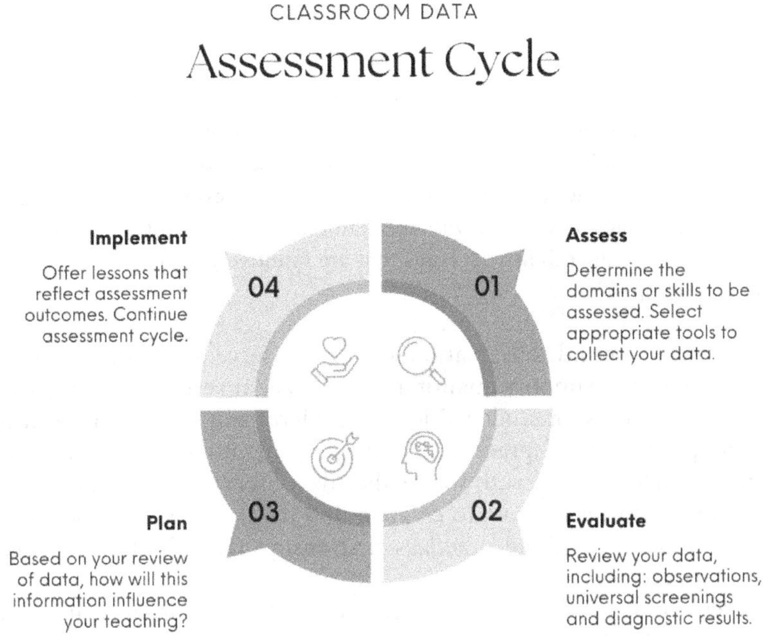

the instructional year begins, what data do teachers need to gain about their students, and how do they obtain those data? This chapter begins with a historical overview of assessment standards, Dr. Montessori's assessment practices, and current BOY assessment protocols used in conventional classrooms that can be melded into Montessori contexts.

ASSESSMENTS AND COMPREHENSIVE ASSESSMENT SYSTEMS IN EDUCATION

As Montessori pedagogy has moved into the public school sector, assessment practices hold a tension between the use of observational (or qualitative) data traditionally collected in Montessori classrooms and the use of quantitative assessment tools used in more conventional classrooms. Public schools are mandated to provide concrete evidence of student growth in a quantifiable manner using valid and reliable assessment tools (*valid* meaning it measures what it says it is going to measure, and *reliable* meaning results are consistent between whoever administers the assessment as shown through national norms). While teachers informally observe students as part of their formative assessment practice, observation is considered subjective and often influenced by personal biases. Seidenberg (2018) makes the point that

> Education as a discipline has placed much higher value on observation and hands-on experience . . . Intuitions about reading do not penetrate very far, and observations are influenced by prior beliefs, including what one has been taught about how children learn and how reading works. Educators are people too, subject to the same cognitive limitations and bias as everyone else. The lack of scientific literacy, combined with deep faith in the validity of personal observation, creates vulnerability to claims that are intuitively appealing but approved or untrue. (p. 11)

With this in mind, observational data can serve as a valuable qualitative component to support quantitative assessment results, offering a more comprehensive view of students' learning. Here may be an opportunity to meld the public school practice of requiring quantifiable data from valid and reliable assessments with the qualitative observation data collected by skilled Montessori educators to create a 360-degree view of students, their learning, and instructional practices that ensure that all children become competent readers.

Given the myriad of data collected related to children's learning and the number of school personnel who interact with students every day, a well-designed assessment plan must be established to create an efficient use of limited school resources. A comprehensive assessment system focused on reading development includes a range of literacy assessment tools used to capture snapshots of students' reading skills at a given moment in time. Results from these tools are especially important to determine specific literacy interventions and ongoing progress monitoring to ensure the forward momentum of all students' learning. Figure 4.2 provides a visual of a possible schedule for implementing a comprehensive assessment plan. Dates will need to reflect your school calendar, and the chart allows for intentional deployment of school staff (reading specialists, classroom teachers, assessment personnel) to meet the plan's objectives.

At the BOY, all students are assessed using a literacy screening tool. For a smaller subset of students who do not yet meet age- or grade-level benchmarks as shown on the screener, an additional diagnostic assessment will be implemented. These data will inform small-group and individual lessons with ongoing weekly and biweekly progress monitoring to support students' reading skills. This cycle is repeated again at the middle of the school year (MOY) and again near the end of the school year (EOY), with enough time still available to utilize the data to design and implement a final round of support to children before the summer break occurs. In addition to these assessments scheduled across the school year, many state departments of education also require end-of-year ELA assessments for certain grade

Figure 4.2. A Proposed Schedule for Implementing a Comprehensive Assessment Plan

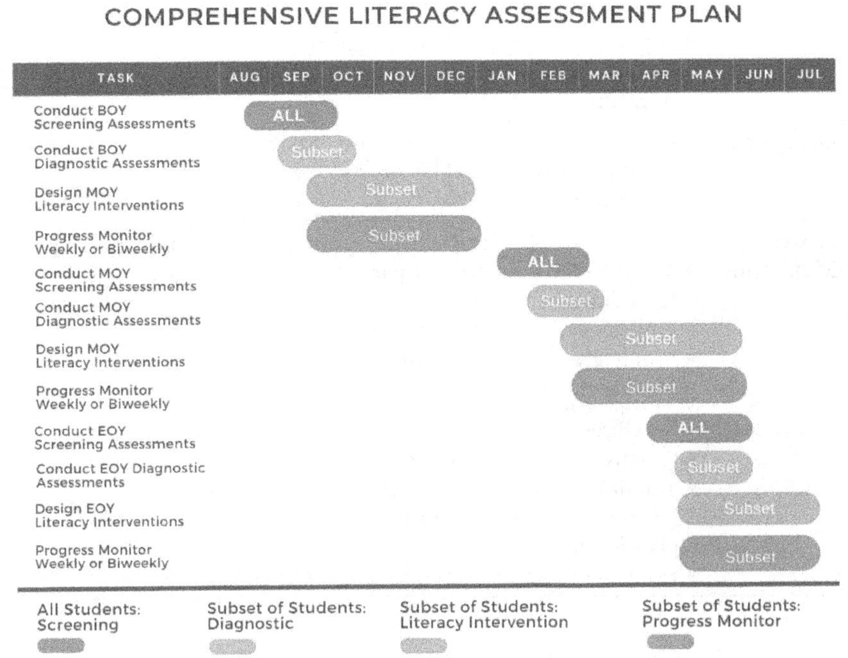

levels. These summative assessments provide an additional look at students' literacy learning, but often do not influence the current year's classroom instruction as scores are usually released in fall of the following school year.

A comprehensive assessment plan will include multiple types of assessments strategically implemented over the course of the academic year (see Table 4.1). Each assessment serves a specific purpose and provides data collected from either all students or a subset of students dependent on results gleaned from this iterative process. *Screening assessments* align with reading research and provide a snapshot of children's discrete literacy skills. A screener is implemented with all students and takes place within the initial weeks of the start of school. The assessment will be repeated as a MOY checkpoint, and once again toward the EOY. For a subset of students who score below developmental or grade-level expectations, a *diagnostic assessment* is given to gain more specific information about the skills that need to be addressed through more focused interventions. These data provide teachers with information to transform classroom instruction to meet the needs of all children. To be sure these focused interventions are guiding students forward in their learning, *progress monitoring* tools are used in frequent intervals, perhaps weekly, biweekly, or monthly. Depending on state or district requirements, there may also be a summative or *outcome assessment*

Table 4.1. Four Types of Assessment

Screening	• Usually given three times a year to the whole class. • Often at least part of it can be given to everyone at once. • Tells if there is a problem or not (in a specific area, usually math or reading).
Diagnostic	• Gets more specific and gives more information. • Tells what particular skills need support. • Is not given to everyone.
Progress Monitoring	• Administered frequently to see if instruction is working. • Might be the same test (or part of test) as the screener, but is used for a different reason. • Is given weekly, every other week, or once a month. • Is only given to students who are receiving an intervention because they scored below benchmark on the screening test.
Outcome	• Measures effectiveness on a broad scale. • Usually given at the end of the year to the whole class. • You don't really do that much with this data; maybe it gives information to next year's teacher or helps the current teacher plan for next year. • Example: High-stakes standardized test like the SAT.

conducted at the end of the school year to all students. Table 4.1 provides an overview of each of the four assessment types.

The next section examines one of the many literacy screening assessments that may be used in an early childhood or Montessori 3–6 classroom. This is followed by an additional screening tool often used in elementary classrooms. Each provides useful data to inform classroom teachers of the students who are mastering literacy skills and those who might need extra reading support.

SCREENING ASSESSMENTS—EARLY CHILDHOOD

Learning what it is young children know and are able to do requires special considerations, as our youngest students often do not yet read, nor can they complete written responses to demonstrate their literacy skills. Assessing pre-readers and writers often requires teachers to assess each child individually. One tool that has been used to gather research-aligned data about children's early literacy skills is the Phonological Awareness Literacy Screening (PALS Pre-K). The next section provides an overview of the tool and use in Montessori classrooms.

Phonological Awareness Literacy Screening

The Phonological Awareness Literacy Screening, or PALS Pre-K (Invernizzi et al., 2004), is a criterion-referenced tool that captures foundational literacy skills necessary for children's reading success prior to entering kindergarten. The assessment is also available to screen more advanced reading and writing skills, so teachers working in kindergarten and 1st through 3rd grade classrooms can utilize the PALS-K and the PALS 1–3 series. According to the National Center for Intensive Intervention (n.d.-a), the tool can be administered as a screening tool, for diagnostic purposes, and as a progress monitoring tool.

The PALS Pre-K assessment battery takes approximately 25 minutes per child and includes several subtests: Name Writing, Alphabet Knowledge, Letter Sounds, Initial Sounds, Rhyme Awareness, and Print and Word Awareness. Prior validation studies reveal that this assessment battery has strong internal consistency across each of the tasks, with reliability estimates ranging from 0.75 (Print and Word Awareness) to 0.95 (Beginning Sound). The following is a brief overview for each of the subtasks of the PALS Pre-K.

Name Writing. The PALS Pre-K administration form has two blank pages labeled as Fall and Spring Name Writing. Children are invited to write their name and to draw a picture of themselves, which are then scored from 0 to 7 using a detailed scale outlined in the PALS Pre-K Teacher's Manual. For those students who scribble or who use pictures to represent both their name and a picture of themselves, Name Writing is scored as 0, while students who correctly write the letters in their name and include a separate picture are scored as 7.

Alphabet Recognition. *Uppercase and Lowercase Letter Names.* The screening tool offers tabbed sections that include 26 uppercase letters randomly displayed on a page and another tabbed section similarly formatted with 26 lowercase letters. Children are asked to point to and name each letter beginning at the top-left corner. Letters identified incorrectly or not known by the child are noted on the administration form. The protocol of the assessment requires students to correctly identify 16 uppercase letters prior to being presented with lowercase letters. Scores are determined by tallying the number of upper- and lowercase letters presented that were correctly identified.

Letter Sounds. If students correctly identify 16 uppercase letters and 9 lowercase letters, they are then presented with the next subtask, Letter Sounds. A practice letter is shown in the upper-right corner of the assessment page to demonstrate that this subtask is different from the previous two administered. The test administrator points to the letter and states, "This is the letter M and it makes the sound /m/," to demonstrate the objective of this task. There are 23 uppercase letters (M, Q, and X are excluded) and three digraphs (sh, th, and ch) formatted in random order for the child to point to and provide the letter sound for each. Children are prompted to provide the letter sound if they instead gave the letter name. This subtask is scored as the number of letter sounds correctly identified out of 26 possible points.

Initial Sounds. Fourteen picture cards are shared one at a time with the child. The test administrator shows the picture, names the image, and then asks the child to identify the initial sound heard at the beginning of the word.

Rhyme and Nursery Rhyme Awareness. Two additional subtests include a section focusing on a child's ability to match rhyming words presented orally and visually by the test administrator, as well as their ability to recite sections of children's nursery rhymes.

Print and Word Awareness. Finally, a child's nursery rhyme is read in a simple book format. The test administrator asks 10 questions related to concepts of print (e.g., directionality of text reading, identifying individual letters and words, etc.).

Results from this assessment tool provide a range of information about children's early literacy development. Some considerations for its use in Montessori classrooms are discussed in the next section.

THE PALS PRE-K ASSESSMENT IN MONTESSORI CLASSROOMS

The schedule and rationale for assessing children using the PALS Pre-K is developmentally appropriate whether a student is enrolled in a Montessori classroom or in a conventional school. However, there are a few protocol items Montessori teachers will want to be aware of before electing to use this tool. Primarily, the protocol for assessing children with the PALS Pre-K follows a prescribed sequence. As noted above, only those children who correctly identify 16 uppercase letters can then be administered the lowercase letter identification subtask. If children are able to identify 16 uppercase letters and 9 lowercase letters, they can then be assessed in letter sound knowledge. However, if a child identifies 15 or fewer uppercase letters, the child may not be administered the lowercase letter recognition nor the letter sounds sections of the PALS, and instead receives a score of 0 for each of these subtasks. This sequence could prove to be an issue for children enrolled in Montessori classrooms, where traditionally there is an emphasis on letter sounds rather than letter names. Thus, when implemented in Montessori programs, it is important to keep in mind the process by which the various subtests of the PALS Pre-K are administered, and a collective agreement to revise certain protocol items might be warranted. When considering the focus on letter sounds through the use of Sandpaper Letters in Montessori classrooms, it may be best to collect data from each of these subtests (uppercase, lowercase, and letter sounds) in their entirety to obtain the most accurate information. Implementation of current reading research recognizes the importance of letter sounds (auditory-only instruction) combined with visible letters (Erbeli et al., 2024) as an approach to increase student learning. This is a standard form of Montessori instruction through the use of Sandpaper Letters (for additional information about the use of Sandpaper Letters, see the early childhood case study in Chapter 5).

Similar to conventional classrooms, PALS Pre-K can be administered at the beginning of the school year as a screening tool and repeated as a midyear and end-of-year screening assessment. Since there are several subsets focused on phonological awareness skills, results from the tool can identify key areas that may need additional support through small-group or individual lessons. And for any areas where students are not yet meeting benchmarks, PALS Pre-K may also be used to measure students' learning through progress monitoring over the course of the school year.

The Preschool Early Literacy Indicators (PELI)

Another tool that can be administered at the beginning of the school year as a screening tool and repeated as a midyear and end-of-year screening assessment is the Preschool Early Literacy Indicators (PELI). The PELI is an assessment tool designed to evaluate essential pre-literacy and oral language skills in children aged 3 to 5. The key skills measured by the PELI include alphabet knowledge, vocabulary, and oral language, similar to the PALS Pre-K. Additionally, it measures vocabulary and oral language as well as listening comprehension, which are also critical for preparing young children for success as they enter kindergarten.

Research and development on the PELI have spanned over a decade, and its reliability and validity have been thoroughly documented, confirming that it serves as an effective measure for early literacy skills in preschoolers. The PELI is embedded in a storybook format and aims to assist teachers in targeting specific instructional support, identifying curriculum needs within early childhood programs, monitoring students receiving additional instruction, and evaluating program effectiveness.

The assessment takes approximately 15 minutes to administer and is conducted three times throughout the school year. Each administration uses different storybooks tailored to the child's age (3–4 years or 4–5 years). These storybooks form the basis of the test, integrating tasks that assess various literacy and oral language skills.

PELI's assessment framework includes the following components:

1. Alphabet Knowledge: Children are shown a page with all 26 letters in random order and asked to name as many as they can. This subtest evaluates their familiarity with the alphabet, an essential pre-literacy skill.
2. Vocabulary and Oral Language: This task includes two expressive language components: Picture Naming and Tell About. In Picture Naming, the child is asked to name 10 pictures, ranging from commonly known items to those less familiar. In Tell About, the child describes five selected pictures, assessing vocabulary depth and oral language use.
3. Comprehension: Comprehension is evaluated through two tasks. In the first, Comprehension Questions, the assessor reads a short story and asks questions about it, focusing on literal comprehension, prediction, and inference. The second task is Shared Retell, where the assessor retells the story, leaving blanks for the child to fill in, assessing the child's memory and comprehension of the narrative.
4. Phonological Awareness: This skill is assessed through a game in which children are shown pictures and asked to identify the first part or first sound of a word. This task helps gauge the child's ability to recognize and manipulate sounds in spoken language, which is vital for later reading success.

The assessment provides benchmark goals for the beginning, middle, and end of the school year, adjusted for different age groups (3–4 years and 4–5 years). These benchmarks are based on research linking early literacy skills to later reading success, helping educators understand whether a child's skills are on track for kindergarten.

PELI generates two key scores for each child:

1. PELI Composite Score: This is a combination of all the subtest scores and provides a comprehensive view of a child's early literacy abilities.
2. PELI Language Index: This combines scores from the Vocabulary and Oral Language and Comprehension subtests, offering an overall measure of a child's language skills.

Teachers can interpret a child's progress by comparing their scores to these benchmarks. Children scoring above the benchmark are likely to continue developing their literacy skills with standard instruction, while children near or below the benchmark may require additional support to ensure their readiness for kindergarten.

In summary, PELI offers a research-based, reliable tool for assessing pre-literacy and oral language development in preschool-aged children as young as 3 years of age. Modifications should not be made to this assessment, as that would skew the benchmark norms provided. Standardization allows data provided by this assessment to be used in comparison to other school settings. By providing educators with actionable data, PELI helps ensure that children receive the early support they need to succeed in their literacy development, paving the way for future academic success (Acadience Reading Pre-K: PELI, 2020).

SCREENING ASSESSMENTS—ELEMENTARY

Similar to assessment practices in early childhood education, screening assessments used in elementary schools are scheduled one to three times a year (usually the beginning, middle, and end of the year) and provide a host of information about students' learning and development. Screening assessments are administered to all students in a class, grade, or school, to determine which students are meeting grade-level expectations in reading and mathematics when compared to a nationally normed recommendation. Perhaps most importantly, especially when considering the needs of children who are not yet meeting literacy benchmarks, results from these tools also guide teachers to recognize which students need additional diagnostic assessments to determine skill areas that require additional support.

At the beginning of the school year, all students are assessed using a nationally normed screening measure. The screener provides the general information regarding whether a child is meeting grade-level expectations, whether they are at, above, or below grade level. A teacher never looks at a single measure as the only piece of data when determining if grade-level expectations are being met. A screener specifies cut scores that determine if a student is above or below grade level, and these expectations tend to err on the side of caution by setting the bar high. Because of this, more students may be identified as needing reading support than actually require instructional intervention. The cut scores necessitate that teachers take a more detailed look at students who did not meet the benchmark. Through additional measures, they determine more precisely whether the child does indeed have a gap in reading skills. In this way, no student should slip through the screening process without receiving needed support.

Two reading screeners commonly used in elementary classrooms are Dynamic Indicators of Basic Early Literacy Skills (DIBELS) and Acadience Reading. These two assessments are freely available online (see Appendix B, available as a PDF online under the Download tab at https://www.tc

press.com/effective-literacy-assessment-in-the-montessori-classroom-9780807786703) and are considered highly valid and reliable. (The NCII Screening Assessment Tools Chart may be accessed online at https://intensiveintervention.org/resource/academic-screening-tools-chart.) It should be noted that both of these assessments include a series of 1-minute assessments that isolate reading skills and provide a snapshot of children's phonological awareness, phonics, fluency, and comprehension skills. While the assessments are given individually, the 1-minute duration of the assessments makes them easily layered into classroom instruction and does not cause a student to be removed from meaningful learning time for extended periods. While the composite scores of these screeners yield an overall ranking of on grade level or not, the individual 1-minute subtests can be analyzed for a deeper understanding of student strengths and weaknesses. Each subtest is discussed in the section "Diagnostic Assessments" later in this chapter and described in Table 4.3.

In older grades (typically 3rd grade and up) screeners may be self-directed by students and completed online. For example, the Star Reading assessment is an online reading test. Originally introduced as the STAR assessment, this test has been rebranded as Star Reading. For this assessment, students log into Star Reading on their computers to read passages and answer multiple-choice comprehension questions. Star Reading provides information on students' literacy skills related to their understanding and analysis of connected text.

Screening assessments include a chart showing the range of possible scores a student may receive. This chart is provided in the assessment materials of valid and reliable screening tests. This chart enables teachers to quickly determine if a student's overall (composite) score is on or above benchmark, below benchmark, or significantly below benchmark. When a student scores below the benchmark on a screening assessment, it signals the teacher to further delve into why the student didn't perform successfully. Teachers do this by administering detailed diagnostic assessments to determine if a student has skill deficiencies that need to be addressed.

Figure 4.3 reviews the initial steps in your comprehensive assessment system. Step 1 requires the selection of a universal literacy screening tool. Because of recent reading legislation described in Chapter 1, it will be important to first review any recommendations made by your state's department of education. In Figure 4.3, universal screeners designated by the Georgia Department of Education (n.d.) are provided. Many of the screeners listed are used in many states. Georgia has also chosen to include their own state-developed screener on this list.

After analysis of data from your screening results, Step 2 is broken down into two pathways. For those students who score at or above grade-level expectations (Step 2a), teachers will continue with Tier 1 instruction—the high-quality language and literacy curriculum found in Montessori classrooms. In Step 2b, the teacher targets specific skills on which the student needs to work either in small groups or individually instructed by the teacher.

Figure 4.3. Beginning of Year (BOY) Screening Process

STEP 1: Select one (state-approved) reading screener to administer to all students within the first 30 days of school.

Step 1: Beginning of Year (BOY)

Universal Screener

*The following are examples of universal screeners. Also, the Georgia Department of Education is designing a free universal screener due August 2024.

- Acadience Reading (K–6)
- ISIP (iStations Indicators of Progress Reading) Reading with RAN (Rapid Automized Naming) and ORF
- mCLASS
- iSTEEP
- Classworks Reading Universal Screener
- MAP Reading Fluency
- aimswebPlus
- Exact Path Diagnostic Assessment
- Predictive Assessment of Reading (PAR)
- FastBridge
- i-Ready Assessment for Reading
- Star Assessments

Step 2a: If student scores **on or above benchmark**, continue with Tier 1 English Language Arts (ELA) instruction. In a Montessori classroom, Tier 1 instruction includes all lessons and materials that support children's language and literacy development, including those located in the Language, Sensorial, and Cultural areas. (See Zoll et al., 2023, p. 107.) Additional ELA curriculum may be required by your state.

Step 2b: If a student scores **below benchmark**, the teacher must intentionally plan to address specific lessons to support learning in this area. For example, if a student scores below benchmark on initial sounds (phonological awareness), the Montessori teacher may invite the student to work with Phonetic Object Box #1 or the Movable Alphabet. These lessons allow students to hear and manipulate sounds within phonetic words.

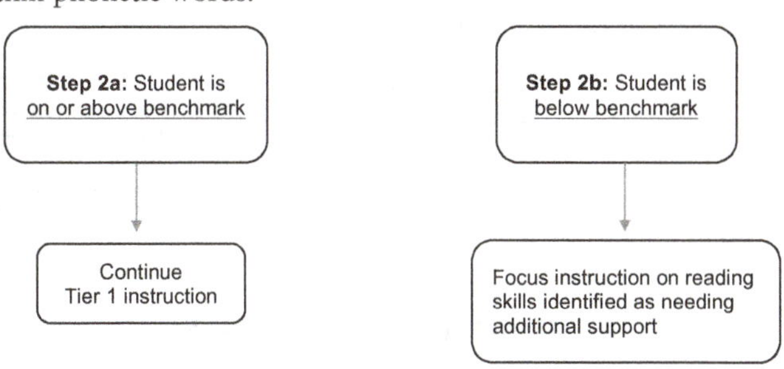

Step 3: The teacher will continue to monitor those students who scored below benchmark, and within 30 days of obtaining screening results an instructional plan will be put in place. The instructional plan can include tiered instruction that outlines differentiated learning opportunities. For example, all students receive

(*continued*)

Figure 4.3. (*continued*)

Tier 1 instruction (Montessori curriculum—and, if mandated by your state, supplemental ELA curriculum). Tier 2 instructional opportunities also include the Montessori curriculum, as well as small-group lessons that focus on needed areas of literacy for those students who scored slightly below benchmark. While Tier 3 instruction is reserved for those students who score significantly lower than benchmark, students assigned to this tier of instruction receive Tier 1 (Montessori curriculum) and Tier 2 (small-group needed literacy skills), as well as Tier 3 individual lessons. This plan can follow your school's RtI or MTSS framework.

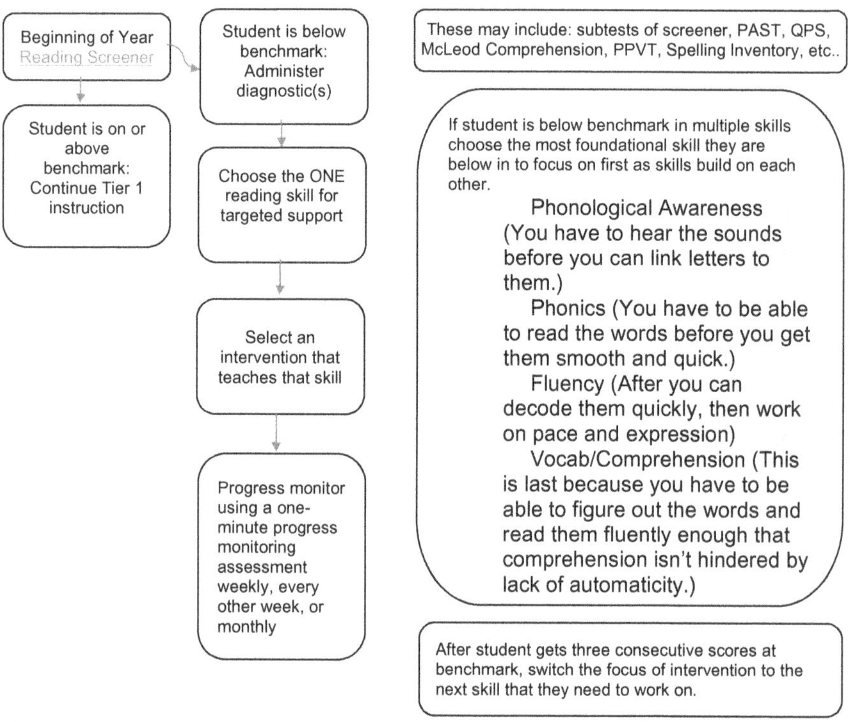

DIAGNOSTIC ASSESSMENTS

Diagnostic assessments provide teachers and programs with critical information about what children know and are able to do, along with their areas of weakness (Bennett, 2011; Black & William, 1998; Harlen & James, 1997). As such, diagnostic assessments can help teachers and programs with lesson planning and pinpointing areas in which children have gained mastery and areas in which they need more support. In a typical traditional classroom, screeners are given to everyone, and diagnostic assessments are just given to those who were below the benchmark on the screener. Decisions to administer diagnostics "are based on developmental benchmarks, prior knowledge of each student's literacy development, and an analysis of each assessment after it is administered" (McAndrews, 2020, p. 17). The diagnostic assessment helps determine exactly which reading skill is weak. Just as you would go to a doctor to determine the cause of an illness, to be *diagnosed*, the teacher must next give specific *diagnostic assessments* to determine what skills need additional instruction.

If students have met the benchmark on the reading screener, the teacher will continue to monitor their progress within the core curriculum. Then, come midyear, the entire class will be screened again.

Many times, the screening assessments can be examined more completely to gain diagnostic information. For example, both DIBELS and Acadience have a series of subtests that work together to give a general composite score. The composite score is used as a screener to determine whether or not the student has met the general benchmark. Further, the teacher can look at the individual subtests to diagnose which areas were below benchmark.

Subtests in a general reading screener usually address the five areas of reading instruction in the report from the National Reading Panel (NICHHD, 2000). This report identified phonological awareness, phonics, fluency, vocabulary, and comprehension as crucial components of reading. For the DIBELS and Acadience assessments, subtests such as First Sound Fluency (FSF) and Phonemic Segmentation Fluency (PSF) test the ability to hear and identify individual speech sounds. Nonsense Word Fluency (NWF), the Correct Letter Sounds subtest, and the Whole Words Read subtest determine whether a student can apply basic phonics rules to make-believe words. This prevents students from reciting a memorized word, and it shows that they can apply the phonics rule to an unknown word. The Oral Reading Fluency (ORF) subtest has students read a grade-level passage aloud. Both accuracy (the percentage of words read correctly) and fluency (the number of correct words read in 1 minute) are measured in this task. Finally, the MAZE subtest (only for DIBELS Grades 3 and up and Acadience Grades 2 and up) addresses vocabulary and comprehension. Considered individually, each of these subtests is actually a diagnostic test. They identify which foundational skills the students struggle with. The composite score gives an overall placement regarding whether or not the child met the benchmark. The subtests break that down into individual areas in which a student can be at or below benchmark.

Additional diagnostic tests add to the student's reading profile. The Phonological Awareness Screening Test (PAST) can be administered one-on-one and is available at no cost (see Appendix B, available as a PDF online under the Download tab at https://www.tcpress.com/effective-literacy-assessment-in-the-montessori-classroom-9780807786703). In this test, students work with

Table 4.2. Subtests From Reading Screener

Subtests From Reading Screener	
LNF/LSF Letter Naming Fluency Letter Sound Fluency	Student says letter names (capitals and lowercase)—1 minute. Student says letter sounds (capitals and lowercase)—1 minute.
FSF First Sound Fluency	Teacher says word, student says the beginning sound—1 minute. e.g., "sun" /s/
PSF Phoneme Segmentation Fluency	Teacher says word, student segments into separate sounds—1 minute. e.g., "cat" /c/ /a/ /t/
NWF (CLS) Nonsense Word Fluency (Correct Letter Sounds)	Student is given a list of nonsense words. Short words can be memorized by sight, and we want to know if the student understands and applies phonics skills, so nonsense words are used—1 minute. e.g., mip Student says /m/ /i/ /p/ or the whole word /mip/ and scores three points for the three sounds.
NWF (WWR) Nonsense Word Fluency (Whole Words Read)	This score is obtained from the test above. This score is how many nonsense words the student reads as a whole word the first try. e.g., mip Student says /mip/. Scored as one whole word read.
ORF (ACC) Oral Reading Fluency (Accuracy)	Student reads connected text for 1 minute. This score is the percentage of words they read correctly. Total words read correctly (divided by) total words read (times) 100. This tests accuracy, whether the student can correctly decode the words. They might do so slowly, but do they get the right answer?
ORF (WPM) Oral Reading Fluency (Words Per Minute = Fluency)	This score is obtained from the test above. The number of correct words read in 1 minute. This shows if decoding has reached an automatic level and if the student reads with prosody.
ORF (Retell)	Student tells what they remember of the story they read above—1 minute. Provides a sense of student's comprehension.
MAZE/DAZE	Student completes a story that has numerous words left out. For each blank, there are three choices. They circle the correct answer—3 minutes. Measures comprehension/vocabulary.

individual speech sounds (phonemes) to add, delete, and substitute phonemes in the context of words.

Phonics diagnostics point the teacher to the phonics skills that have been mastered and which ones still need to be mastered. The Quick Phonics Screener (QPS) does this nicely, as do many other phonics diagnostics.

It should be noted that the National Center on Intensive Intervention includes anecdotal information and observations under the umbrella of diagnostic assessment (American Institutes for Research, n.d.). In this book, we are generally referring to more formal diagnostic measures, while acknowledging that observational data contribute to the teacher's understanding of their students. Formalizing observational data collection in some type of protocol may be helpful.

The triangulation of data is a method of research for determining whether data are valid. If a teacher takes a child's screening data, diagnostic data, and observation data and analyzes the information, the data should reflect the same results across assessment type, proving that the conclusions being drawn are true. Substantiating that those data are valid is important. We all know that everyone can have an off day, and assessment results may not accurately represent what it is children know and are able to do. By reviewing outcomes from multiple sources, the teacher is cross-checking the results. One Georgia Montessori teacher reported that her observations, cross-checked with the diagnostics the LETRS phonics and word reading surveys and the PAST assessment, help "determine groups for literature/phonics work and determine interventions" (K. Bordeaux, Elementary 1, GA, personal correspondence, August 31, 2024).

It is worth noting that whether you are a Montessori teacher seeking to prove that your observations are correct or a public school teacher seeking to prove that your screening assessment is correct, triangulation of data will meet your goal, and using multiple data points to approach the same entity is empowering irrespective of pedagogy.

AMS 2023 School Accreditation Standards support the use of formal data collection through an assessment system in Standard 4: "The quality Montessori school enacts an ongoing assessment system that monitors and documents learner outcomes that are based in equitable practices and uses these results to improve educational effectiveness." In criterion 4.2, the use of both observation (qualitative) and other quantitative assessments is required.

Appendix B (available as a PDF online under the Download tab at https://www.tcpress.com/effective-literacy-assessment-in-the-montessori-classroom-9780807786703) contains a chart with a sampling of screening and diagnostic assessment options. It notes the type of assessment (screener, diagnostic, or progress monitoring), whether the assessment is currently available at no charge, and how the assessment can be accessed.

USING FORMAL ASSESSMENT IN THE MONTESSORI SETTING

Teachers everywhere are grappling with the best way to teach reading, determining how they can use the vast knowledge we have gained through the science of reading. The classroom settings are varied. Some teachers are situated in public schools and are responding to their state's reading legislation and high-quality curriculum initiatives. Some are in public Montessori schools. These individuals are seeking to find the balance between the Montessori pedagogy and state requirements. Other teachers working in private and independent Montessori schools are searching for ways they can better their reading instruction. All are working diligently to meet the needs of their students to ensure their reading success. In the following section, we show how the beginning-of-year assessment could look in a classroom that has not emphasized this aspect of instruction in the past. There are three action steps for change that teachers should consider when transitioning to BOY assessment practices:

1. Utilize a reading screener.
2. Formalize protocol for observational data.
3. Implement at least one diagnostic assessment for a small number of students.

Action Step #1: Utilize a Reading Screener

If you are already in a public school setting, there is a good chance this is a requirement for your classroom, most likely at the beginning, middle, and end of the school year. If you are not, we strongly suggest you administer a screener at least once in the school year. If you are not provided with a specific screening instrument that you must use, the aforementioned DIBELS and Acadience are readily available, free, and easy to administer (see Appendix B [available as a PDF online under the Download tab at https://www.tcpress.com/effective-literacy-assessment-in-the-montessori-classroom-9780807786703] for links to these tools). The 1-minute length of each subtest allows you to meet with a child quickly and send the student back to their learning.

The amount of information received from these brief sessions is significant and relevant, enabling teachers to individualize instruction and providing school administrators with information to make data-informed personnel and curriculum adjustments needed to ensure successful instructional interventions. Assessment results provide a snapshot of students' literacy skills, highlighting strengths and areas that need additional support. Data analysis will include disaggregating the data to review results of each subtest separately. These data will help with the identification of which Montessori activities will best help each student move forward. In our last book, *Powerful Literacy in the Montessori Classroom,* we included a chart that matched Montessori materials to specific literacy skills that are tested by the subtests. This chart is available in Appendix A (available as a PDF online under the Download tab at https://www.tcpress.com/effective-literacy-assessment-in-the-montessori-classroom-9780807786703).

Action Step #2: Formalize Protocol for Observational Data (Turn Your Qualitative Observations Into Quantitative Data)

Observation as an assessment tool remains a valuable data source. As you seek to strengthen your classroom assessment protocols, begin the year by implementing a formalized procedure to record and report on your student observations. If you already do this, kudos to you! If not, keep in mind that it is our desire to show those outside the Montessori world that Montessori pedagogy is successful. Take your observations to the next level by making the qualitative data more quantitative. There are numerous methods for doing this. It is possible, for example, to choose a teacher-generated tally sheet of literacy skills where the teacher simply checks off and dates when that skill has been observed.

Action Step #3: Implement at Least One Diagnostic Reading Assessment

Diagnostic reading assessments truly allow the educator to see students' strengths and weaknesses. Over time, teachers can build up a repertoire of diagnostic assessments that they use with individual students as they seek to gain a deeper knowledge about students' literacy needs. One diagnostic assessment that is particularly fitting to the Montessori pedagogy is the Peabody Picture Vocabulary Test (PPVT). The PPVT tests students' receptive vocabulary knowledge. Vocabulary knowledge is indicative of future reading success and also is correlated to students' prior background knowledge and literacy knowledge. Vocabulary, background knowledge, and literacy knowledge are all key elements of strong literacy instruction. Knowing more about a student's understanding in these areas will enable the teacher to build stronger literacy experiences for them.

CONCLUSION

It is clear that from the very start of her career, Dr. Montessori recognized that to meet children's unique interests and developmental needs, assessment and observations in early childhood were necessary. Indeed, in the decades since its inception, the Montessori philosophy has been well recognized for its grounding in scientific observation. And even with the differences in educational philosophies across educational programs, Montessori educators—like all educators—need to be aware of students' individual needs, beyond what can be observed, so as to know when to step in for guidance and when best to challenge their students. Accordingly, we discussed how the implementation of classroom assessments (e.g., PALS and the PPVT) and observational tools (e.g., the CLASS) are not only grounded in the writings of Dr. Montessori and aligned with Montessori standards, but also can be readily used in combination with current practices to assist Montessori educators in effectively guiding children so that children reap the maximum benefit from their classroom experiences. By implementing these tools, Montessori educators will have a common language across classrooms and programs about student achievement and their classroom experiences.

CHAPTER 5

Schedule/Logistics

MONTESSORI SCHEDULES

The 2-hour uninterrupted work period is essential to the Montessori schedule. This 2-to-3-hour block of time should be protected from outside interruptions such as itinerants, enrichment classes, or large-group instruction. According to the AMS accreditation 2023 guidelines, infants and toddlers should have access to a 2-hour work cycle on a daily basis. For early childhood and elementary levels, a 3-hour work cycle, 5 days a week, is "optimal" and a 2-hour work cycle, 4 days a week, is a minimum requirement.

The accreditation information continues to encourage independence in learning, while recognizing the place for explicit instruction. Standard 3.24 states that the Montessori teacher "provides for a balance of uninterrupted, self-directed, self-teaching, and collaborative activities with the presentation of individual, small-, and large-group lessons."

WORK PLANS

Montessori work plans are tools that support the development of executive function and self-directed learning skills. These plans serve as personalized schedules that help students outline the activities they intend to work on over a specific period, whether it be daily or weekly. By incorporating work plans into their routine, students gain experience in setting goals, managing time, and organizing their tasks. This structured yet flexible approach encourages them to take an active role in their own learning, fostering independence, responsibility, and intrinsic motivation.

Work plans are not typically used in the earliest stages of a Montessori education. However, in the kindergarten year, work plans are sometimes used to provide a basic framework for children to choose activities and materials in their classroom environment. As students grow and advance to elementary and middle school levels, work plans become more sophisticated, evolving to meet their developmental needs. They are introduced to more complex planning processes and begin setting personal academic goals with their teachers' guidance. Through regular consultations, students learn to balance their workload and prioritize tasks, becoming increasingly independent in managing their educational journey.

Work plans are not, however, universally applied in Montessori classrooms. For some Montessori educators, there is controversy as to "how to balance this structured plan with the spontaneity of student-chosen subjects" (Oesting, 2022)—though work plans do offer students authentic planning opportunities. Oesting (2022) describes one effective approach applied in an upper elementary Montessori classroom, where the teacher (guide) re-created a student planner on the whiteboard:

> Every week, the guide would schedule all the lessons they planned to give that week, and any class business such as class meetings or events and the students would in turn copy them down on their weekly plan. Additionally, on the "To Do" section of the planner, the guide would list consistent student-driven materials that students were expected (to complete) such as word study, math fact practice, and writing prompts. Another column was provided for students to track what they accomplished. For some, there was a place to enter the time they began and completed the task. Rather than just tick off what they did, there was a place for the student to record their work and use for feedback or reflection during a one-on-one conference/meeting/chat with the student. The plan for the next week can then be dynamically built off of this work record.

The use of work plans also nurtures self-assessment and reflection. With varying degrees of teacher support, students regularly review their progress, identify areas for improvement, and adjust their work plans accordingly. This reflective practice helps students develop a growth mindset and resilience when facing challenges. Over time, they gain the confidence and skills necessary to handle more demanding academic environments, making them well prepared for future academic work.

TRADITIONAL SCHEDULES

Research compiled in the report from the National Reading Panel (NICHHD, 2000) made evident that successful readers require a daily minimum of 90 minutes of reading instruction. That 90 minutes is considered "Core" or "Tier 1" instruction. This is the reading instruction to which *all* students must have access. It is to be systematic and explicit in nature. The 90 minutes can incorporate large-group, small-group, and individual learning experiences. Most typically in public schools, a large portion of this is used for whole-group instruction, followed by differentiated guided practice. In the early childhood and elementary settings, this core instruction hits upon the five main areas of reading: phonological awareness, phonics, fluency, vocabulary, and comprehension. Instruction in foundational skills, engaging with complex texts, and writing are woven into this schedule.

Many states currently have legislation that requires that high-quality instructional materials (HQIM) be used for Tier 1 instruction. The Reading League (n.d.) has published a tool, Compass, that can be used to determine if a curriculum is based on the Science of Reading. This tool will be discussed at length in Chapter 6.

Current research supports a 90-minute Tier 1 (core instruction) time dedicated daily to reading instruction. Any intervention time is in addition to the 90 minutes of core Tier 1 instruction. In public school settings, many times schoolwide schedules are created. Teachers have choices to make within the larger schedule, but the 90 minutes of Tier 1 core instruction are required for all their students. Best practice recommends no students receive other services such as speech, special education, reading, or occupational therapy during this Tier 1 instructional block of time.

MELDING A MONTESSORI CLASSROOM WITH OUTSIDE SCHEDULING REQUIREMENTS

There are fundamental differences in instructional approaches that must be considered when discussing literacy instruction in Montessori and conventional elementary classrooms. For Montessorians, these differences can seem like fitting a round peg into a square hole. For example, there can be great variation between each approach in how instructional time is scheduled or the degree to which there is student agency and choice in learning.

One hallmark of a Montessori classroom is the 3-year age span of its students. Children between the ages of 3 and 6 years of age are enrolled in primary classrooms. And children from 6 to 9 years of age and 9 to 12 years of age are enrolled in lower and upper elementary classrooms, respectively. Where instruction in conventional classrooms is frequently delivered to the whole class simultaneously, Montessori educators are trained to deliver lessons in small groups or with individual students. Activities that support students' reading skills are differentiated and individualized based on ability, with small-group instruction used to share introductory lessons with a particular group of students.

Though some public school classrooms offer 2-year "looping" cycles, most classrooms are identified by a single age group (e.g., kindergarten, 1st grade). High-quality commercial curricula are designed to support developmental expectations for a particular age group identified by grade-level standards, Common Core State Standards, or Early Learning and Development Standards.

Current trends in ELA instruction point to delivering solid Tier 1 curriculum aligned to reading research as a way to abate the number of children who do not yet meet grade-level ELA benchmarks. Tiered instruction refers to a 3-Tiered model, where each tier reflects certain criteria (Gersten et al., 2008, p. 5).

These fundamental instructional approaches greatly influence teaching and learning. The following sections provide a view of how instructional time focused on literacy development is scheduled in both Montessori and public school classrooms. Special attention is warranted for publicly funded Montessori schools situated in states impacted by recent reading legislation, especially those mandating that the selection of a commercially produced ELA curriculum be implemented with fidelity, in addition to the Montessori curriculum.

ELA INSTRUCTION IN PUBLIC SCHOOLS

With more attention given to improving children's reading scores in the United States (National Assessment of Educational Progress, NAEP, 2023), there is uniformity in instructional scheduling with "most U.S. schools allot[ting] between 90–120 minutes for reading instruction across grades K-5" (Reading Rockets, 2024a). But how these scheduled time blocks are parsed out for specific literacy instruction will vary based on the design and requirements of individual commercial ELA curricula. ELA curricula must be evidence-based and include dedicated time to each of the main areas of language and literacy development—phonological awareness, phonics, fluency, vocabulary, and comprehension—as well as writing skills. During this 90–120-minute time block, teachers will dedicate some time to review previous content, as well as present new ELA content primarily delivered through whole-group instruction. Depending on the curriculum, additional learning may take place in small groups or in individual lessons.

Table 5.1 provides an example of Tier 1 ELA instructional patterns across K–5 classrooms, noting time dedicated to whole-group and small-group reading instruction. This is considered all Tier 1 instruction, even the small-group time. Many public school systems have encouraged teachers to devote small-group or one-on-one time to all students, not just those who need help. So when it is part of the 90–120 minutes, the teacher is offering a small-group option to all. Table 5.2 gives an example of an ELA schedule at an early childhood (K–1) grade level.

The example schedule in Table 5.3 is one way that traditional classroom teachers may divide their 90-minute block of literacy instruction. The first 45 minutes is dedicated to a whole-group lesson. Frequently this is around a shared reading of grade-level text with a focus on language comprehension skills such as vocabulary, comprehension, background knowledge, and verbal reasoning. The second 45 minutes is used for small focus groups

Table 5.1. ELA Instructional Block (90–120 minutes) Grades K–5, Adapted From Reading Rockets, 2024c

ELA Block (90–120 minutes)—Reading Instruction Grades K–5			
	Grades K–1	Grades 2–3	Grades 4–5
Whole-Group Reading	15–20 minutes	10–15 minutes	10–15 minutes
Small-Group/Partner Reading	30 minutes	30–40 minutes	30–40 minutes
Whole-Group Writing	15–20 minutes	10–15 minutes	10–15 minutes
Small-Group/Partner Writing	15–20 minutes	20–30 minutes	20–30 minutes
Total	**120 minutes**	**90–120 minutes**	**90–12 minutes**

Table 5.2. Example of a Kindergarten or 1st-Grade Whole-Group ELA Schedule, Adapted From Reading Rockets, 2024c

Sample Kindergarten/1st-Grade Tier 1 ELA Schedule		
Literacy Topic	Instructional Time (estimated)	Possible Activities
Oral Language Concepts of Print	10–12 minutes	Shared reading of big book or projected text; echo or choral reading or shared texts
Phonological Awareness	5–10 minutes	Select one area of phonological awareness to work on with students; daily use of systematic curriculum (example: blending and segmenting 2-, 3-, and 4-letter phonetic words)
Alphabet Knowledge Phonics	10–12 minutes	Daily cumulative review (1–2 minutes) Read or write letter-sound targets
Oral Language Vocabulary Reading Comprehension	15–20 minutes	Teacher read-alouds (dialogic reading); introduce and practice target vocabulary
Writing Instruction	15–20 minutes	Daily handwriting Dictated words or sentences Sentence construction exercises
Total Daily Whole-Group Time	**30–40 minutes**	Total time

Table 5.3. Example of an ELA Schedule, Adapted From Reading Rockets, 2024b

Instruction	Time	Class Configuration				Notes
Tier 1/Core Reading Instruction	45 minutes	Whole Group				
Small groups	45 minutes 15 min. each	M	Intervention	Skill Group	Skill Group	Chart to the left shows the teacher-led station. While the teacher meets with these groups, the other students may be working on independent practice and activities.
		T	Skill Group	Intervention	Skill Group	
		W	Skill Group	Skill Group	Intervention	
		Th	Intervention	Skill Group	Skill Group	
		F	Intervention	Skill Group	Skill Group	

continuing the Tier 1 (Core) instruction. These groups rotate through to see the teacher. When not with the teacher, the students have independent activities they are completing. No child misses any of the core instruction to have a targeted intervention. All students are given the opportunity to meet with the teacher whether or not they are on grade level. Students on or above grade level are given small-group instruction in an area that grows them in their literacy learning.

In the next sample public school schedule (Table 5.4), the classroom teacher realized that they needed additional intervention time for a small group of students. The shaded areas show where that teacher could add in more literacy intervention time without subtracting from the students' Tier 1, Core, instruction.

In the traditional classroom, schedules are frequently schoolwide. Often, the administration assigns specific times for literacy instruction so that teachers can have flexible groups between classrooms.

MONTESSORI CLASSROOMS MELDING COMMERCIAL ELA CURRICULUM

As you read the previous section, you might have begun to wonder, "So how do we make this work?" For a public Montessori classroom, there will have to be some elements of compromise as teachers meet requirements that private Montessori classrooms do not have. Part of being a public Montessori school means that there must be adaptations to the Montessori framework. As Shonkoff (2024) observes, teachers are adapters. Public Montessori

Table 5.4. Example of an ELA Schedule With Added Intervention Times, Adapted From Reading Rockets, 2024b.

Instruction	Time	Class Configuration				Notes
Intervention	20 minutes	Class is having breakfast, making lunch choices, doing independent practice. Intervention group meets.*				Having a routine for class entry at the beginning of the day makes this possible.
Core Reading Instruction	45 minutes	Whole Group				
Small groups during workshop model	45 minutes 15 min. each	M	Intervention	Skill Group	Skill Group	Chart to the left shows the teacher-led station. While the teacher meets with these groups, the other students are working on independent practice and activities. An additional small group could be added with a paraprofessional, grandparent, or community volunteer to review intervention.*
		T	Skill Group	Intervention	Skill Group	
		W	Skill Group	Skill Group	Intervention	
		Th	Intervention	Skill Group	Skill Group	
		F	Intervention	Skill Group	Skill Group	
Intervention	15 minutes	Whole Class: Silent reading or independent activities upon return from lunch. Intervention group meets*				
Intervention	15 minutes	Whole Class: Buses are called. Intervention group meets.*				

*Potential daily intervention times are designated with an asterisk. One would be selected. The teacher, classroom aid, or foster grandparent could deliver the added intervention.

teachers must be adapters to the highest degree. These teachers also have the opportunity to bring Montessori education to a population of students who otherwise would not have access to this type of instruction. When many people think of Montessori education, they think of the rich, white elite paying top dollar for their children to engage in this nurturing, individualized learning experience filled with beautiful materials. Dr. Montessori wanted this type of education for all children. Dr. Montessori actually dedicated much of her work to supporting children living in poverty. She believed that every child, regardless of their background, had the potential to learn and thrive when given the right environment. In 1907, she opened her first Casa dei Bambini (Children's House) in a poor district of Rome, where she implemented her revolutionary educational approach.

By offering a nurturing environment, hands-on materials, and freedom within limits, she helped children develop self-discipline, concentration, and a love of learning. Even children who were previously considered disadvantaged or unable to learn began to excel. Many of these children surpassed expectations, not only mastering basic skills but also exceeding the performance of their more affluent peers in traditional settings. Montessori's work showed that children's abilities were not limited by their circumstances but rather shaped by the opportunities they were given. Her success with children from impoverished backgrounds highlighted the power of education to transform lives, advocating that high-quality education should be accessible to all, regardless of socioeconomic status.

Let's look more carefully at the flexibility within the Montessori curriculum. According to the AMS accreditation report (2023), "A 3-hour uninterrupted work cycle, 5 days per week is optimal. The school allocates and protects, at minimum, a 2-hour work cycle, 4 days per week." Right there, teachers have some flexibility, and they will probably need to adapt the work cycle within this given range. The guidelines go on to say, "Enrichment programs, recess, transition times, group snack, and full-class lessons are not part of the uninterrupted block of student work time." While classwide instruction is not a part of the work cycle, the differentiated and flexible practice time of many high-quality instructional materials could be worked into this work period. If you are situated in a public school setting, there is a strong likelihood that you are mandated by your district or state department of education to fit the 90-minute ELA requirement into your schedule. Some possibilities to address this challenge might include working within the AMS accreditation standards by offering the minimum 2-hour Montessori work period and then using the additional hour to implement other ELA requirements. Or, as the AMS guidelines say, the work cycle may be completed four times a week; this could be a place where the public school requirements are adaptive and allow you to have one day a week for additional ELA time. Qualitative results from the survey previously discussed also provided insight as to how teachers were managing these competing elements of literacy instruction time. The following is a sample of those responses:

- "Everything is still done in small groups or individual lessons. I'm not yet required to implement the other curricular materials with fidelity so that I can use whatever works within our Montessori environment."

- "For me, the other ELA curriculum is embedded in my language lessons as an extension to work being done or as follow-up work."
- "In my classroom we do Orton-Gillingham in the afternoon and Montessori in the morning."
- "We use the ELA curriculum as an intervention tool to give struggling students more systematic practice . . . it's given me more resources to meet my students' needs."

Teachers should be applauded for their resourcefulness in meeting Montessori pedagogical tenets, as well as district and state science of reading mandates, in an effort to meet the needs of all students. There are multiple approaches to meeting this challenge as it best fits your classroom context. The objective is to keep the needs of the students at the center of the decision-making.

CASE STUDY DISCUSSION AND ANALYSIS WITH ANSWER KEY (BOY)

Case Study—Early Childhood

As described previously, a case study provides an opportunity to explore ways to manage challenges. For the early childhood case studies, we'll follow a single teacher over the course of an academic year to better understand how assessments and their results are used to improve student outcomes. The case study will begin with a brief overview of the classroom and language and literacy assessment tools that were implemented. Results will be shared, along with opportunities for you to interact with the data, analyze and discuss outcomes with your colleagues, and determine possible next steps in classroom instruction. Each case study will conclude with recommendations to offer the reader further support in applying these protocols in their own schools.

Scenario

Khadija, a Montessori-trained (3–6) teacher, was hired to lead a new classroom recently opened at Laurel Heights Elementary School, a Montessori charter school located in an underresourced urban community. Working in collaboration with the school's reading coach and other support staff, she has assessed all of the newly enrolled students to gather a baseline of young children's language and literacy development. Results from the Phonological Awareness Literacy Screening (PALS Pre-K) and the Peabody Picture Vocabulary Test (PPVT-IV) provided useful data to inform Khadija's teaching at the beginning of the school year.

Khadija appreciated the snapshot of her students' understanding of emergent literacy skills. She and her colleagues selected three subtests of the PALS Pre-K to review: name writing, uppercase letter recognition, and letter sound recognition (see Table 5.5). Note that PPVT results will be reviewed in the middle of year (MOY) early childhood case study.

There are two points of clarification when using the PALS Pre-K. Khadija works in a multi-age classroom (3–6-year-olds), and PALS Pre-K is meant to capture the emergent literacy learning of 4-year-old children. Knowing she wanted to have data from all her students, she opted to use the screening tool with all 18 children enrolled in her classroom. Doing so will mean that they will need to interpret any outcomes for 3-year olds and 5-year-olds differently than would be recommended. For 3-year olds, the results may simply be information about what the children already know, such as which letter sounds they can identify. However, for 5-year olds, results may indicate a more focused plan, especially if children at this age do not yet meet 4-year-old benchmarks. The second point, the PALS Pre-K protocol, requires that letter sound data only be collected if children are first able to identify 16 uppercase letters and 9 lowercase letters. She and her literacy coach decided to collect data on all subtests so that Khadija would have the most relevant data to inform her instructional time. One additional consideration for amending the protocol is specific to Montessori classrooms, as early literacy begins with letter sounds using the Sandpaper Letters rather than letter names, which are typically taught in commercial ELA curricula. In Montessori classrooms, students may be more successful with identifying letter sounds than they are recognizing letter names, but we would not know this if we followed the protocol of requiring students to recognize 16 uppercase letters and 9 lowercase letters before giving them the opportunity to identify any letter sounds. Why would this matter in literacy instruction? If we offer a child three letter names, c, a, and t, they are simply able to say the names of the letters. But if we offer the letter sounds /c/, /a/, and /t/, the child is now ready to slide those sounds together to read the word /cat/. The reading process has begun!

Below are prompts to help guide your thinking as you review the BOY screening results for three subtests of the assessment: name writing, uppercase letter recognition, and letter sound recognition. This is followed by recommendations to deepen your understanding of working with the data. All data tell a story; we just have to be willing to really look for the insight they offer about our students.

Reflections/Dialogue Prompts

- Even if you are not familiar with the screening tool, what information can you gather by analyzing data in Table 5.5:
  - » Name writing scores?

  - » Uppercase letter recognition scores?
  - » Letter sound recognition scores?
- Identify the two students who have the strongest name writing skills. Identify the one student who has the least skill in name writing.
- Identify the two students with the strongest uppercase letter recognition skills. Now look at their letter sound recognition skills—are there similar outcomes?
- For the students you identify as needing extra support, what activities will you add to your instruction in a Montessori classroom?

Fall BOY PALS Pre-K Assessment Data—Kadija's 3-6 classroom

Responses to Prompts

- Even if you've not used the PALS Pre-K in your own teaching, a quick review of scores can give you a snapshot of students' literacy skills. For example, if we look at *name writing* scores, we know the highest score is 7 and can identify that about a third of the children scored between 0 and 1 on this subtest (students a–e, g, and k). Two-thirds of the children only identified between 0–3 *uppercase letters* (students a–l) and 16 of the 18 children identified 0–3 *letter sounds* (students a–m, o, p, and r).
- Two students who have the strongest name writing skills are i and j, with a score of 6 out of a possible 7. And the student who has the least skill in name writing is g with a score of 0 out of a possible 7.
- Two students with the strongest uppercase letter recognition skills are o and q (knowing 18 and 23 uppercase letters, respectively). Now when you look at these students' letter sound recognition skills, student o knew no letter sounds (score 0 out of 26), while student q knew 13 letter sounds.
- Since PALS Pre-K was developed for use with 4-year-old children, if you are working in a multi-age classroom, you will want to consider looking at results based on age group (e.g., students a–e are 3-year-old children, while students n–r are 5-year- olds). When you are planning your instruction, you may well provide greater frequency for 5-year-old children to increase their name writing skills, while also planning for authentic name writing activities for the 3-year-olds but within the context of traditional Montessori work period rather than additional instructional interventions.

Applying Tiered Instruction to Your Data

There's another approach to analyzing data that will provide additional clarity to your assessment results. Below are the same student scores from

Table 5.5. PALS Pre-K Results From BOY Screening (3 Subtests)

Name Writing (max score 7)		Uppercase Letter Recognition (max score 26)		Letter Sound Recognition (max score 26)	
Student	Score	Student	Score	Student	Score
a	1	a	3	a	3
b	1	b	2	b	0
c	1	c	0	c	0
d	1	d	0	d	0
e	1	e	0	e	0
f	5	f	0	f	0
g	0	g	1	g	0
h	3	h	1	h	0
i	6	i	1	i	0
j	6	j	1	j	0
k	3	k	3	k	0
l	5	l	3	l	1
m	5	m	6	m	0
n	3	n	9	n	6
o	4	o	18	o	0
p	4	p	5	p	0
q	4	q	23	q	13
r	4	r	11	r	1

the three PALS Pre-K subtests, only now the scores have been highlighted to reflect which students would benefit from additional instructional time beyond the usual language materials offered during morning work time. First, Khadija and the school's literacy coach reviewed benchmarks outlined by the tool and developed their own legend to help organize the data to inform tiered classroom instruction (Table 5.6).

For example, if a child was able to recognize 6–12 letter sounds, they were assigned to Tier 2. Instruction in Tier 2 includes the Montessori language curriculum offered to all students (Tier 1) and additional small-group or individualized lessons focusing on only those letter sounds the child does not yet know.

Then they applied this code to their fall assessment results to identify which children were already meeting end-of-year benchmarks and which children could benefit from additional support; see Table 5.7.

Table 5.6. Tiered Instruction/RtI Legend

Tiered Instruction / RtI Legend			
PALS Pre-K scores have been placed in one of three tiers to identify instructional needs			
Tiers	Name Writing	Uppercase Letters	Letter Sounds
3	0–3	0–4	0–5
2	4–5	5–15	6–12
1	6–7	16–26	13–26

Table 5.7. Tiers of Instruction and PALS Pre-K Results From BOY Screening (3 Subtests)

Name Writing (max score 7)		Uppercase Letter Recognition (max score 26)		Letter Sound Recognition (max score 26)	
Student	Score	Student	Score	Student	Score
a	1	a	3	a	3
b	1	b	2	b	0
c	1	c	0	c	0
d	1	d	0	d	0
e	1	e	0	e	0
f	5	f	0	f	0
g	0	g	1	g	0
h	3	h	1	h	0
i	6	i	1	i	0
j	6	j	1	j	0
k	3	k	3	k	0
l	5	l	3	l	1
m	5	m	6	m	0
n	3	n	9	n	6
o	4	o	18	o	0
p	4	p	5	p	0
q	4	q	23	q	13
r	4	r	11	r	1

Fall BOY PALS Pre-K Assessment Data—Identifying Tiers of Instruction

As this is the beginning of the school year, and all of the children are newly enrolled in the school, it may not be surprising to see so many scores aligned to Tier 3 outcomes. You may recall that only 5% of the students are expected to fall in this range, yet it appears that almost 89% of the students are assigned to Tier 3 for Letter Recognition. Though additional diagnostics may be used to further clarify these outcomes, at the early childhood level, this type of imbalance is not a learning gap, but an *opportunity* gap. Children have not yet had the opportunity to receive lessons to increase the number of letter sounds or letter names they can identify. These data, reviewed in this way, will reinforce teachers' classroom observations and lesson recordkeeping data and further ensure that each child receives the very lessons needed to move their learning forward.

And in response to the final prompt:

- From this initial review of the data, we can see trends for the students you identify as needing extra support. Below are some possible activities you might add to your instruction in a Montessori classroom.

Montessori Activities to Support Name Writing, Uppercase Letter Recognition, and Letter Sounds

Name Writing—Independence is a key outcome for children enrolled in Montessori 3–6 classrooms. One simple task to support children's name writing skills is to simply allow them to write their names—on artwork, their metal inset tracings (Figure 5.1), or phonetically written notes about the work they completed in class that day. Each of these are authentic opportunities for children to reinforce their name writing skills and letter recognition.

Puranik and Lonigan (2012) highlight that "learning to write one's name has both a personal and social significance . . . (that it provides) children with their first opportunity to connect oral and written language . . . (and that it) may thus serve as a foundation on which to build other literacy skills" (p. 2). The outcome of their study demonstrated that children "who were most proficient name writers showed superior performance on all emergent reading-related tasks, including alphabet knowledge, phonological awareness, and print concepts" (p. 11).

Sandpaper Letters (Figures 5.2 and 5.3)—Given the importance of children's name writing on a multitude of emergent literacy skills noted above, an additional consideration is to select the letters in a child's name for introductory lessons to Sandpaper Letters. Though Montessori training programs often promote a specific sequence for their instruction and letter sounds are

Figure 5.1. Metal Insets

Photo courtesy of Nienhuis Montessori

Figure 5.2. Sandpaper Letters

Photo courtesy of Nienhuis Montessori

Figure 5.3. Cursive Sandpaper Letters

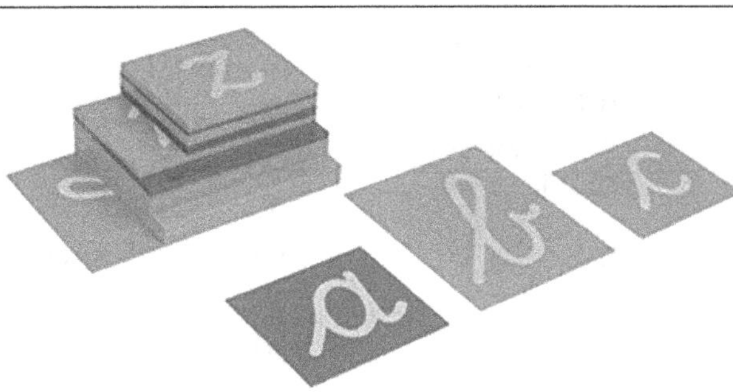

Photo courtesy of Nienhuis Montessori

Table 5.8. Elementary Case Study Assessment Information

Assessment Name	Sarah's Score 8/21	Benchmark Beginning of 2nd Grade
PAST-Phonological Awareness Screening Test	13/22 Mastery through level F	No formal norms. May be a concern if below level I
Author Notes: The student scored below level I. Therefore, phonological awareness skills may need bolstering. It is worth keeping in mind that if a student has dyslexia, this is often where their disability shows difficulty: the ability to hear the individual speech sounds. Also, sometimes students have difficulties in phonological awareness because they have not practiced these skills. Traditional public schools may use a published intervention. An intervention such as Heggerty (Heggerty.org) offers Pre-Kindergarten, Kindergarten, Primary, and Primary Extension support that can be implemented in just 10 minutes a day. Montessori activities that support phonological awareness include: I Spy Game, Phonetic Object Boxes What are your next steps?		
QPS—Quick Phonics Screener	Letter Names: 26/26 Letter Sounds: 26/26 VC & CVC: 6/10 and 18/20 Consonant Digraphs: 5/10 & 6/10 Blends: 8/10 & 9/10 Silent e: 0/10 & 2/10	Diagnostic, no formal norms Usually, by the end of 1st grade, students should have mastered through the Silent e phonics rule.
Author Notes: Student is need of support in early phonics skills such as digraphs (sh, ch, th, wh) and Silent e words (e.g. cake, rate). Traditional public schools may use a published intervention such as Vanderbilt PALS. Montessori activities that will strengthen foundational phonics skills: I Spy Game, Sandpaper Letters, Movable Alphabet, Phonetic Object Boxes What are your next steps?		
Acadience Reading Nonsense Word Fluency (NWF)	**Correct Letter Sounds (CLS):** 17 **Whole Words Read (WWR):** 1	**Correct Letter Sounds (CLS):** At Benchmark—54–71 Below Benchmark—35–53 Well Below Benchmark—0–34 **Whole Words Read (WWR):** At Benchmark—13–20 Below Benchmark—6–12 Well Below Benchmark—0–5

(continued)

Table 5.8. *(continued)*

Author Notes: While the student can sound out three letter words, linking the letter with its sound, she does so very slowly. She also does not blend the sounds automatically in her head so that she can just read the whole word without individually saying the separate sounds first. Traditional public schools may use a published intervention such as Vanderbilt PALS. Montessori activities that will strengthen foundational phonics skills (short vowels, consonant-vowel-consonant word decoding, blending): CVC word cards, Decodable Books, Phonogram Activities. What are your next steps?		
Acadience Reading Oral Reading Fluency (ORF)	Words correct: 9 64% accuracy Words correct: 9 60% accuracy Words correct: 14 74% accuracy	**Words Correct per Minute:** At Benchmark—52–67 Below Benchmark—37–51 Well Below Benchmark—0–36 **Accuracy:** At Benchmark—90%-95% Below Benchmark—81%-89% Well Below Benchmark—0%-80%
Author Notes: In all cases, first a student must be able to decode the words in the short passage they are reading, then they work to become fluent in their reading (to read at an appropriate speed with expression). This student reads very slowly, decoding only 9–14 words in a minute, and gets many of them incorrect (60–74% accuracy). She should first build phonics (decoding) skills that allow her to correctly figure out the words with 90–95% accuracy. Then, she should work on building fluency, knowing those phonics skills with a high level of automaticity so that her reading is smooth and at a comfortable pace. . . . Traditional public schools may use a published intervention such as Vanderbilt PALS or UFLI. Emphasize decodable texts and stories in reading practice times. Montessori activities that will strengthen foundational phonics skills: I Spy Game, Sandpaper Letters, Movable Alphabet, Phonetic Object Boxes. What are your next steps?		
McLeod Assessment of Reading Comprehension	0	1–4 words Grade 1 and below 5–8 words early 2nd grade

Table 5.8. (*continued*)

Author Notes: The student could not decode enough words to be able to fill in any blanks. Therefore, this cannot be used as a comprehension measure. How else can you gather data to see if the student has grade-level comprehension skills? What are your next steps?		
Spelling Inventory	29 feature points, 5 words correct	40 feature points, 11 words correct
Author Notes: Writing (encoding) abilities seem to align with reading skills. Montessori activities that support transcription (spelling, grammar, letter formation) skills: CVC word cards organized by medial (vowel) sound, Phonogram Cards and Activities, Grammar Activities		

the primary focus of this lesson, there is compelling research that should encourage Montessorians to consider two variations in the presentation. The first would be to individualize all initial Sandpaper Letter lessons to reflect the letters in the child's name. All subsequent letters could then follow the sequence recommended in training or by the Montessori school. As Sandpaper Letter lessons usually present three letters within one lesson, it may mean offering two or three lessons to successfully present the child's full name. Also worth considering would be adding the name of the letter to the presentation: "This is the letter s, it makes the sound /s/." This simple variation may extend the isolation of difficulty, but given the research and its connection to state early learning standards, it may also positively influence other areas of children's emergent literacy development.

CASE STUDY—ELEMENTARY

In the following case study, consider the role of a 2nd-grade teacher who is learning about her students at the beginning of the school year. Note which data she is reviewing to better understand one student's literacy development and to identify where additional support may be needed.

Scenario

At the end of 1st-grade, Sarah's teacher observed she was having significant reading difficulties. Sarah's teacher reported to her parents that she seemed to be the only pupil in the class struggling. Her parents immediately hired a tutor.

Sarah demonstrates a high level of social-emotional awareness. She appears very focused. When reading, she does not give up on the task. Her desire to please the teacher is evident in her work ethic.

At the beginning of 2nd grade, her teacher gave her the following set of reading assessments (Table 5.8). Sarah's scores are listed in the middle column. For comparison purposes, the beginning of 2nd grade benchmarks for each assessment are listed in the column at the right.

Part II

ALL SCHOOL YEAR LONG

Integrating Data, Progress Monitoring, and Instruction to Maximize Reading Success for All Students

While Part I highlighted key practices that must occur during the first month or so of school, Part II shares practices that are implemented as soon as initial data have been reviewed and then continue over multiple months. The title for Part II is intentional, because it is important that the reader understand that these "next steps" in the assessment cycle do not just occur at the middle of the school year. While some items will indeed occur at the midyear point in the schedule (e.g., middle-of-year screening administration), the majority of the actions recommended in this part center on the continuous implementation of iterative, skill-based, data-based decision-making.

Figure II.1 and Figure II.2 chart how you will progress after the review of your BOY results. For those students who *meet or exceed* the literacy benchmarks, they will continue their work in the Montessori classroom, demonstrating agency with the materials with continued guidance from their teacher (this is referred to as Tier 1 instruction in many state ELA requirements). For those students who meet *only some* of the literacy benchmarks, you should review results further to identify which areas of literacy will require additional support. You can plan small-group and individual lessons to support this learning. And for those students who *do not yet meet any* grade-level benchmarks, reviewed data will highlight the specific areas of literacy that need support. It will be important that your planning, particularly for these students, begin with a focus on foundational literacy skills.

A second decision tree has been developed to help you decide next steps in classroom instruction for those students who are not yet meeting

Figure II.1. Middle of Year (MOY) and Ongoing Progress Monitoring Decision Tree

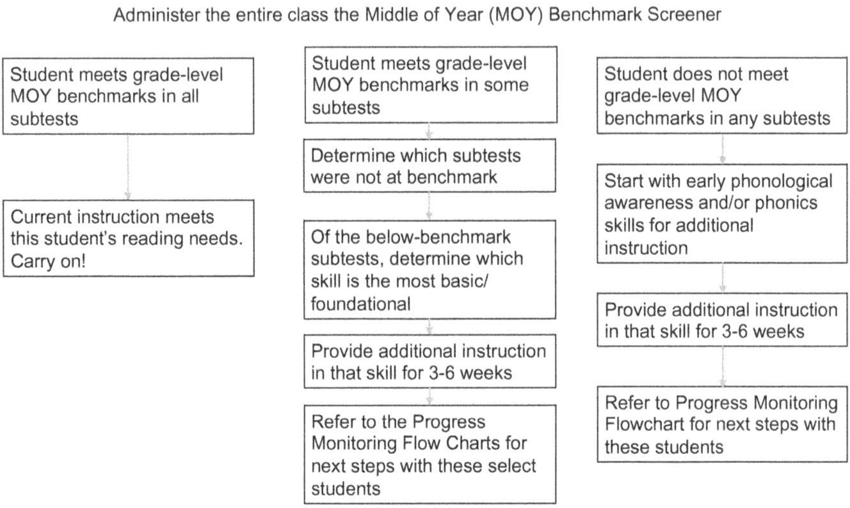

developmental benchmarks. Figure II.2 highlights the management of instructional interventions in conventional classrooms. Consider how you might adapt this procedure to work in your particular context. Once you review the data, you'll have a sense of which children need support with which literacy skills. For example, if the data reveal a small group of children who are struggling with decoding skills, you could plan additional lessons using Sandpaper Letters, the Movable Alphabet, or the Phonetic Object Box. If some students are struggling with fluency or comprehension, additional lessons encoding words with the Movable Alphabet and additional attention to building vocabulary and background knowledge through the multitude of lessons supporting biology, geometry, geography, and literature may be warranted. These lessons may take place in small groups or with individual children. If your school has a literacy coach, they may be able to support some of these lessons as well. Children continue to have agency in their learning. What this protocol offers is a form of clear, decisive record-keeping that efficiently supports all learners to move forward in their literacy development.

Remember, any data you collect are only worthwhile if it informs your work in the classroom. If they are solely collected to determine where students are in their learning or to satisfy a state assessment mandate, these data are static and has only a short-lived value. Rather, we know that

Figure II.2. Middle of Year (MOY) Progress Monitoring Flowchart

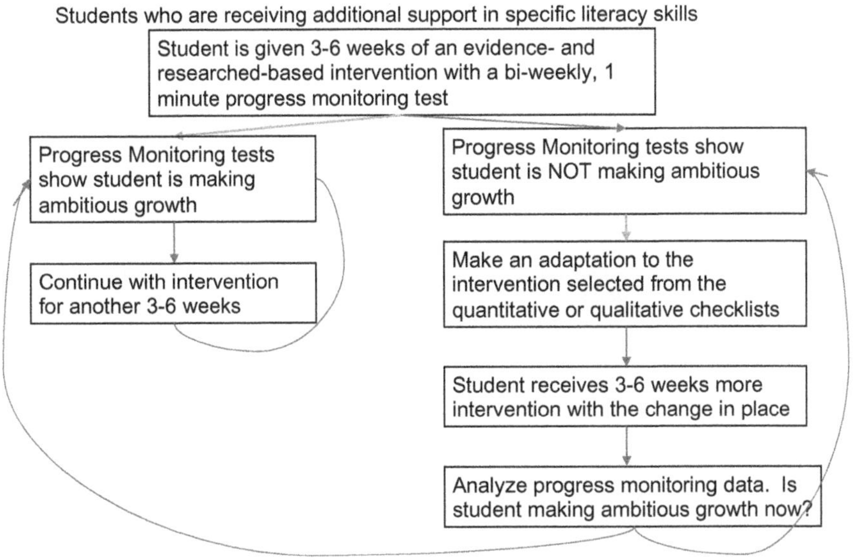

learning is a dynamic experience, and that most students will demonstrate growth in learning when offered authentic and engaging learning experiences that meet them where they are in their reading development. The use of data to influence classroom planning and instruction is what makes data dynamic and purposeful, and perhaps serves as the very crux of liberatory practice. A student is not defined by a score. Rather, data provide educators and literacy coaches with evidence and a map to know where to effectively place their attention and instructional time in the classroom to meet the needs of all students.

CHAPTER 6

Lesson Application

In consideration of the previous chapter's case studies, it is important to consider the data that you have collected and analyzed. Using these insights, you decided that some of the early childhood students would benefit from instruction with the Montessori Sandpaper Letters, whereas the elementary students would benefit from lessons with the Movable Alphabet (see Figures 6.1 and 6.2). In both cases, the lessons would align with the children's current abilities and ensure that the lesson is both engaging and appropriately challenging. As you will notice, the lessons incorporate tactile and hands-on elements to encourage interest, while providing opportunities for independent practice. (See Tables 6.1 and 6.2.)

The same structure for this lesson could be extended for students ready to explore higher-level phonics skills.

Teachers must keep some instructional considerations in mind. Once the lesson is complete, the teacher will reflect on the student's understanding of the learning objective. In the case of the Movable Alphabet lesson, students are expected to accurately select the correct letter symbols that match the corresponding sounds when encoding words. The teacher's observation notes will then document the child's mastery of this literacy skill. However, if the student struggles to identify the correct letter symbols when composing words, the teacher will often elect to return to the same lesson the following day. If a consistent pattern emerges highlighting that the student does not yet have automaticity of foundational phonics skills, the teacher

Figure 6.1. Sandpaper Letters

Photo courtesy of Nienhuis Montessori

Figure 6.2 Movable Alphabet

Photo courtesy of Maitri Learning

then may choose to return to additional work with Sandpaper Letters. Or the teacher may continue with this same lesson and extend the second period of the lesson over multiple days, offering extended shared practice time ("We do"). This instructional strategy is a key attribute of the Montessori pedagogy that teachers (and those who prepare teachers) would be wise to emphasize in classroom practice. A decision tree related to a Montessori teacher's thinking while delivering a Three-Period Lesson can be found in Chapter 7.

If after these strategies have been implemented the student continues to struggle, then the situation may warrant adding selected activities, materials, or instructional approaches to further support that student's learning. For example, for students needing additional phonemic awareness practice, ETC Montessori has created manipulatives that can bring Elkonin boxes into the Montessori classroom. Picture cards of objects are provided, and children use tokens to represent the number of sounds in the object pictured. Figure 6.5

Table 6.1. Lesson Example 1

Name of Activity	Sandpaper Letters
Area	English Language Arts
Materials	A set of cutout sandpaper letters glued to boards
Aims	Direct: To teach letter sounds and their symbols and to develop fine motor skills and correct directionality for letter formation Indirect: To prepare children for reading and writing, and to foster their love of language and learning
Preparation	**Sensorial lessons** that teach rough and smooth (Tactile Boards), prepare the hand for the pincer grasp (Knobbed Cylinders) **Language lessons** (I Spy game and oral language activities for initial, ending, and medial sounds)
Age	3–4.5 years (depending on the child's age and skill level)
Presentation	1. Select the Sandpaper Letters: Choose three sandpaper letters and bring them to a mat or table. Stack the letters face-down, positioning the stack in the upper-right corner of the work area. 2. Introduce the First Letter: Take the first sandpaper letter from the group and place it face-up in front of you. Using your index and middle fingers, trace the shape of the letter, starting at the point where you would begin when writing the letter. 3. Model Proper Tracing: Follow the exact path you would use to write the letter, ensuring you maintain smooth, continuous strokes as you trace its shape. 4. Say the Letter Sound: As you trace the letter, say the corresponding sound aloud (focus on the sound the letter makes, not its name). 5. Student's Turn: Invite the student to trace the same letter with their index and middle fingers. Encourage them to say the sound of the letter as they trace it, following the same procedure you modeled. 6. Move the First Letter: After the student has traced and said the sound of the letter, move that letter to the upper-left corner of the workspace, making room for the next letter. 7. Repeat with the Next Letters: Go through the same steps (tracing, saying the sound, and giving the student a turn) with the remaining two letters from the stack. 8. Three-Period Lesson: Once all three letters have been introduced, lay them out together in front of the student. Conduct a Three-Period Lesson to reinforce recognition and understanding of the letter sounds. (See the section "The Montessori Three-Period Lesson Decision Tree" in Chapter 7 for a full description of the Three-Period Lesson.) 9. Reinforce Tracing and Sounds: Throughout the lesson, make sure to have the student frequently trace the letters and repeat the sounds to solidify their understanding and retention of each sound.

(*continued*)

Table 6.1. (*continued*)

Points of Interest	The different colors of the vowels and consonants and the feel of the rough sandpaper when tracing the letters
Control of Error	If the child's fingers slip off the sandpaper, they can feel the difference in texture between the smooth surface and the rough sandpaper, helping them become more aware of the letter formation.
Variations	Incorporate different textured materials, like velvet or felt, to create letters that offer a diverse tactile experience. Have the child trace a letter and then write the letter in a sand tray.
Extensions	Say the Letter Name: As you trace the letter, say the corresponding name of the letter that makes the sound (the name of the letter that makes the sound /s/ is "s"). Select three sandpaper letters and place them face-down. Gently knock on the back of one and ask, "Who's there?" Then flip the letter over and excitedly announce which letter and sound are revealed.

shows the sound (Elkonin) boxes and cards. When a teacher identifies that a student needs to build their phonological awareness at the phoneme (individual speech sound) level, and the teacher has already used the phonological awareness instruction included in the Language curriculum, an activity like this further brings specific skill work to the individual needs.

There should be clear connections to students' learning and any extra activities brought into the Montessori classroom. First, the materials should clearly address students' identified literacy needs. Any outside activities must provide ample time for the repeated exposures some students require to learn a skill. The material should support a gradual release of responsibility noted in the "I Do, We Do, You Do" approach of explicit instruction. Evidence shows that different individuals take more or less exposures and/or "We do" work than others before reaching a level of skill mastery. And beyond the benefit of additional practice within a particular literacy skill that some students will benefit from having, teachers can also consider these additional activities to support any students with specific interests and/or for those working above grade level, too.

Maitri Learning has developed numerous supportive manipulatives that follow the Montessori thought process and provide supplemental learning, such as the vocabulary development cards related to botany. For a student who needs additional vocabulary intervention, or a student with a high interest level in the natural world, or for an advanced student who just craves learning and collecting ever more precise vocabulary, the vocabulary cards provide targeted and explicit vocabulary work using the Three-Period

Table 6.2. Lesson Example 2

Name of Activity	Movable Alphabet
Area	English Language Arts
Materials	A set of lowercase letters with blue vowels and red consonants A container of small phonetic objects (i.e., cat, mop, pin, flag, etc.)
Aims	Direct: To associate the printed letters of the alphabet with sounds of spoken language Indirect: To prepare children for building words and for reading
Preparation	**Language lessons** that provide experience with phonemic awareness and letter-sound knowledge (Sandpaper Letters)
Age	3.5–5 years (depending on the child's age and skill level)
Presentation	1. Take the Movable Alphabet (Figures 6.3 and 6.4) and the container of phonetic objects to a mat. 2. Choose one object from the container and place it on the mat. 3. Say the name of the object out loud. Identify the first sound in the word and find the corresponding letter from the Movable Alphabet. Place the letter next to the object. 4. Repeat the word slowly to identify the middle sound, and then the final sound. Place the matching letters for each sound next to the object as you go. 5. Select another object from the container and follow the same process.
Points of Consciousness	When the child understands that alphabetic sounds have specific symbols and that these symbols can be put together to form words
Points of Interest	The different colors of the vowels and consonants and the small objects
Control of Error	The teacher's observations
Variations	Incorporate different objects.
Extensions	As ready, have the child write noun phrases (i.e., black cat, wet mop, red pin, etc.)

Figure 6.3. Movable Alphabet

Photo courtesy of Maitri Learning

Figure 6.4. Child With Movable Alphabet

Photo courtesy of Maitri Learning

Figure 6.5. Sound (Elkonin) Boxes With Materials

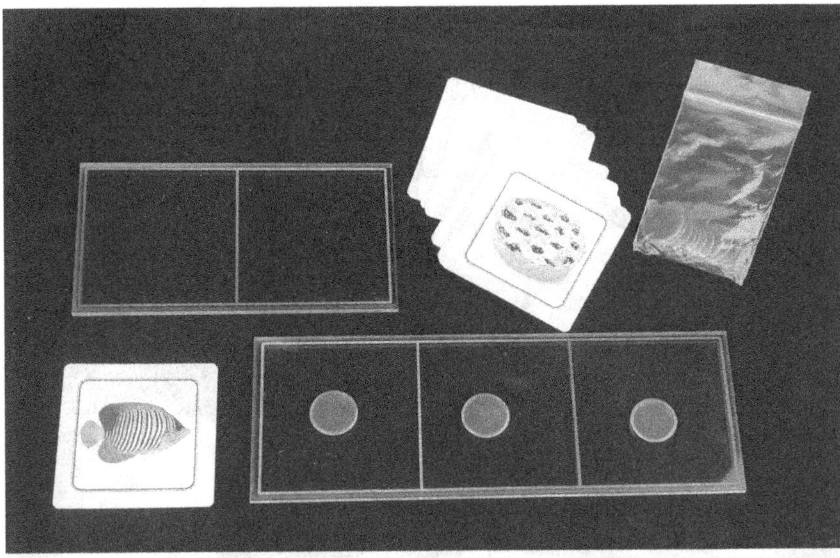

Figure 6.6. Parts of Books by Maitri Learning

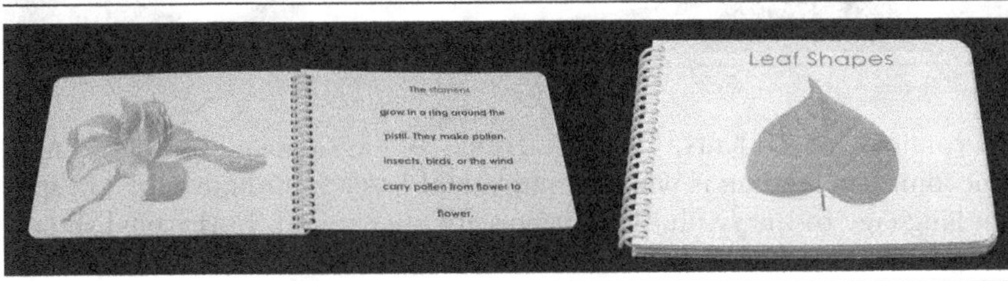

Lesson. Maitri Learning includes a brief summary of what this instruction would look like, with the teacher naming the specific parts of the flower, the student working with the teacher to recall the names, and ultimately, the student independently naming the flowers (see Figure 6.6).

For older students, Maitri's "Parts of Books" provide vocabulary support and extension with terms, definitions, and pictures that can be read about and practiced using the coinciding matching cards (Figure 6.7).

THE ROLE OF ENCODING IN LESSONS

The Montessori Language curriculum recognizes the importance of encoding, and Dr. Montessori included this translation of speech into print for

Figure 6.7. Three-Part Cards by Maitri Learning

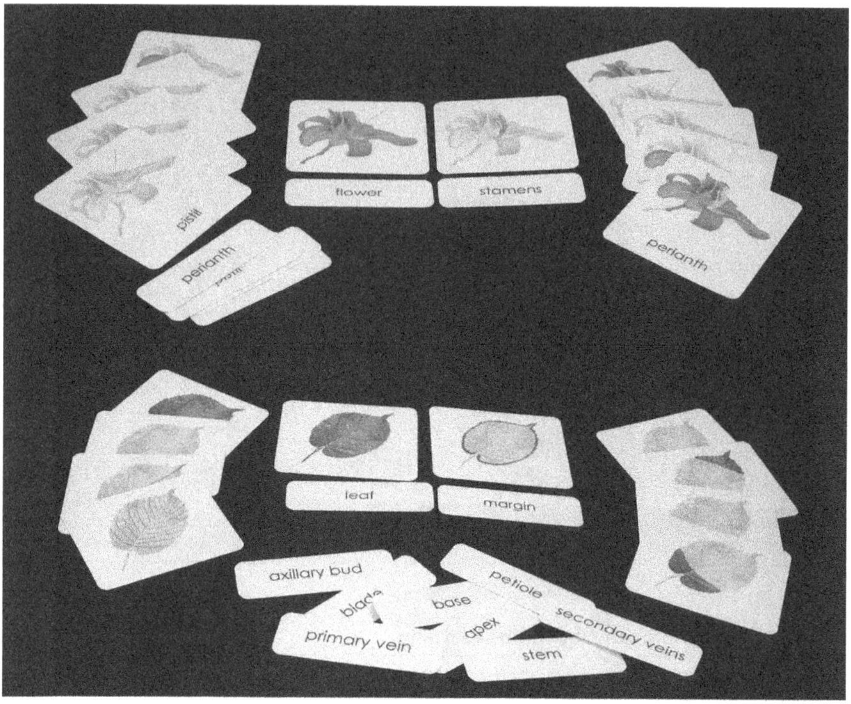

the youngest of students. Often described as the opposite of "decoding," "encoding" in reading is when an individual links the sounds heard in spoken language to the symbol that represents that sound. In the English language, this means linking specific sounds to letters and then writing those letters. While reading, a child must recognize the symbol and the letter, and link a sound(s) to it. When writing, the child must summon the symbolic representation of the sound and re-create it to share with others, thus taking the knowledge of letter-sound correlation to a deeper level and moving the letter-sound knowledge from a receptive understanding to an expressive level. This is a strength of the Montessori curriculum: children write early on in their education and create a strong letter-sound correlation. As soon as the Movable Alphabet is used to create words and sentences, the children are encouraged to practice those words by copying them in writing.

Just as there is the Simple View of Reading, there is the Simple View of Writing. Attributed to Berninger et al. (2002), the Simple View of Writing consists of coming up with ideas and getting them down on paper (ideation and text generation). As with the Simple View of Reading, writing is not quite that simple. Berninger and colleagues revised their concept by adding the component of executive functioning to their framework. There are fewer formal assessments used for writing than reading in public schools, and in many curricula, writing has been secondary to reading. However, with structured literacy lessons and the current reading research, the importance of interweaving strong writing opportunities and instruction is moving to the forefront. Writing makes the connection between the phonics rules and how the words are actually built.

A writing component that demonstrates the application of phonics skills strengthens students' learning. In the Montessori classroom, make sure that emphasis is placed on the wonderful writing materials available.

For students struggling with grammar (language structures), additional work with Key to Writing and Reading in English materials (Figure 6.9) and the Montessori method of sentence diagramming (Figures 6.10 and 6.11) might be added to students' work time.

The Simple View of Writing (Figure 6.8) involves generating ideas (ideation) and expressing them in written form (text generation). This framework can be effectively integrated into Montessori classrooms. In terms of ideation, Montessori classrooms are filled with rich content. Using an evidence-based methodology such as the Hochman Method, which emphasizes explicit and carefully sequenced instruction, curriculum content can enhance the rigor of writing activities, and grammar is most effectively taught within the context of students' own writing (Hochman et al., 2017). However, Montessori teachers often guide students through lessons with rich content only to have them copy the text verbatim from definition or content cards. Instead, a more effective approach would be for teachers to

Figure 6.8. Adapted From the Simple View of Writing

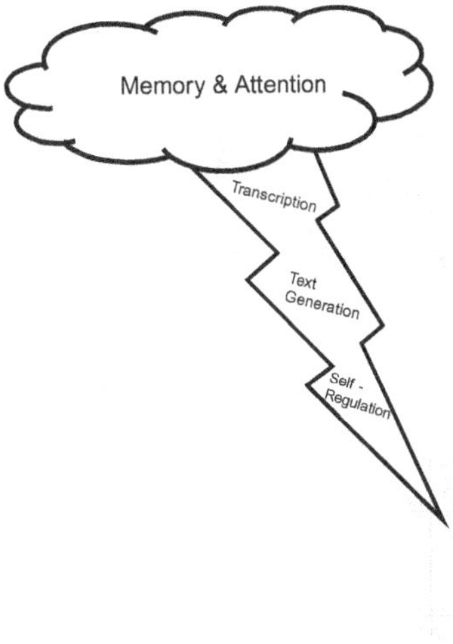

Berninger, 2002

Figure 6.9. Key to Writing and Reading in English

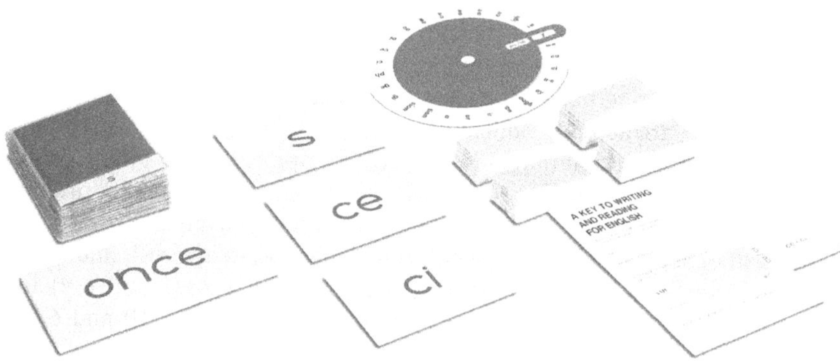

Photo courtesy of Nienhuis Montessori

Figure 6.10. Sentence Analysis

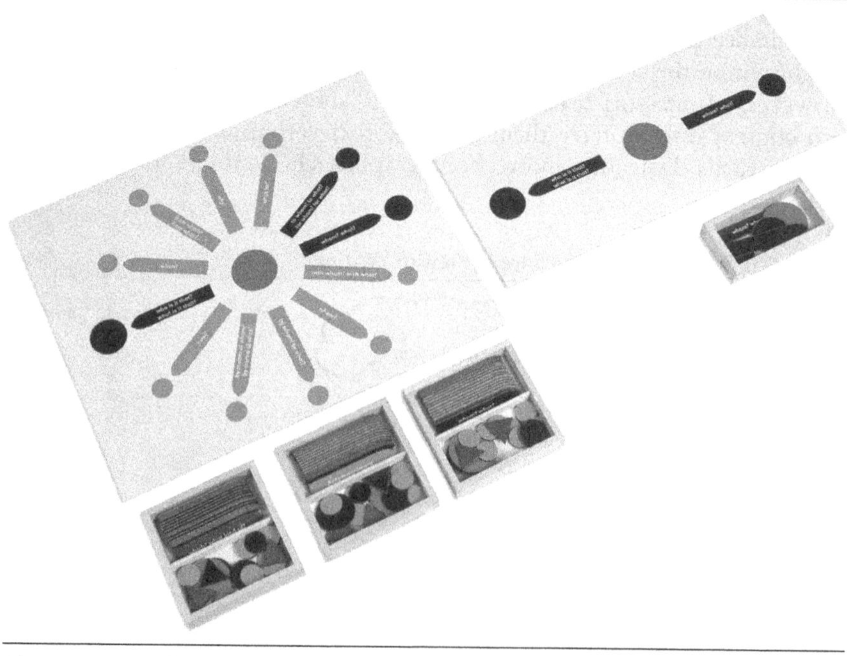

Photo courtesy of Nienhuis Montessori

Figure 6.11. Identifying Parts of a Sentence Through Grammar Analysis

Photos courtesy of Maitri Learning

encourage students to leave their work out, move to a designated writing space, and capture what they remember in their own words. The examples below, featuring Maitri's "Parts of Books" (Figure 6.6), demonstrate such implementation. Table 6.3 shows how curriculum content can enhance the rigor of writing activities, and Table 6.4 shows how grammar is most effectively taught within the context of students' own writing.

CURRICULUM EVALUATION GUIDELINES

Throughout the year, as you are teaching, it is worthwhile to consider how the curriculum being used reflects reading research, whether one is considering the Montessori practice or the public school curriculum. At a national level, the Reading League has created a document that can be applied to any literacy curriculum. This document is called the *Curriculum Evaluation Guidelines* and is part of the Reading League Compass, a collection of materials that support the implementation of the Science of Reading (Reading League, 2023). These guidelines provide a list of language and reading practices that are aligned to the science of reading and a list of "red flag" items that might be clues that the curriculum does not reflect current reading research. For example, a red flag that the curriculum practices are not aligned with the science of reading is if "students are not exposed to rich vocabulary and complex syntax in reading and writing materials" (Reading League,

Table 6.3. Vocabulary Lesson

Name of Activity	Parts of a Flower
Area	Science & English Language Arts.
Materials	"Parts of" books for the flower. Photos include the featured part in full color while the rest of the image fades into muted shades of gray. Books should be sized for the child's hand. Three-part card set that matches booklet and includes photos, labels, and control cards (word and label put together).
Aims	Direct: To learn about the parts of the flower To recall information about the parts of the flower through writing Indirect: To develop an understanding and appreciation of the natural world To build comprehension and writing skills
Preparation	Science lessons that provide experience with learning about plants. Word recognition practice.
Age	6–9 years (depending on the child's age and skill level).
Presentation	1. Introduce the Concept: Begin by explaining the parts of the flower. 2. Model with Photo Cards: The teacher will place the photo-only cards on the work surface in one row, leaving space below for the label card. 3. Model with Label Cards: The teacher will select and place label cards under the appropriate photo, sounding out the words for clarity. 4. Use Control Cards for Checking: The teacher will lay out the control cards for each match and compare them to verify the placements. 5. The teacher will use the booklet to read to the students and describe the parts of the flower. 6. The teacher will model recalling the parts of a flower (without looking at the book) and then writing about the parts either with the Movable Alphabet or in print. 7. Student Activity: Direct students to complete the work on their own, including recalling the parts of a flower (without looking at the book) and then writing about the parts either with the Movable Alphabet or in print.

Points of Consciousness	When the child further develops an understanding and appreciation of the natural world. When the child further builds comprehension and writing skills.
Points of Interest	The topic and beautiful pictures.
Control of Error	Control cards and teacher review of student writing.
Variations	Further work with other botany topics.
Extensions	Children can be supported with teacher-directed research on the following questions: Not all flowers are the same. Find other examples. Can we find the same parts?

2023, p. 14). If "students are exposed to rich vocabulary and complex syntax in reading and writing materials and orally, including but not limited to read alouds, at language levels beyond students' reading levels" (p. 18), the Curriculum Evaluation Guidelines list that as a practice aligned with the science of reading.

Table 6.6 is an excerpt from the checklist.

This tool can be used at the classroom level, at a schoolwide level, or at the district level. Consider how our first book illustrated the alignment between Scarborough's Reading Rope and Montessori practices. This chart takes analysis of literacy instruction a step further. We know that there is no perfect literacy curriculum. Using this checklist, however, you can pinpoint the instructional pieces of *any* ELA curriculum that is present and strong in your classroom, as well as bring to light very specific areas that may need instructional adjustments.

The entire *Curriculum Evaluation Guidelines* document can be accessed at no charge on the Reading League website, www.thereadingleague.org/wp-content/uploads/2023/03/The-Reading-League-Curriculum-Evaluation-Guidelines-2023.pdf.

Table 6.4. Symbolizing Sentences Lesson

Name of Activity	Symbolizing Sentences
Area	English Language Arts
Materials	"Parts of" books for the flower. Photos include the featured part in full color while the rest of the image fades into muted shades of gray. Books should be sized for the child's hand. Paper Grammar Symbols according to the chart below: Noun: Black triangle Article: Light blue equilateral triangle Adjective: Blue equilateral triangle Verb: Red circle Preposition: Small green crescent Adverb: Small orange circle Pronoun: Light gray isosceles triangle Conjunction: Pink rectangular symbol Interjection: Thin gold oval or shape, similar to an exclamation point
Aims	Direct: To identify the roles of words Indirect: To develop skills in understanding, the structure of our language
Preparation	Understanding of the parts of speech, and the roles of each part.
Age	6–9 years (depending on the child's age and skill level).
Presentation	1. The teacher writes a sentence based on what the students have learned from the booklet. 2. Each part of the sentence is written on a small piece of paper. The teacher lays these out, in order, on the work surface. 3. The teacher then identifies each word and its part of speech, and labels it accordingly. 4. The teacher models writing this on a sheet of paper and drawing the symbols above. (See Table 6.5.) 5. The teacher will go through this again, and enlist the students in the activity. 6. Student Activity: Direct students to complete the work on their own.
Points of Consciousness	When the child further develops skills in understanding the structure of our language.
Points of Interest	The symbols.
Control of Error	Teacher review of student work.
Variations	Further work with other botany sentences.

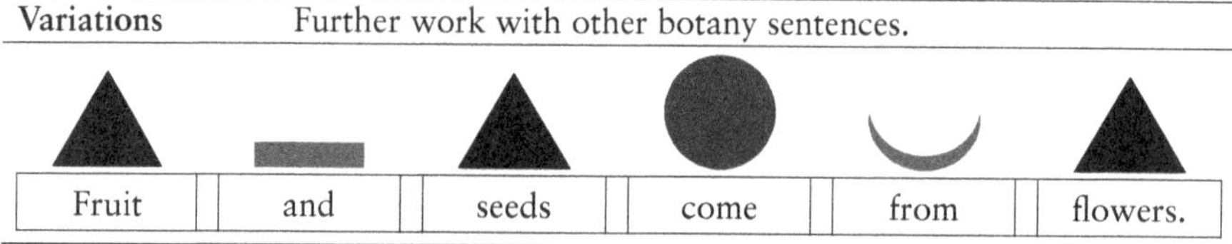

Table 6.5. Grammar Symbol Definitions (Zoll, Feinberg et al., 2023, p. 82)

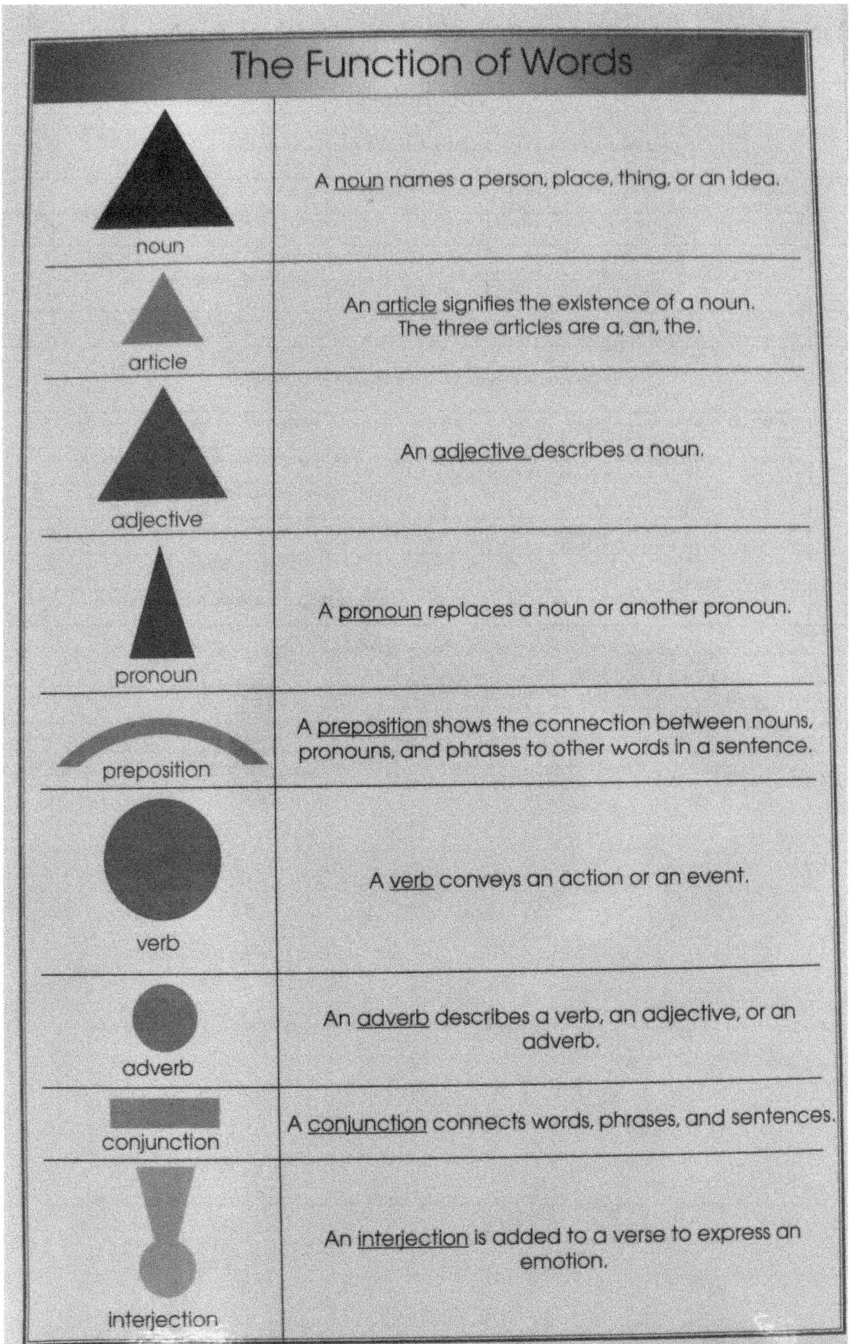

The Function of Words	
noun	A noun names a person, place, thing, or an idea.
article	An article signifies the existence of a noun. The three articles are a, an, the.
adjective	An adjective describes a noun.
pronoun	A pronoun replaces a noun or another pronoun.
preposition	A preposition shows the connection between nouns, pronouns, and phrases to other words in a sentence.
verb	A verb conveys an action or an event.
adverb	An adverb describes a verb, an adjective, or an adverb.
conjunction	A conjunction connects words, phrases, and sentences.
interjection	An interjection is added to a verse to express an emotion.

Table 6.6. Excerpt From the *Curriculum Evaluation Guidelines* (Reading League, 2023)

Vocabulary		
	Red Flags: Practices Not Aligned With the Science of Reading	**Red Flag ✓**
2.7	Vocabulary worksheets and activities are used with little opportunity for deep understanding of vocabulary words.	
2.8	Instruction includes memorization of isolated words and definitions out of context.	
2.9	Tier 2 words are not taught explicitly and practiced; students are not given opportunities to use them in their speech, see them in print, and use them in writing.	
2.10	Students are not exposed to and taught Tier 3 words.	
2.11	Explicit instruction in morphology is not present and/or not taught according to a scope and sequence (i.e., simple to complex) consistently throughout K-5 instruction.	
	Practices Aligned With the Science of Reading	
2.12	Instruction includes robust teacher-student and student-student conversations in order to support a clear understanding of vocabulary words.	
2.13	Vocabulary words are taught deeply by using concept maps or other devices that help students understand multiple layers of the word. (Anderson & Freebody, 1981)	
2.14	Explicit instruction in vocabulary for Tier 2 and 3 words is evident, as well as instruction in the context of texts (most Tier 1 words).	
2.15	Tier 2 words are taught explicitly, and students are given opportunities to use them in their speech, see them in print, and use them in writing (when appropriate).	
2.16	Explicit instruction in morphology is provided with numerous opportunities for students to read and write words with these morphemes	
2.17	For Multilingual Learners, instruction in ELD is included to support continued vocabulary development.	

Glossary

English Language Development (ELD): Instruction that is specially designed for Multilingual Learners to help develop their listening, speaking, reading, and writing skills in English.

Morphology: The system of meaningful parts, or morphemes, that make up words.

Tiered Vocabulary Words: A means of classifying words due to their level of difficulty and frequency of use. It is important to note that these tiers are *not* related to tiers of instruction in a Multi-Tiered System of Supports.

Tier 1 Vocabulary Words: Words students already know the meaning of (e.g., house, car, dog, school).

Tier 2 Vocabulary Words: Words that are not likely to be familiar to young children but reflect a concept they can identify with and can use in conversation (e.g., shiver, excitement, remarkable). Tier 2 words can appear in multiple domains and content areas.

Tier 3 Vocabulary Words: Words that are low frequency and domain or content-area specific (e.g., words from math, science, history, music, art).

CHAPTER 7

Assessment

Beginning-of-year screeners determine which students need additional support and point us toward additional diagnostic assessments that will further pinpoint instructional foci. The beginning-of-year screener is, in essence, assessing the child's response to the previous year's instruction and potentially identifies learning loss that might have occurred over the summer. As the year progresses, assessment continues to be important. At the midyear point, the screener is administered to the whole class once again. It is vital that this midyear screener be administered to *all* students for two main reasons. First, this assessment shows the child's response to the current instruction. The new structures, materials, and teachers of the current year may be working (or not working) for the child, and the teacher needs to know this. Skipping the midyear screening assessment because the child met the benchmark at the beginning of the year is not valid reasoning. A student who is not responding strongly to the current instruction could be overlooked without this assessment. Waiting until the end of the year for the screener does not give time for instructional adjustments that could allow the student to reach the benchmark before graduating that grade. Without a midyear screening assessment, a student might not be flagged as needing support until the end of year. The student could be passed on to the next class with a problem for next year's teacher to deal with, missing an opportunity to make the most of the current year's instruction.

Additionally, midyear student data may track students' improvement toward moving them out of tiered interventions. The new dataset will also identify students who now need additional support who didn't at the beginning of the year. These students can begin targeted interventions to address these needs. Screening assessments (beginning, middle, and end of year) are given to all students.

Additional assessments are given to selected students who are not meeting benchmarks on the screening assessments. Thinking back to Chapter 4, recall that screening assessments are given universally, to all students, and diagnostic assessments are given selectively to students who perform under the benchmark scores on the screeners.

DETERMINING WHERE TO START—ANALYZING DATA RESULTS

Knowing how to use the data that have been collected is key to successful literacy instruction. Perhaps this is also the most daunting task. Using data requires decision-making skills that influence the future of the child. We feel Dr. Montessori would have encouraged teachers to meet this challenge, to analyze the data, and to use the data for the good of the individual. A true research scientist, Dr. Montessori exemplified how the instructor examines a situation and makes choices with concrete evidence supporting their choice.

Once the assessments are complete, the teacher must determine which skill that is not mastered is most foundational learning to reading. A child might not be able to decode words (meaning additional phonics-based activities may be warranted), read with fluency (perhaps requiring additional support with reading pace and expression), or remember what is read (continued focus on comprehension). Rather than intervene in all three of these areas, the teacher should choose the area that is most foundational. In this case, that is the decoding/phonics instruction. Instruction will of course continue in all areas of literacy development through day-to-day Tier 1/core curriculum taught in the classroom, but specific attention will be given to the skill that assessment results point to as having the greatest need. A child must first be able to slowly decode the word before they can read that word with speed or comprehend what that word means. Once that skill is up to benchmark, the teacher may move on to the next foundational skill in need of intervention. So once the skill of decoding a word is mastered, fluency is addressed. Students must practice decoding with a level of automaticity that leads to fluency, reading with speed and prosody.

The decision-making flowchart in Figure 7.1 is available on the Rhode Island Department of Education website and can help in this work.

This flowchart guides the teacher through the hierarchy of literacy skills, so the most foundational area of need can be easily determined and targeted.

THE MONTESSORI THREE-PERIOD LESSON DECISION TREE

In conventional classrooms, teachers implement pre- and post-tests or exit tickets to capture students' understanding. In Montessori classrooms, authentic assessment practices are implemented, including observations conducted by educators in early childhood settings to contextualize student responses or more student-centered practices in elementary and middle school settings where educators guide students' reflections and self-assessment of completed work.

Figure 7.1. Intervention Decision-Making Flowchart (Courtesy of the Rhode Island Department of Education)

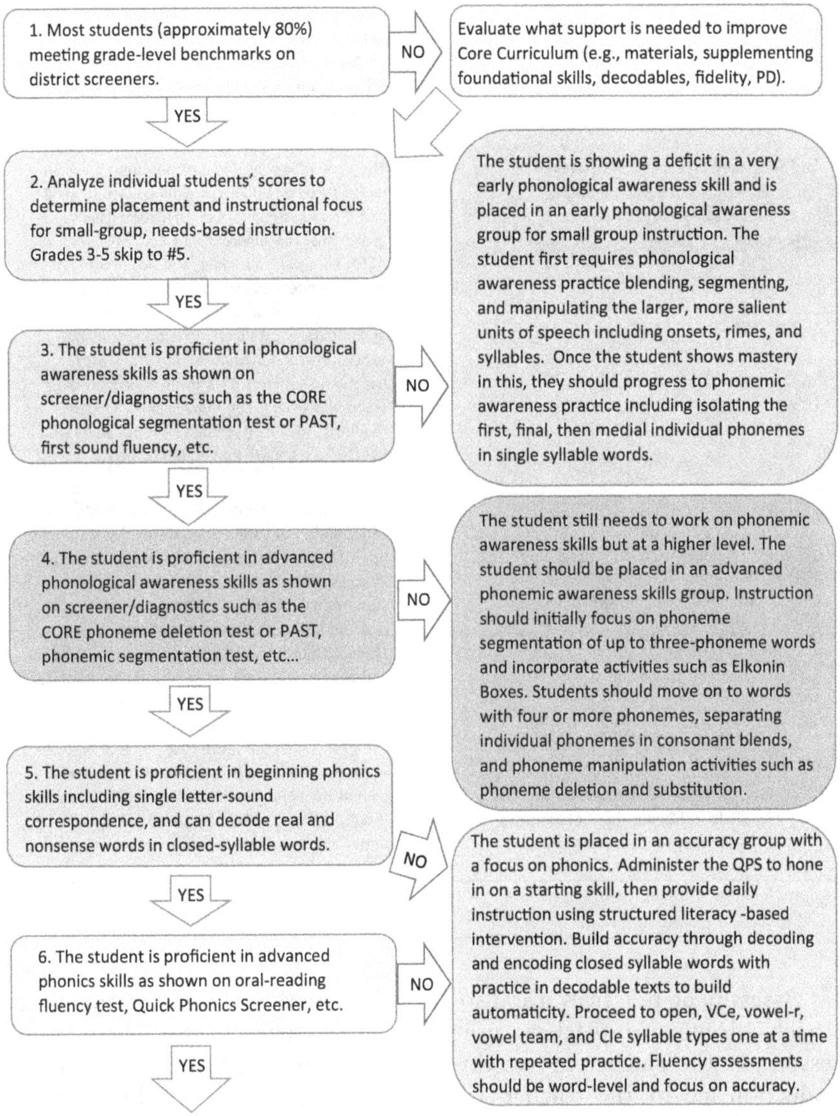

Source: https://ride.ri.gov/sites/g/files/xkgbur806/files/IAC/StructuredLiteracy/MTSS-Reading-WhitePaper.pdf

(continued)

Figure 7.1. (*continued*)

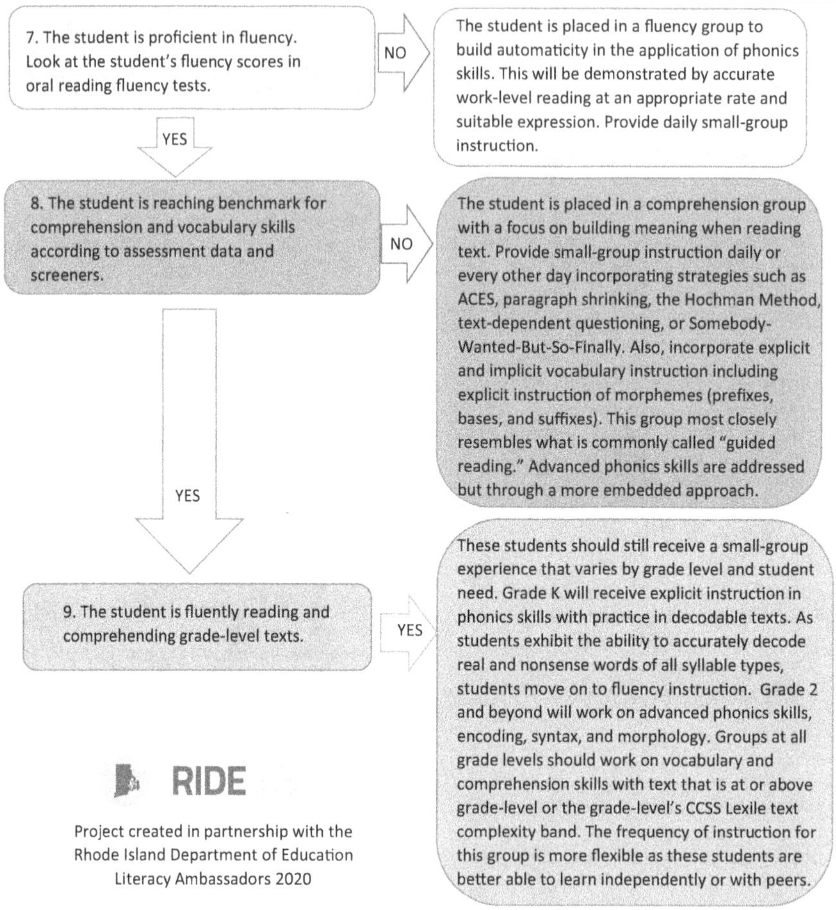

Assessment practices are also embedded within the instructional approach Montessori teachers use when implementing the Three-Period Lesson. As the teacher moves through each period of the lesson—an introduction led by the teacher, practice with the material collaboratively engaging both the teacher and the student, and then to the gradual release of responsibility during the activity, which will ultimately be led by the student—many real-time decisions are made by the teacher (see Figure 7.2). For example, if the child remains engaged as the teacher models the activity during the introductory period of the lesson, then the teacher will often make the decision to move on to the second period of the lesson. Here, the child transitions from being an observer to directly engaging and practicing

Figure 7.2. Montessori Three-Period Lesson—Decision Tree

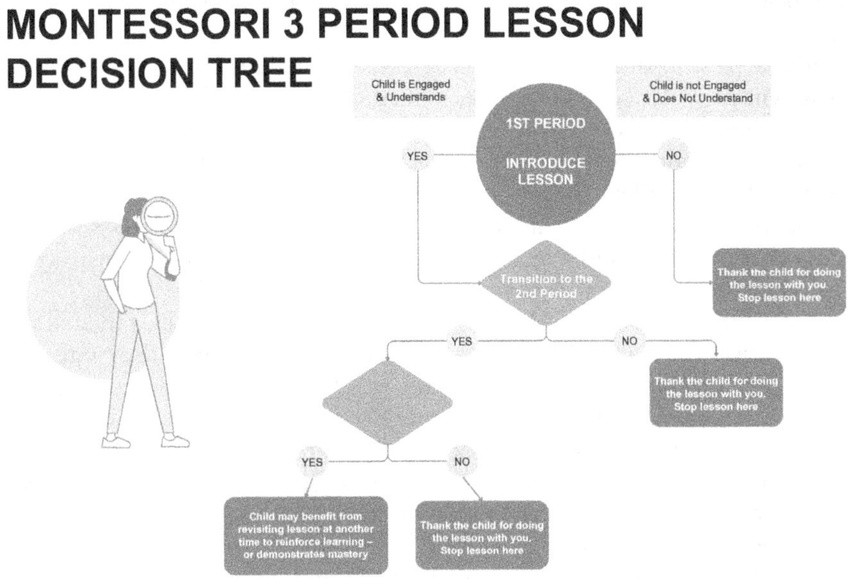

with the materials. If the child does not yet demonstrate understanding of these concepts, then the teacher will graciously stop the lesson here and thank the child for working with them today. However, if the child demonstrates their understanding of the lesson's objectives and they remain engaged, then the teacher may opt to progress to the third period of the lesson. At this stage of the lesson, either the child demonstrates their mastery of the lesson, or it's clear that they would benefit from additional opportunities to practice with the particular activity. For an example of the Three-Period Lesson using the Sandpaper Letters, see Chapter 4 of Zoll et al., 2023.

PROGRESS MONITORING

Implementing a three-times-a-year screening assessment is the first step in a complete and successful assessment plan. Once the screener is in place, the next step is to consider the implementation of progress monitoring assessments for selected students. Progress monitoring is defined as conducting short assessments on a regular schedule to examine students' performance and to evaluate the effectiveness of instruction (National Research Council, 2008). Results of these assessments then inform further adjustments to classroom instruction. Throughout the course of the year, students who are below benchmark and who are receiving additional support need to be given progress monitoring assessments. While teachers are always observing evidence of student learning and progress, a formal progress monitoring assessment provides concrete evidence of student growth that shows whether instruction and interventions are successful. Progress monitoring assessments also inform teachers as to when intervention and instruction needs to be adapted. When those outside of your classroom need evidence that students are making reading growth, the progress monitoring tests provide data that move beyond anecdotal evidence to demonstrate that instruction is working.

A progress monitoring tool is a short (usually 1 minute), targeted test that focuses on the specific skill the teacher is addressing in their intervention. For example, if the student did not reach the benchmark score in their beginning-of-year DIBELS assessment, the teacher looks at the areas in which they struggled. They then focus on the earliest skill in the literacy progression that needs support and provide additional support in that area (see Chapter 6). But teachers need to know if what they are doing is working, so on a regular basis (weekly, biweekly, or monthly), the 1-minute progress monitoring assessment is given to the child and charted. The teacher can graph the progress monitoring data to create a sloped line. The National Center on Intensive Intervention (NCII) provides a free graphing tool that charts student data compared to nationally normed growth rates (https://intensiveintervention.org/resource/student-progress-monitoring-tool-data-collection-and-graphing-excel). If the student's progress monitoring scores are above the aim line, the student is improving at an appropriate rate. If their scores are below the aim line, the intervention is not working and adaptations to the intervention may be needed. (See the adaptation checklists later in this chapter.) The graph in Figure 7.3 shows a student making ambitious growth on their progress monitoring assessments, represented by the dotted line on the bottom. The top dotted line depicts the growth needed to meet the benchmark.

The graph in Figure 7.4 shows a student's progress monitoring assessments that are tracking below the ambitious growth rate (top dotted line). This is a signal to adjust the intervention.

A growth rate is the amount one would expect the reading score to increase per week. For example, if students are identifying letter sounds using the Vanderbilt Letter-Sound Fluency progress monitoring test, we know a student should be increasing the number of correct letter sounds they can identify by 1.8 letter sounds per week. Usually, the weekly growth rate is provided in the administration manual; this is not a number a teacher needs to know off the top of their head. It is provided in the progress monitoring tool.

Figure 7.3. A Student Making Ambitious Growth on Their Progress Monitoring Assessments (NWF CLS Nonsense Word Fluency; CLS= Correct Letter Sounds)

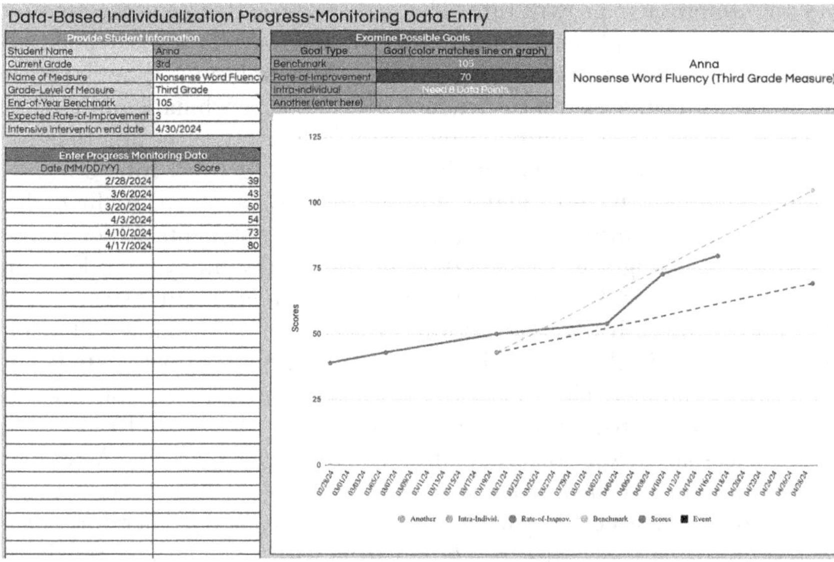

Graphing tool created by Devin Kearns (www.devinkearns.com)

Figure 7.4. A Student Not Making Ambitious Growth on Their Progress Monitoring Assessments (NWF CLS)

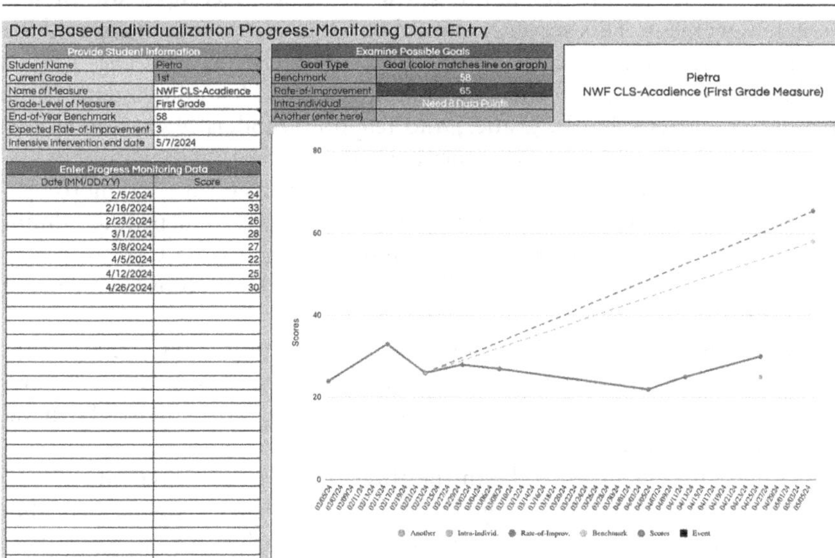

Graphing tool created by Devin Kearns (www.devinkearns.com)

Many times, two growth rates are given, a "realistic" growth rate and an "ambitious" growth rate. The realistic growth rate is the amount of increase that students who are already at grade level must make to remain at grade level as the year continues. The ambitious growth rate is the amount of increase that a student below the benchmark must make to close the gap and eventually be at grade level. This means that the ambitious growth rate is larger than the realistic growth rate; students below benchmark have to make more growth to catch up. At first, this may seem counterintuitive. How can the struggling students achieve more than those meeting the benchmark? But this is absolutely true. Keep in mind that the below-benchmark students are receiving extra instruction in their area of need. If the intervention instruction is working, it will result in more growth in that particular area. The ambitious growth rate is not an arbitrary number. This number is normed using thousands of students and is the reason progress monitoring assessments are chosen from a pool of evidence-based tests that have this research behind them. A teacher cannot develop a formal progress monitoring tool on their own, because they do not have access to such a large normative group. Therefore, progress monitoring tools must be chosen from assessments that are trialed and accepted on this large scale. NCII provides a list of valid and reliable measures at https://intensiveintervention.org/resource/academic-progress-monitoring-tools-chart.

It is beneficial when school districts have selected a uniform screening assessment for all students to allow for a direct comparison of student achievement. This screener should be given at the beginning, middle, and end of the year. Typically, the districts assign testing windows (a range of dates) when these screeners are administered. This allows data to be compared across schools, grades, and teaching models (e.g., Montessori vs. traditional). Screening assessments need to be both valid and reliable. An assessment is considered valid if it tests what it says it is going to test. It is reliable if a comparable score is received if different people administer it (inter-rater reliability) or if different forms of the test are given. So, forms A, B, and C should all result in similar findings (test-retest reliability).

The National Center on Intensive Interventions (NCII) has published a tools chart that rates reading and math screeners (https://charts.intensiveintervention.org/ascreening). This tool may be useful for the initial selection of screeners.

While all students partake in the three-times-a-year screening assessments, other assessments are given to select students. This ensures that valuable instruction time is used effectively. Further testing should be done with purpose and falls into two categories: diagnostic and progress monitoring.

Diagnostic tests may continue to be given throughout the school year as the need arises to gain more information about specific students. If a teacher observes that a child appears to be struggling, they may administer one or more diagnostic assessments to determine the specific skill with which the child is having trouble. Once that area is determined, the teacher can provide an intervention that gives additional instruction in this area. This may be done one-on-one or in a small group with students who all need support in this area. At this point, it is to the teachers' benefit to progress monitor students receiving the extra intervention. Teachers do not need to progress monitor all students. If screening assessments show that a student is meeting grade-level benchmarks, then there is no need to progress monitor those students. The Tier 1 instruction is meeting their needs and can be continued as usual. Students who are not meeting benchmark(s) should be given a progress monitoring assessment (weekly, every other week, or monthly) that tests the focus skill of the intervention. In this way, growth in that skill is documented. Many screening tests provide coinciding 1-minute progress monitoring tests (DIBELS, Acadience, iReady). Once a student scores at the benchmark level or above on three consecutive progress monitoring tests, the focus of instruction should change to the next reading skill in which the student is below benchmark.

Throughout the school year, assessments should look like Figure 7.5.

Progress monitoring allows the teacher to have empirical measurements that show whether or not the instruction is working. If the instruction is not successful, it can be modified before an extended period of time has passed. Adaptations to instruction show that the teacher is responsive to the individual learner. This aligns to the Montessori philosophy being reflective of and responsive to individualized learning plans. When students have not yet met developmental milestones in their learning, it may be that the teacher has not yet found the instruction to which they will best respond. It may take the teacher multiple tries of various interventions until the child makes growth, but this model demonstrates that the teacher believes all students can learn—the teacher just needs to discover how they learn best. Using the screening and progress monitoring data to support instructional adjustments provides the needed concrete evidence that may be required by public school systems.

FURTHER INDIVIDUALIZING TIER 1 (CORE INSTRUCTION) AND TIERED INTERVENTIONS

As progress monitoring tracks students' growth, modifications to the intervention instruction may be needed to elicit a stronger student response. The teacher may also find they need to make adjustments to Tier 1 instruction

Figure 7.5. Classroom Data Assessment Cycle

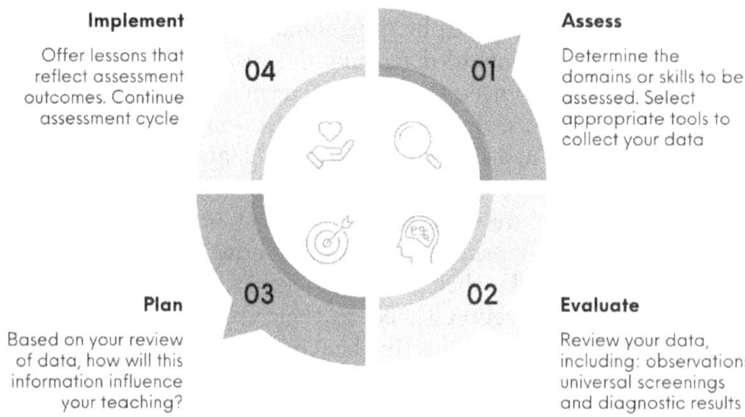

ZOLL & FEINBERG 2025

so that instruction is more individualized and better meets students' needs. These modifications may be either quantitative or qualitative in nature.

Quantitative Changes

A quantitative change is a concrete, measurable adjustment made to the intervention and/or implementation of the intervention itself. Usually, qualitative adaptations include time/frequency and group size. If progress monitoring does not show ambitious growth, an adjustment to one of these areas can be made. Here is how this would look in the classroom.

Time. Time can be adjusted in three main ways. First, the daily time period devoted to the intervention/instruction may be increased. For example, if the intervention was being implemented for 15 minutes a day, the teacher may increase that to 30 minutes a day. Second, the duration of time over which the intervention will be implemented may be increased. Perhaps the intervention was going to be implemented for 4 weeks, and now that time is adjusted to 6 weeks. Finally, the number of intervention sessions per week may be increased. Instead of having an intervention time 3 times in the week, now the intervention will be implemented 5 times a week. Or instead of once a day for 10 minutes, now it will be twice a day for 10 minutes.

Environment. Another quantitative adaptation that can be made is in the individualization of the environment. Moving to a small group from a larger group or even to individual instruction is a strong change that can benefit a student who is still not mastering a specific literacy skill.

Figure 7.6 shows the quantitative considerations.

Qualitative Considerations: Adjusting Instruction

Qualitative adjustments refer to changes in how the intervention/instruction is delivered. Earlier we discussed explicit instruction in the "I Do, We

Figure 7.6. Quantitative Adaptations

Quantitative Adaptations: Adjusting the Intervention

If the student is not making ambitious growth (according to nationally normed growth rates), ask yourself:

Is the intervention…
Yes No
☐ ☐ being implemented with fidelity? (If not, implement with fidelity and collect 3 more data points)

What prevented the student from receiving the intervention as intended?

What changes can be made to ensure fidelity is maintained?

Is the intervention…
Yes No
☐ ☐ focused on the skill that showed as the student's need on the assessments?

What data show that the skill of focus is the student's need?

Does the progress monitoring assessment test this skill?

What do you think…
Yes No
☐ ☐ Is progress not being made due to TIME or LEARNING ENVIRONMENT?

Does the student need:
additional practice?
more feedback?
a smaller group size?
more time with the intervention?
to be more engaged?
to attend more to intervention?

Possible next steps…

Adapt TIME:

-increase instructional time
-increase # of days intervention is given
-increase # of sessions per day

Adapt LEARNING ENVIRONMENT:

-change size of group
-change group to be more homogenous
-change setting
- add motivation system

Do, You Do" model. The checklist in Figure 7.7 targets important elements of explicit instruction that the teacher can double-check are being used.

UTILIZING OBSERVATIONAL DATA

In the following section, you'll learn about assessment protocols that meld practices from traditional and Montessori education as a way to enrich educators' understanding of assessment methodologies to inform classroom practices. We begin with a historical reference to Dr. Montessori's teaching about observation practices and then provide an overview of three literacy assessment tools, protocols for each, and additional information specific to implementation in Montessori programs. We conclude by proposing a comprehensive assessment system, as it applies to children's language and literacy development, that can be used to inform continuous improvement across early childhood systems.

We briefly highlight the forms of assessment below.

Two types of assessment play an integral part of a teacher's world on a daily basis: formative assessment and summative assessment. During Dr. Montessori's training sessions, she also described other assessments used to determine children's "attention, memory, and imagination" (Montessori, 1913/2013, p. 42). In these sessions, Dr. Montessori recommended data protocols that would be recognizable to many educators and researchers today. She prescribed a pre- and post-assessment methodology, whereby teachers collect student data at the beginning and end of the school year. She recognized that collecting only one observation, as a snapshot of the child's development, was not adequate. Rather, it was important to follow their growth over time because "the life of the child is nothing but rapid transformation" (Montessori, 1913/2013, p. 62).

In addition to collecting longitudinal data, Dr. Montessori required teachers to "know how to compare these with other data and to analyse them" (Montessori, 1913/2013, p. 63) using established standards of her era as comparison data. To help organize teachers' observations, Dr. Montessori provided the *Diary of Individual Psychology*, a simple notebook that would include daily observations that would be filed in the child's individual Biographical Chart at the end of each day. "And because they are data, the teacher or anyone who would wish to consult them afterwards will be able to form a picture of the psychic development of the child" (Montessori, 1913/2013, p. 43).

Dr. Montessori was also greatly influenced by advancements in technology in the early 1900s as she developed new strategies that included the use of photography and cinematography to enhance her work with children:

Figure 7.7. Qualitative Adaptations

Qualitative Adaptations: Adjusting Explicit Instruction

If the student is not making ambitious growth (according to nationally normed growth rates), ask yourself:

Model ("I Do")

Did you…

- ☐ Focus on a single objective
- ☐ Explain with clear, concise, and consistent language
- ☐ Show the thinking
- ☐ Model the performance of a skill or strategy
- ☐ Model additional examples (use multiple models)

2. Guided Practice ("We Do")

Did you…

- ☐ Provide lots of guided practice
- ☐ Give immediate, targeted feedback
- ☐ Provide an opportunity for each student to demonstrate grasp of new learning
- ☐ Work through an activity or exercise under the teacher's direct supervision.
- ☐ Provide visual, physical, and verbal prompts

3. Independent Practice ("You Do")

Did you…

- ☐ Provide opportunity to reinforce skills
- ☐ Provide opportunity to apply new knowledge
- ☐ Provide opportunity to complete a task on their own away from the teacher's guidance
- ☐ Make certain independent practice demonstrates understanding of the learning objective

4. Student Engagement

Did you…

- ☐ Elicit frequent student responses
- ☐ Maintain a quick pace (engage and maximize content covered and amount of student practice)
- ☐ Provide immediate, targeted feedback
- ☐ Monitor student responses
- ☐ Ask questions from all levels of Bloom's Taxonomy

A modern teacher . . . should have a camera to take instantaneous photographs because at a certain point in the development of the class, when the children are working by themselves, come in by themselves, take their places by themselves, arrange the tables and get out the didactic materials all alone, when in a word they do everything by themselves, then what else has the teacher to do but to observe?

> It is important that she should record and keep her observations. (1913/2013, p. 44)

In time, classroom observations were also represented in other formats, allowing Dr. Montessori to demonstrate her data more clearly (Montessori, 1917/2013). For example, while observing students during a 3-hour work cycle, she would graph her observations along three horizontal lines representing (1) a child's restful state of inactivity along the "state of quiescent" line listed in the middle of the graph, (2) their disorganized activity in the classroom represented below the quiescent line, and (3) a child's attention and sense of order while engaged with classroom material. Figure 7.8 illustrates the working curves of two children. In this example, only the line of quiescence is visible and children's activities are noted as either above the line (engaged activity) or below the line (disorganized or distracted activity). The first represents the activity of a child "in whom order has not yet been established" (Montessori, 1917/2013, p. 100). According to the graph, we can see the child falls below the "state of quiescent" line while waiting to enter the classroom, but becomes quickly engaged in a frame activity, followed by a greater sense of disorder (noted by how far below the line of quiescence the graph line is drawn). Next, the child works with plane insets, followed by a much shorter episode of disorder; returns again to the frames, followed by a short period of disorder; and then, the entire class comes together where the child remains along the line of quiescence before engaging in a period of recreation.

By comparison, the second chart highlights the working curve of a child as they select more advanced work and maintain focused concentration, even electing to "choose an intelligent pastime, such as looking at illustrated books" for recreation (Montessori, 1917/2013, p. 106). Dr. Montessori highlighted the stability of the line, pointing out that it remained straight and parallel to the line of quiescence for much of the morning work cycle.

According to Chappuis and colleagues (2011), sound assessment practices should include clear purposes, clear targets, sound design, effective communication, and student involvement. Whether an assessment is diagnostic, formative, or summative in nature, it should be sound in practice if it is to inform teachers and programs about how best to support children. Each form of assessment emphasizes a different aspect of student performance and takes place at different stages of the instructional cycle.

Assessment, especially in early childhood education, can raise challenges requiring special consideration. For example, some children are not ready to respond to written text, as they cannot yet read a set of directions to successfully complete an assessment task. Adult support, along with consideration for the delivery of assessments (how will the assessments be conducted and by whom), and expectations of children's time and attention require that assessment tools be carefully selected and reflect developmentally appropriate expectations of young students.

Figure 7.8. Observation Diagram, Working Curves

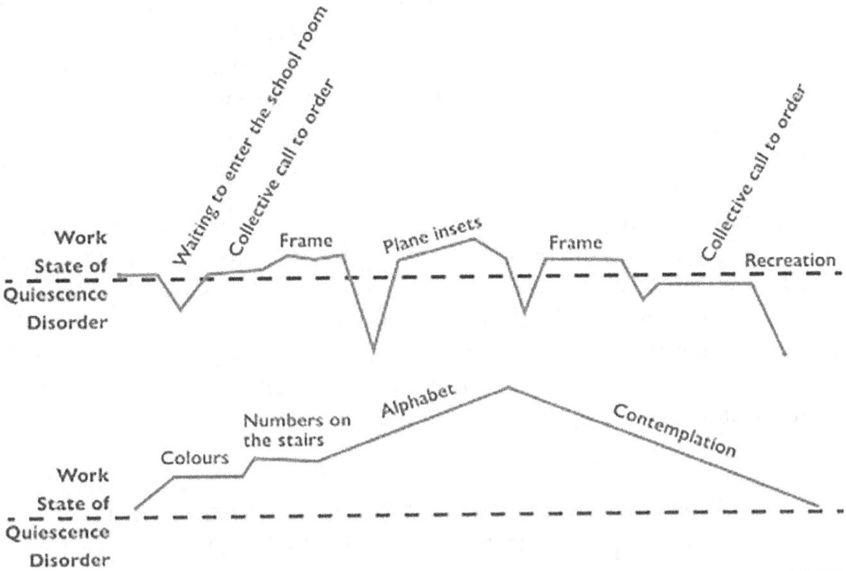

From Zoll et al., 2023, p. 224; Courtesy of the National Center for Montessori in the Public Sector adapted from Spontaneous Activity in Education, Maria Montessori 1917.

As discussed above, for some children, midyear screening data and observational notes will highlight gains in their language and literacy development, whereas for other children the data may indicate that the child has not made satisfactory improvement over the previous 4–5-month period. Observational assessments of teacher-child interactions can help document improvements in the effectiveness of teachers and their interactions with children in their classroom as well as contribute to a rich narrative that tracks a student's learning over time.

In 2019, an assessment survey conducted by the American Montessori Society identified school administrators implementing the Stanford Achievement Test, DIBELS, AIMSweb (Achievement Improvement Monitoring System), and MAP (Measures of Academic Progress) to translate student outcomes using conventional assessment tools. DIBELS, AIMSweb, and MAP are screening assessments frequently employed in public school settings. Most screening assessments begin at the kindergarten level. Before kindergarten, different tools such as PALS Pre-K may be utilized. Given the inherent constraints of assessing very young children who may not yet be able to read or write, educators should include developmentally appropriate assessments that rely on observations, documentation, and portfolios to more holistically and accurately capture children's development. As part of this effort, checklists and rating scales, as well as norm-referenced tools that are verbally administered to young children, should be considered when developing a program-wide assessment system. To support today's Montessori educators and administrators in meeting the needs of all learners, especially as it relates to their language and literacy development, we will review the following tools: (1) PPVT, the Peabody Picture Vocabulary Test (Dunn & Dunn, 2007); (2) PALS Pre-K, the Phonological Awareness Literacy Screening (Invernizzi et al., 2004); and (3) CLASS, the Classroom Assessment Scoring System (Pianta et al., 2008). These are three examples of tools and assessments available in the field that could support Montessori educators and children. The first two tools capture individual children's language and literacy development, and the third tool, the CLASS, is a systematic observation assessment that provides a means of understanding the ways in which educators engage with children to support their early learning and development, including in areas of language and literacy.

THE IMPORTANCE OF LANGUAGE INSTRUCTION AND ITS APPLICATION IN MONTESSORI CLASSROOMS

One criticism of the Science of Reading movement is the public perception that strong reading outcomes will be realized when greater attention is given primarily to phonics instruction. However, a review of state legislation contradicted this perception, showing that 34 states actually refer to a range of literacy pillars required of effective reading instruction. Yes, legislation referred to phonics instruction, but it also identified phonemic awareness, vocabulary, fluency, and comprehension (Neuman et al., 2023) as mandated instructional strategies. What was of note in this same legislative review was that although oral language and background knowledge were written into some legislation, overall, these aspects of reading instruction received the least attention in state mandates (Neuman et al., 2023).

Here is an overly simplified example of why both phonics and vocabulary instruction are needed to achieve comprehension. A student reading a phonetically accessible book may be able to decode the word "cast," sounding out each of the individual phonemes: /c/ /a/ /s/ /t/. But to comprehend what was read, the student will need to know if the word represents the *cast* you would wear on a broken arm, or if the character in the story was part of a *cast* for a school play, or if they *cast* their fishing line into a pond. Whether it is content that is read to us or that we read ourselves, "the knowledge we bring to a text is the key determinant in how much we understand that text" (Anderson & Pearson, 1984, in Cabell & Hwang, 2023, p. 175). That is because to read with comprehension is to "simultaneously extract and construct meaning from text" (RAND Reading Study Group, 2002, in Cabell & Hwang, 2023, p. 176).

Whether we follow the Simple View of Reading model (Gough & Tunmer, 1986) or Hollis Scarborough's Reading Rope (Scarborough, 2001), a child's vocabulary and background knowledge play an integral role in their becoming successful readers. A team of reading researchers who formed the Knowledge Matters Campaign, "an equity movement, pointing a path to supporting all students as readers, writers, thinkers, and learners" (2022/2024), also noted the importance of developing students' language skills:

> The Science of Reading has often been interpreted far too narrowly as exclusively focused on foundational skills. Reading success requires much more than foundational skills. There are other factors critical for literacy development, including those that address language, meaning, and communication. Among the most important is knowledge. Knowledge is necessary to comprehend what we read. Foundational skills are literally meaningless unless readers can make sense of words and texts. This sense-making requires knowledge that must be systematically built (not just activated!) through instructional experiences and curricula that evoke curiosity and the desire to learn more. In short, knowledge matters.

Recognizing the role of policy in influencing reading instruction in schools, the Scientific Advisory Committee of the Knowledge Matters Campaign (2022/2024) drafted model language for policymakers to use when developing reading legislation highlighting the importance of building content knowledge.

> Comprehensive, coherent literacy instruction must begin in the earliest grades—Pre-K and Kindergarten—so that as students are learning to read, they are also building their reading comprehension.
>
> Instruction aligned to the science of reading should be designed around the research on reading comprehension, which includes the important role that content knowledge plays in literacy.
>
> Prioritizing the acquisition of knowledge across a broad range of topics should be the focus of instruction and will require high-quality curricula in, and daily time devoted not just to English language arts, but also to science, social studies, and the arts. English language arts curricula should be rich in content about the natural and social world, with topics sequenced to provide opportunities to build oral and academic language so that students can make meaning of the words and sentences they encounter in print.

It may be that there's a notable instructional imbalance in some classrooms. where there's a greater emphasis on other literacy skills, which can diminish time spent on language development. Perhaps this imbalance exists because instruction mirrors state legislative expectations. Perhaps it's due to the focus of the ELA curriculum selected by the school district; there's often an instructional imbalance with a greater emphasis on a single literacy strand rather than addressing the wider scope of literacy instruction. What is clear from the research is that to ensure students become successful readers, significant instructional time must be devoted to building children's language skills. Hwang and colleagues (2023) in their longitudinal investigation noted the positive relationship between domain knowledge and reading ability in the elementary years. Outcomes of the study indicated that "stronger earlier domain knowledge would lead to stronger later domain knowledge and reading, and stronger earlier reading would lead to stronger later reading and domain knowledge" (p. 13), with background knowledge serving a more important role in reading development than reading does on domain knowledge development.

Daniel Willingham (2021), in his book *Why Don't Students Like School?*, offers additional insight about the importance of background knowledge and its positive influence on students' reading comprehension. As students build background knowledge on a particular topic, they simultaneously build vocabulary. As described earlier, phonics instruction helps students decode a word, but background knowledge supports their understanding of its meaning. Since writers cannot include all information on a topic, readers' background knowledge allows them to bridge logical gaps in texts, helping to clarify what may be ambiguous. Also, when more background knowledge is stored in long-term memory, it allows for greater mental space to be available in working memory so readers can integrate and tie together different pieces of information (Willingham, 2021, pp. 30–37).

Maryanne Wolf (2017) describes this as "the acme of deep reading represent(ing) that 'fertile miracle of communication' that happens when readers use all of their cognitive and linguistic capacities to 'go beyond the wisdom of the author' to generate their own best thoughts" (Voyager Sopris, n.d.). Like Willingham, she also highlights the interactive nature of language, background knowledge, and reading comprehension:

> The word-rich get richer and the word-poor get poorer, a phenomenon (cognitive psychologist, Keith Stanovich) called the "Matthew Effect" after a passage in the New Testament. There is also a Matthew-Emerson Effect for background knowledge: those who have read widely and well will have many resources to apply to what they read; those who do not will have less to bring, which, in turn, gives them less basis for inference, deduction, and analogical thought and makes them ripe for falling prey to unadjudicated information. (Wolf, 2018, p. 56)

So when should we begin to build vocabulary and background knowledge? The short answer is, immediately. This can apply to educators who work with the youngest of students. For example, the infant or toddler

Figure 7.9. Geographic Landforms Nomenclature

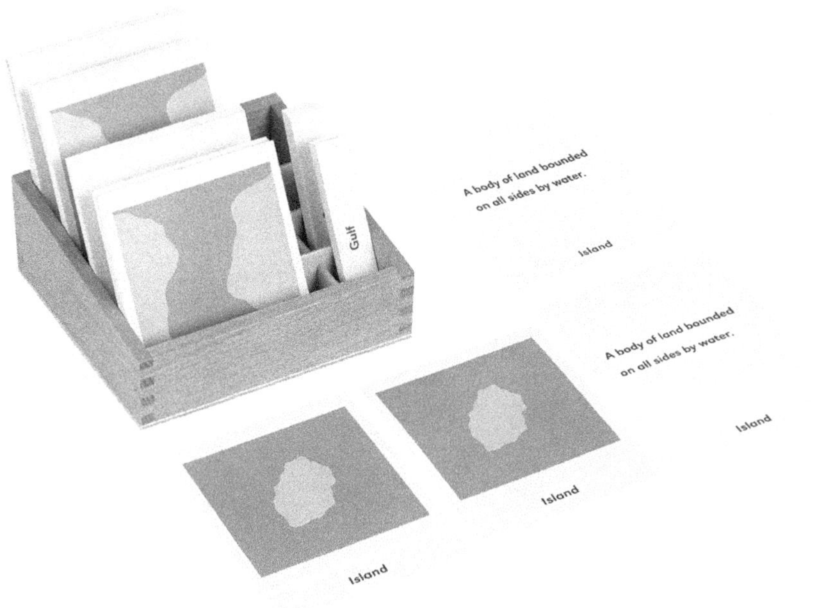

Photo courtesy of Nienhuis Montessori

teacher can simply narrate the child's day: labeling the clothing the child is wearing, the weather outside their door, the types of birds singing while on their walk in the park—these are all authentic and foundational learning opportunities. When a child enters a Montessori classroom, they are offered rich language opportunities through an integrated approach Cabell and Hwang (2023) refer to as content-rich ELA instruction that "integrates literacy and science and/or social studies within the ELA instructional setting" (p. 175) to build students' academic language. They define integrated literacy and content-area instruction as reading or writing activities that are aligned to the science or social studies content being learned. This type of integrated learning is found throughout the Montessori curriculum. Examples of this include when a teacher presents geography and botany lessons to teach about different landform types (Figure 7.9) or parts of a flower (Figure 7.10), respectively. Initially, these lessons are taught with landform models and real flowers for students to explore, and students are offered the correct terminology (i.e., island, isthmus, archipelago, or stamen, pistil, corolla).

Young children build background knowledge about the people and things that are directly in their home and school environment. They are

Figure 7.10. Leaf shapes

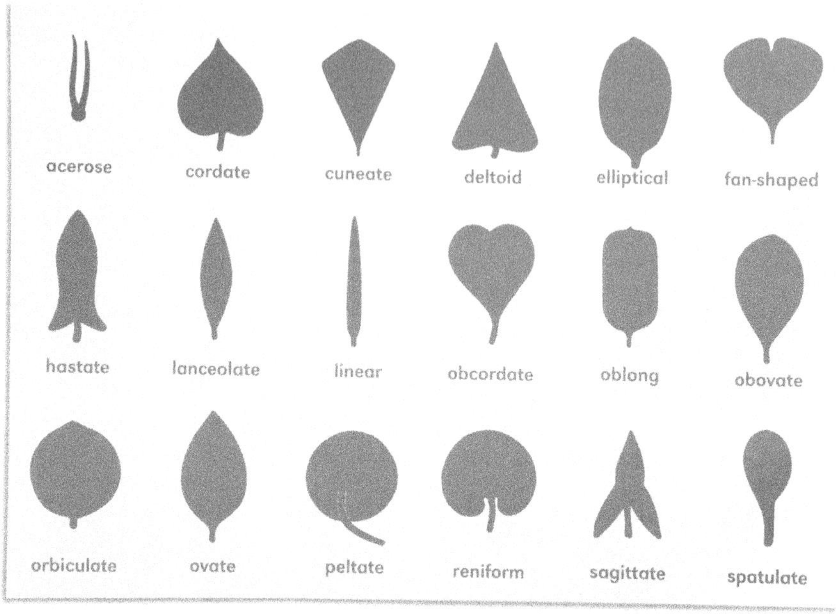

Photo courtesy of Nienhuis Montessori

offered rich children's literature to further build their understanding of what is in their local ecosystem. As students move into elementary classrooms, learning extends into what Dr. Montessori called the *cosmic curriculum*. At this age, students are ready to learn about the wider world, including all that can be found in the universe. Through narratives called the Great Stories, students learn about history, language, and science. They come to understand the universe and their place in it through timelines, self-directed research, trips into the community, and hands-on experiments (Duffy & Duffy, 2016). Through it all, a particular emphasis in the Montessori curriculum is to build children's vocabulary and background information about all that is relevant in the child's life. This information then becomes stored in their long-term memory and can be referenced and further refined in future learning.

As part of progress monitoring, having an understanding of students' language skills—vocabulary, background knowledge, language structures—will be an important next step. Students come to school with varying degrees of knowledge of the world and background knowledge related to science, history, geography, the arts, and the humanities. One assessment that informs the teacher of prior knowledge and vocabulary is the Peabody Picture Vocabulary Test (PPVT).

PEABODY PICTURE VOCABULARY TEST

The PPVT (Dunn & Dunn, 2007) is a widely used norm-referenced assessment tool recommended for use in educational and clinical settings to measure an individual's English receptive (listening) vocabulary and can serve as a proxy for their oral language skills.

Although not discussed here, parallel Spanish versions of this assessment that capture Spanish receptive vocabulary are also available (Dunn et al., 1986). Since the PPVT does not require a person to write or speak, this assessment tool has been used with individuals as young as 2.5 years of age through adulthood.

The tool's protocol generally takes 10–15 minutes for completion and begins at an age-specific level of difficulty. As part of this assessment, a child is required to look at four images displayed on a tabletop easel (black-and-white line drawings, PPVT-III, or color line drawings, PPVT-IV). As an example, the test administrator asks, "Show me *ball*," and the child looks at each of the images on the page and then points to the picture that best represents the orally presented word. This procedure continues for the duration of the assessment, until both a baseline and a ceiling score are established that describe the range of known words. There are two forms of this assessment. Form A is typically used at the beginning of the school year to determine baseline data, and Form B is used either during the middle or end of the year for program monitoring of the literacy curriculum, which in turn can inform site-based professional development, or more generally, for post-assessment of change in receptive vocabulary knowledge.

The PPVT is an age-norm-referenced assessment tool and has a mean standard score of 100 and a standard deviation of 15. This assessment has a very high and successful rate of measuring children's receptive vocabulary knowledge.

THE PPVT IN MONTESSORI CLASSROOMS

The language materials in a Montessori preschool classroom provide a diverse range of concepts and rich vocabulary opportunities for children. Using three-part cards, Montessori teachers offer lessons on topics ranging from (but not limited to) objects in a home, types of transportation, and parts of flowers. Throughout the day, children learn the language of math and the names of two- and three-dimensional shapes as well as continents, countries, and states. Teachers' observational notes can document which topics and materials have been shared and ultimately mastered by the child. In addition to teachers' notes and checklists, the PPVT offers teachers additional insight specific to children's receptive language development. For example, in one early literacy project, the PPVT was administered to all preschool children at the beginning of the school year, which provided teachers and program administrators with valid and reliable data in an efficient time frame (Zoll, 2012; Zoll & Rosenquest, 2011). For those children who scored well below national averages (a score of 85 or lower), teachers and literacy coaches provided additional authentic language experiences to augment children's learning so that they could catch up with their more skilled peers. The assessment was implemented again in January of the same academic year, with only those children who scored at 85 or lower on the original assessment taking part. The PPVT allowed teachers to track individual children's language development during the school year and reconsider their work with those children who needed additional support. As part of this effort, a final or post-assessment was also implemented with all of the children at the end of the school year. These pre- and post-data analysis provided evidence of children's learning through increased vocabulary knowledge over the course of the academic year. This protocol was especially useful for children who needed additional language support, including dual-language learners, as they were working toward mastery of English language skills.

The Montessori pedagogy is particularly strong in vocabulary development. Receptive and expressive language is fostered in many lessons and activities in the early childhood classroom. Administrators, parents, and education departments desire data to see the strengths of Montessori instruction. The PPVT is an assessment that will showcase this strength.

CHAPTER 8

Schedule/Logistics

MELDING A MONTESSORI CLASSROOM WITH OUTSIDE SCHEDULING REQUIREMENTS

Montessori teachers who are operating in the world of public school mandates may find that some outside requirements feel more comfortable to them than others. Many public Montessori classrooms find they are required to implement a reading screener. Consider the options for reading screening tools; some are more aligned to Montessori than others. Star Reading and iReady screeners are computer-based assessments, a modality of testing that is infrequently used in typical Montessori classrooms. DIBELS and Acadience are individually administered screening assessments. The individual administration is more closely aligned with Montessori philosophy and may feel easier to layer into the Montessori classroom. While flexibility will be necessary to meet scheduling and assessment requirements, the Montessori teacher may be able to select options that are aligned to Montessori practice. This is especially true if teachers and administrators are aware of the options that are available to them.

HISTORY OF RtI AND MTSS

In order to have a deeper understanding of how the logistics and scheduling of a Montessori classroom may occur with less disruption to Montessori practice, it is important to understand the national public school movement to a multi-tiered system of support (MTSS).

In response to No Child Left Behind (NCLB) legislation, response to intervention (RtI) was initiated in public schools. RtI was a process that identified students who were not making adequate academic growth and sought to remediate the problem. RtI frequently appears more reactive to students not meeting benchmarks, rather than proactive to set up schoolwide systems to ensure all students' success. Unfortunately, in most places RtI was rolled out without adequate professional development and monetary resources. As it developed from work in special education, it frequently focused on students' disabilities and was seen by many as a pathway to receiving an

IEP, or individualized education program (Massachusetts DESE, 2015). Additionally, when teachers attempted to add instructional supports for struggling students, they sometimes replaced core (Tier 1) instruction with their interventions. This supplanted or replaced the classroom curriculum. Legally, all students deserve a Free and Appropriate Public Education (FAPE). If Tier 1 instruction was not provided to *all* students, FAPE was not being upheld. Teachers were trying their best to meet the needs of the students but were sometimes not given the resources necessary to do so.

With the implementation of the Common Core Standards in 2012 and the development of new educator evaluation systems, the system began to change. Educators looked at which systemic components of RtI needed to remain and which components needed to be altered so that all students would retain access to Tier 1 instruction and receive the additional supports (in Tier 2 and 3 instruction) they needed. The Every Student Succeeds Act (ESSA) was passed in 2015. The underlying theme of this act was that every child deserves to be as successful as possible. According to ESSA (2015), a multi-tiered system of support is "a comprehensive continuum of evidence-based, systemic practices to support a rapid response to students' needs, with regular observation to facilitate data-based instructional decision making." This resulted in a switch from response to intervention (RtI) to the multi-tiered systems of support (MTSS). Both are three-tiered systems that provide a core curriculum (Tier 1) to all students, a Tier 2 of targeted interventions to selected students, and a Tier 3 of intensive interventions to select students. While RtI had mainly an academic focus, MTSS addresses the "whole child," recognizing that student needs include academic, behavioral, and social emotional components.

Instead of focusing on the deficit of the student if they are not meeting benchmarks, MTSS shifts the focus to problem-solving regarding the many components of learning—curriculum, instruction, the learner, and the learning environment—that can be altered to better fit the needs of the child. Similar to Dr. Montessori's approach to thinking as a researcher, today's teacher must continue to recognize children's social and emotional growth and serve as a detective to determine how to best individualize instruction so all learners' needs are met.

There are three main foci of MTSS that are important to keep at the forefront of thought. First, focus on successful student outcomes. Not only is this positive focus celebrating the child as a whole, it also emphasizes the importance of being able to provide evidence of these successful outcomes through data collection.

Second, the MTSS process, and teaching in general, revolves around data-based decision-making. Data-based individualization, the instructional implementation of knowledge gained from data-based decision-making, "shows evidence of improving student outcomes—in alignment both with prior studies of Data-Based Individualization and with the broader literature on

Data-Based Decision Making" (Kearns et al., 2021, p. 369). This use of data focuses on how data influences teachers' decision-making. Decisions based on measurable data prove more effective for a student's academic achievement.

Third, universal screening and continuous progress monitoring are integral to this process. The iterative cycle of an assessment schedule is integral to the MTSS process.

The Massachusetts Department of Education uses the analogy of the dentist to explain the tiers of intervention. (If you just cringed, at least you will remember this!) We all know that everyone should be seeing the dentist every 6 months for a cleaning and check-up. This is like Tier 1 instruction. Everyone gets their Tier 1. Sometimes the dentist determines that an individual needs something extra (Tier 2). Perhaps this is a filling for a cavity. The dentist (the teacher) can handle this themselves. Just because a person gets a filling, we don't take away Tier 1 (the general cleaning/instruction that everyone gets). Likewise, the dentist does not throw up their hands when they find a person has a cavity and exclaim, "Oh my! I better fill everyone's second molar today just in case they need it!" You only give the extra intervention to the person who needs it. Sometimes, an individual needs more than the dentist can give them, and they are referred to a specialist (Tier 3). The person goes to see someone else with expertise in a specific need. Maybe they go to an orthodontist for braces. It is not expected that they are treated by the orthodontist for the rest of their life; it is an intensive intervention that occurs only as needed. In MTSS, flexible Tier 2 and 3 instruction is important. Once a student is given Tier 2 or 3 instruction, it does not continue forever. The needed skill is bolstered, and then the child is released back to only Tier 1 instruction.

As a Montessori teacher, perhaps you are thinking, "I already do this. I see a student struggling, and I intervene and model and support as needed." Terrific! If this is the case, it is the added layer of formal assessment that offers the data to track this intervention time that is needed. The research and evidence-based 1-minute progress monitoring assessments give us the quantitative data needed in the data-based decision-making model.

In general, Tier 1 (Core Instruction) is considered the responsibility of the classroom teacher(s). Tier 2 instruction is the interventions that are put in place as a first step to addressing specific student needs that have held the student(s) back from reaching benchmarks. Usually, this is also the responsibility of the classroom teacher. They may meet with individuals or small groups to provide short lessons that address needed skills. Usually these are short interventions of 15–20 minutes. Students could also receive Ter 2 support from other individuals such as paraprofessionals and other teachers in the building. Tier 3 interventions are intensive interventions that are usually provided by a special educator or reading specialist. These interventions are more intense in duration of time (often 30–60 minutes per day) and even more individualized.

LAYERING INTERVENTION INSTRUCTION INTO THE MONTESSORI CLASSROOM

Interventions do not change the core curriculum, so Montessori instruction is not altered. Instead, Tier 2 instruction can be layered into the classroom, guiding the teacher as they individualize instruction to meet the needs that have surfaced through both formal assessments and observation. Responding to individual needs and tailoring instruction to each child is a strength of Montessori education, and assessment gives added information that will make the teacher's individualization that much more effective, focusing instructional time on what each student needs the most.

EXPLICIT INSTRUCTION AND ELICITING RESPONSES

As discussed previously (see Archer, Chapter 3), explicit instruction calls for the gradual release of responsibility through the "I Do, We Do, You Do" model. Explicit instruction is needed in Tiers 1, 2, and 3. It is important to keep in mind that individual students will vary in the amount of "We Do" or supported practice they must have before a skill is mastered. Figure 8.1 shows the roles of the teacher and student throughout explicit instruction until mastery is reached.

For explicit instruction to be successful, the students must be actively engaged in the instruction. How does a teacher know if the students are engaged? There is a constant give-and-take between the teacher and students.

Figure 8.2 is a reminder of two questions that should be foremost in the teacher's mind no matter what subject area they are instructing or what tier of instruction they are teaching: "Are the students engaged right now?" and "Are the students understanding?" The only way to know the answer to these questions is to elicit responses from the students. The more responses a student makes, the more engaged they are in the lesson and the more formative and observational assessment data you have to guide instructional decisions.

A national center called IRIS, which is an acroynym for IDEA (Individuals with Disabilities Education Act) and Vanderbilt University's Research for Inclusive Settings, seeks to promote the use of evidence-based instruction and intervention for all students, especially those with disabilities. IRIS provides professional development for educators that supports inclusive education. According to IRIS, every student should be given approximately 3–5 opportunities to respond every minute (Vanderbilt University, 2024b).

Table 8.1 contains a checklist that is based on Anita Archer's Explicit Instruction, the IRIS modules (Vanderbilt University, 2024b, and the NCII Explicit Instruction Module 6, National Center on Intensive Intervention, n.d.-b), and Himelee and Himelee's *Total Participation Techniques* (2017).

Figure 8.1. Explicit Instruction

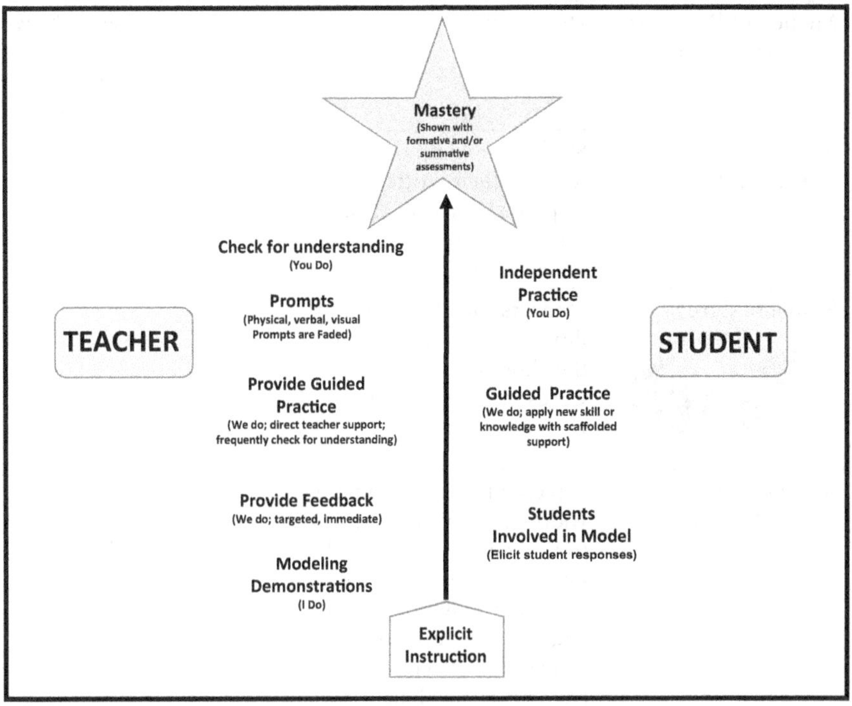

Based on Archer & Hughes, 2011; Pearson & Gallagher, 1983

Figure 8.2. Engaging Students Through Frequent Responses

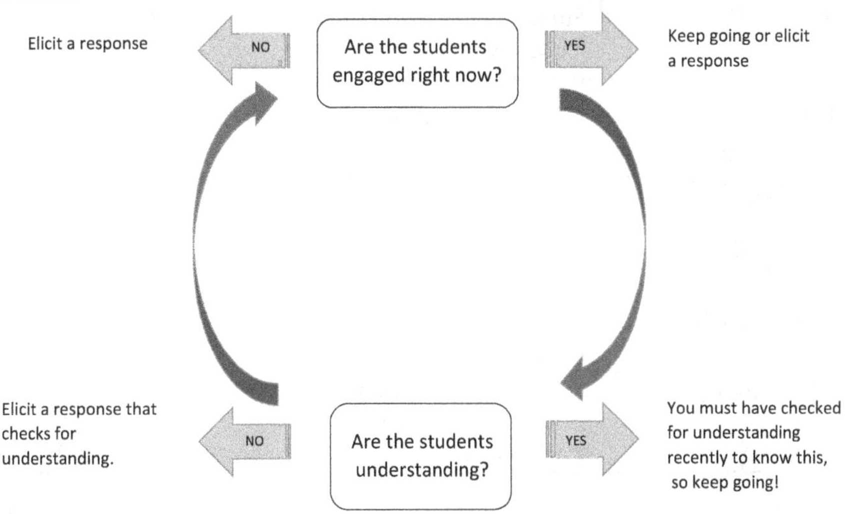

Table 8.1. How to Increase Student Engagement With a Lesson

Consider the techniques listed here. Which do you already use in your instruction, and which could be added to increase engagement and understanding?

Method of Response and Engagement	Definition	I use this method.	When/how could I add this method?
Individual Whiteboards	Students hold up their boards to show their written response. Teacher can scan the class/group for understanding		
Response Cards 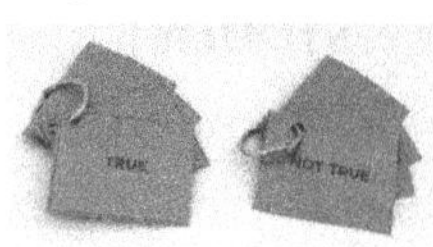	Students each have a set of flip cards on a key ring that they hold up to respond. Cards may be labeled A, B, C, D; True/False; etc . . .		
Agree/Disagree	A piece of yarn spanning the width of the room is attached to the ceiling or a piece of tape runs along the floor. Opposite ends are labeled "agree" and "disagree." A statement is given and students move along the continuum to denote their level of agreement and are ready to tell why they chose to stand where they are.		
Thumbs Up/ Thumbs Down	Students show thumbs to gauge their level of agreement or understanding.		
Fingers as a Number 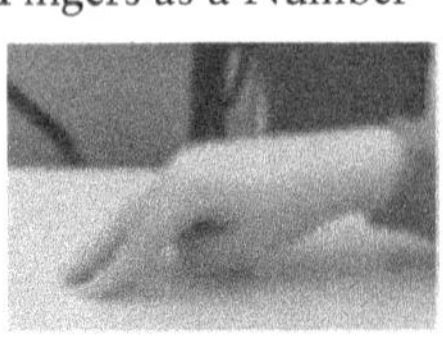	Given numbered choices, students show on their fingers which answer is correct.		
Partner Retell	Partner Turn-and-Talk to summarize learning.		
Choral Response	Group responds together, usually in response to teacher's signal.		

(*continued*)

Table 8.1. *(continued)*

Echoed Response	Teacher says something, group repeats back.
Turn and Talk	Students respond to a prompt in a short paired discussion.
Whip Around	Students are given a prompt (e.g., What is your favorite color?). They are given wait time to think of an answer. Teacher has students quickly go around the room to each say their answer. Answers can be repeated.
Stop and Jot	Students respond to a prompt in a short written response.
Individual Response 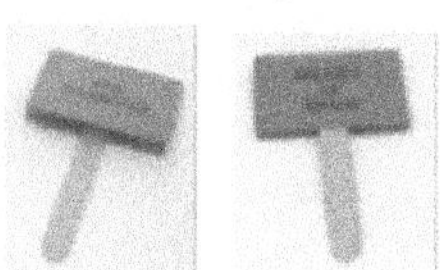	Teacher calls on specific student for answer (cold call).

MONTESSORI THREE-PERIOD LESSON ALIGNED TO EXPLICIT INSTRUCTION

Similar to Archer and Hughes's (2011) Explicit Instruction model, Montessori educators use an instruction approach known as the Three-Period Lesson. As detailed in the section above, explicit instruction is purposeful and structured around three key moments in classroom instruction. This is also true for the Montessori Three-Period Lesson as the teacher moves from modeling the lesson for students, to providing extended student practice opportunity, and ultimately having students demonstrate mastery by replicating or recalling the lesson in its entirety. Figure 8.3 illustrates a comparison of each of these instructional strategies.

In the Montessori classroom, the Three-Period Lesson serves as both an instructional approach and a formative assessment strategy. When working with an individual or a small group of students, the teacher monitors learning at each stage of the lesson and gauges whether to move forward or revisit at another time—all in response to their observation of the student.

> . . . during the first period, the educator models the language (naming) as they demonstrate each step of the lesson to the student. Then, during the second

Figure 8.3. Explicit Instruction Aligned to Montessori Three-Period Lesson

Both instructional models are structured to include clear modeling, guided practice, and independent practice,.

	I DO:	WE DO:	YOU DO:
EXPLICIT INSTRUCTION	• The teacher introduces the lesson, modeling and explicitly highlighting key portion of the activity. • Instruction is usually to the whole class or to a small group of students. • Teacher narrates their thinking using consistent language.	• The student leads the guided practice portion of the lesson. • The teacher closely monitors and offers guidance as needed. • Feedback from the teacher is direct and immediate.	• The student now engages in independent practice of lesson. • Students offered new activities that replicate lesson learning objectives. • Teacher support is minimal.
	1ST PERIOD:	**2ND PERIOD:**	**3RD PERIOD**
MONTESSORI 3-PERIOD LESSON	• The teacher introduces the lesson, modeling and explicitly highlighting key aspects of the activity. *Naming period.* • Instruction is usually with one student or a small group of students. • Teacher focuses on concise, deliberate modeling and naming	• The student moves from observer to active participant, replicating the lesson as it was modeled. *Recognition period.* • Often the materials contain a 'control of error' that guide students' use of materials. • The teacher is now an observer, monitoring student progress.	• The student now engages in independent practice of lesson. *Recall period.* • Student replicates same lesson. • Extension activities may be new to the student, but reflect same learning objectives. • Teacher support is minimal.

Zoll, Feinberg, Saylor, 2023; Archer & Hughes, 2011; AMS n.d.

period, the teacher assesses learning by asking the student to point to a correct response (recognition). Last, in the third period, the teacher asks the student to respond with the correct name when asked (recall). Simultaneous with conducting the lesson, the teacher notes the student's level of success at each stage and makes in-the-moment decisions regarding the progression of the lesson. This authentic assessment practice formatively guides the teacher's work with each child. Rather than completing a lesson that is not yet understood, the teachers can conclude the lesson at any stage when they determine the child has experienced an appropriate level of challenge while not yet demonstrating mastery. (Zoll et al., 2023, p. 223)

There is an additional feature inherent in the design of many Montessori materials that facilitates students' learning known as a "control of error." The control of error serves to inform the student of their progress in the lesson rather than needing to rely solely on direct feedback from the teacher. Instead, the control of error provides students with "instant feedback about (their) progress . . . allowing (them) to recognize, correct, and learn from an error without adult assistance. Putting control of the activity in the child's hands strengthens (their) self-esteem and self-motivation as well as (their) learning" (AMS, n.d.-b).

One example is Sandpaper Letters, which provide tactile feedback if the child's fingers leave the rough sandpaper letter and instead slide along the wooden surface of the material. This simple design encourages the young child's hand movement to kinesthetically follow the shapes of each letter. Depending on the classroom materials that have been selected by the teacher, students will learn the shapes of letters written in cursive or in print—and in some classrooms, instruction is provided in both writing styles.

Another example are the many three-part cards found in the Language, Sensorial, and Cultural areas of the classroom. Three-part cards consist of three items: (1) photo cards, (2) the corresponding labels, and (3) control cards that pair the photo with the label for self-checking. In the Cultural area of the classroom, there may be three-part cards related to types of flowers found in the neighborhood. In this example, there may be images of a sunflower, rose, tulip, marigold, and so forth. One set of cards have just the image, whereas another set has the same images but also includes the correct label. In introductory three-part card lessons, students begin by first matching the two image cards. Later, they will then add the corresponding label. The control card provides immediate feedback to the student if they have matched the correct labels, allowing them to self-select a different response, if needed.

These didactic materials, just like Montessori teachers, are purposed with facilitating independent learning—a hallmark of Montessori classrooms. They serve as instructional tools to help children explore concepts through hands-on experiences. And they are visually appealing, as well as self-correcting, enabling children to recognize and correct their own mistakes, fostering autonomy and self-mastery. The materials offer a structured framework that guides children to understand and internalize concepts at their own pace, supporting both cognitive development and a sense of order.

CASE STUDY DISCUSSION AND ANALYSIS (MOY)

Case Study—Early Childhood

Scenario—We're returning to Khadija's classroom to examine how her students have progressed since the start of the school year. As they did with the screening tool they used at the beginning of the school year, Khadija and the school's reading coach assessed children again using the PALS Pre-K, as well as implementing the Peabody Picture Vocabulary Test (PPVT-IV) to determine students' receptive language skills.

Khadija was excited to see if her classroom observations aligned with data from PALS Pre-K and the PPVT-IV. Over the past 4 months, she had created both individualized and small-group literacy activities that reflected

Table 8.2. Tiered Instruction/RtI Legend

Tiered Instruction/RtI Legend *PALS Pre-K scores have been placed in one of three tiers to identify instructional needs*			
Tiers	Name Writing	Uppercase Letters	Letter Sounds
3	0–3	0–4	0–5
2	4–5	5–15	6–12
1	6–7	16–26	13–26

specific skills children demonstrated as needing additional support. She and her colleagues again selected the same three subtests of the PALS Pre-K to review (name writing, uppercase letter recognition, and letter sound recognition) and compared outcomes between this point in the school year with students' initial benchmark scores that were captured at the start of the school year (see Table 8.2). Since the use of tiered instruction was helpful to Khadija in her planning, they reviewed the data using the same legend they had collaboratively designed and were comfortable with the benchmarks they had set, as all of her 3-year-olds had now turned 4 years old by the start of the new calendar year.

Prompts:

- Begin with **Name Writing scores** at the beginning of the school year (BOY).
    - » How many students were assigned to Tier 1? __________
    - » How many students were assigned to Tier 2? __________
    - » How many students were assigned to Tier 3? __________
- Now look at **Name Writing scores** from the middle of the school year (MOY).
    - » How many students were assigned to Tier 1? __________
    - » How many students were assigned to Tier 2? __________
    - » How many students were assigned to Tier 3? __________
- What do you notice about these outcomes? Has Khadija's instruction been successful in supporting her students' name writing skills?
- Which children will benefit from continued support in this area?
- Now, in the same way, review **Uppercase Letter** scores at the beginning of the school year (BOY).
    - » How many students were assigned to Tier 1? __________
    - » How many students were assigned to Tier 2? __________
    - » How many students were assigned to Tier 3? __________

Table 8.3. Looking Across Two Points in Time: Beginning of Year (BOY) Screening and Middle of Year (MOY) Progress Monitoring (3 Subtests of PALS Pre-K)

Name Writing (max score 7)			Uppercase Letter Recognition (max score 26)			Letter Sound Recognition (max score 26)		
Student	Score BOY	Score MOY	Student	Score BOY	Score MOY	Student	Score BOY	Score MOY
a	1	6	a	3	4	a	3	14
b	1	7	b	2	26	b	0	24
c	1	7	c	0	9	c	0	11
d	1	4	d	0	10	d	0	17
e	1	3	e	0	26	e	0	23
f	5	6	f	0	9	f	0	16
g	0	6	g	1	6	g	0	11
h	3	6	h	1	14	h	0	23
i	6	6	i	1	2	i	0	5
j	6	7	j	1	24	j	0	14
k	3	5	k	3	26	k	0	24
l	5	7	l	3	24	l	1	11
m	5	6	m	6	21	m	0	17
n	3	7	n	9	18	n	6	23
o	4	7	o	18	26	o	0	16
p	4	6	p	5	26	p	0	11
q	4	7	q	23	25	q	13	23
r	4	7	r	11	15	r	1	5

- Now look at **Uppercase Letter** scores from the middle of the school year (MOY).
    - » How many students were assigned to Tier 1? ___________
    - » How many students were assigned to Tier 2? ___________
    - » How many students were assigned to Tier 3? ___________
- What do you notice about these outcomes? Has Khadija's instruction been successful in supporting her students' uppercase letter recognition skills?
- Which children will benefit from continued support in this area?

- And finally, review **Letter Sound** scores at the beginning of the school year (BOY).
    - » How many students were assigned to Tier 1? ________
    - » How many students were assigned to Tier 2? ________
    - » How many students were assigned to Tier 3? ________
- Now look at **Letter Sound** scores from the middle of the school year (MOY).
    - » How many students were assigned to Tier 1? ________
    - » How many students were assigned to Tier 2? ________
    - » How many students were assigned to Tier 3? ________
- What do you notice about these outcomes? Has Khadija's instruction been successful in supporting her students' letter sound recognition skills?
- Which children will benefit from continued support in this area?

Khadija also wanted to review outcomes from the PPVT, so that she has an understanding of her students' growing receptive language and vocabulary. Since the PPVT assesses an individual's English language skills and knowledge from a family survey conducted at the beginning of the year, and almost half of her students spoke a language other than English at home, the school's reading coach helped separate scores reflecting this information. Table 8.4 demonstrates PPVT scores from Khadija's classroom at the beginning of the year and again at the middle of the school year.

Table 8.4. Peabody Picture Vocabulary Test

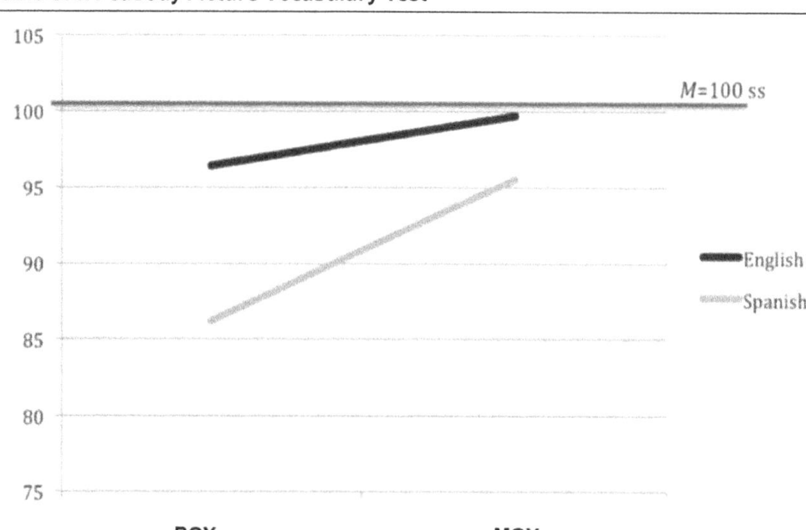

Test (PPVT-IV) BOY and MOY Average Scores by Home Language (English or Spanish)

The BOY scores demonstrate that on average all children in her classroom, regardless of the language that was spoken in the home, would benefit from a strong focus on language development. When the same assessment was given again in January (MOY), Khadija and the school's ELA team were thrilled to learn that language instruction in this classroom was positively influencing all students' language learning. And while the outcomes for children who were noted by their families as speaking Spanish at home did not yet meet those of their same-age peers, on average their receptive language skills grew at a very strong rate, as noted by the trajectory of change between their pre- and midyear scores.

Prompts:

PPVT Beginning of Year (BOY) Scores

- The line M=100 demonstrates the standardized score of the assessment, indicating children who have a receptive vocabulary representative of a same-age English-speaking individual. With this in mind, what can you determine about the English-speaking students' receptive vocabulary at the **beginning of the school year?** On average, did English-speaking students meet the standardized score, meaning their receptive vocabulary was similar to their same-age peers?
- Now compare the same line (standardized score) with data from the line for Spanish speakers. What can you determine about the Spanish-speaking students' receptive vocabulary at the **beginning of the school year?** On average, did Spanish-speaking students meet the standardized score, meaning their receptive vocabulary was similar to their same-age peers?

PPVT Middle of Year (MOY) Scores

- Again, the line M=100 demonstrates the standardized score of the assessment, indicating children who have a receptive vocabulary representative of a same-age English-speaking individual. With this in mind, what can you determine about the English-speaking students' receptive vocabulary at the **middle of the school year?** On average, did English-speaking students meet the standardized score, meaning their receptive vocabulary was similar to their same-age peers?
- Now compare the same line (standardized score) with data from the line for Spanish speakers. What can you determine about the Spanish-speaking students' receptive vocabulary at the **middle of the school year?** On average, did Spanish-speaking students meet

the standardized score, meaning their receptive vocabulary was similar to their same-age peers?

- Overall, have children in Khadija's classroom demonstrated growth in their receptive vocabulary? Of the two groups (English- and Spanish-speaking children), which has demonstrated the greatest growth during this time? What informed your decision?

After reviewing these data and as you think about your own classroom—regardless of the age group you are working with—which materials will you focus on to intentionally influence your students' vocabulary development?

Case Study—Elementary

Third-grade student Bella began as a 4-year-old Montessori student in the Casa (preschool) classroom. Last year, her teacher added extra phonics support for Bella in a small group because Bella's accuracy rate when reading grade-level material was about 75–80 percent. When the teacher analyzed Bella's mistakes, it appeared that Bella frequently guessed at words using the first letter. She also substituted words that seemed to "make sense," rather than attempting to read the words letter by letter or sound by sound. Daily reminders to look at the word and read the word through appeared to keep Bella focused on decoding.

At the beginning of 3rd grade, Bella's accuracy (ability to decode the text correctly) was greatly improved. On her BOY screener (Acadience), Bella correctly decoded the majority of words she read in 3-minute Oral Reading Fluency passages, receiving scores between 93 and 98 percent. The BOY benchmark was a rate of 95 percent accuracy, so her teacher was quite happy. Bella read between 32 and 38 words per minute on these assessments, with a benchmark of 70 words per minute. So although Bella was figuring out the words correctly, the decoding process was not automatic for her, which slowed her down.

The teacher decided to give Bella the first few months of school with no additional support in reading. When given choice in the classroom, Bella did not choose reading or writing activities. However, she was an active participant in discussions, had a wide vocabulary, and verbally expressed content knowledge and learnings at a high level of understanding.

When the MOY screener was given at the beginning of January, Bella did not show improvement in her fluency (number of correct words read per minute). She did not make many decoding errors, but she read a limited number of words in the 1-minute time span. Her comprehension of what she read was at grade level. She could easily retell all the main ideas and details from the Oral Reading Fluency passages.

Table 8.5. Middle of Year Oral Reading Fluency Scores

Middle of Year 3rd Grade Acadience Oral Reading Fluency (ORF)		
	Bella's Score	MOY Benchmark
Accuracy	98%	96%
Fluency (Words per Minute)	43 wpm	86 wpm
Retell	26	26

Bella's scores on the MOY Acadience Reading assessment are shown in Table 8.5.

The teacher decided to give Bella a Quick Phonics Screener to determine if there were particular decoding skills that were slowing Bella down. Bella showed mastery of all phonics sections, getting between 8 and 10 out of 10 in each section correct. In all phonics areas, except for letter names and sounds, Bella worked slowly and methodically. As this is an untimed diagnostic to see if the student knows the phonics skill, her slow pace did not impact her score. However, the teacher noted her speed was consistently labored.

Identify Bella's strengths and weaknesses in reading:

What additional support could the teacher provide Bella?

How could this intervention be implemented in your classroom?

What materials would you use to provide this support?

Author's note: Bella's data show she understands and applies phonics/decoding skills but does so in a slow manner. This means that she has not reached a level of automaticity with these skills. It is recommended that Bella be supported in a manner that provides ample opportunity to use her decoding skills until she can apply them fluently. Consider practice with decodable texts. These texts would allow Bella to use her decoding skills again and again, but in the context of connected text. Consider echo readings, where Bella repeats the reading after the teacher reads it out loud in an attempt to match the teacher's rate and expression. Repeated readings, timed readings, and readers' theater are also beneficial for students who are working to build their fluency skills.

Part 3—Wrapping Up the School Year: Prioritizing, Keeping on, and Defining Next Steps

We have now come to the conclusion of the academic year. Through a series of assessments that included observations, universal screeners, and diagnostic tools, you successfully identified key areas of literacy and aligned language lessons that were offered to students. Instruction included intentional small-group and individual lessons. Progress was monitored, with special attention given to those students who were not yet meeting developmental expectations. As you reviewed these data points over time, growth in children's learning became visible. The data also provided authentic opportunities to engage teaching staff in professional dialogue about their work in the classroom, supports or materials needed to enhance student learning, and meaningful connections with families to understand and support their child's literacy learning at home.

One recommendation the authors make as you review the End of Year Decision Tree: Aim to complete these assessments a good 6–8 weeks before the actual end of the school year. Why would timing be an important consideration? Because for those children who have demonstrated some growth over time, but still demonstrate need to increase their vocabulary skills, or phonological awareness, or need to improve their fluency in order to build their comprehension in reading, we still have precious time through the remainder of the year to engage them in lessons that meet their specific needs. But some will say,

"The children will come to understand reading in their own time."

"We push academics too soon on children."

"In Finland, children do not begin to read until age 7."

Though these comments may hold some truth, for many children they will be statements of oppression. These beliefs can reflect bias and privilege. They infer that we carry expectations that all children have access to books, literacy materials, and rich conversations outside the classroom; that all children engage in learning experiences in their community; that they frequent their local library and children's museum; that they can identify the trees in their park, and can name the fruits and vegetables in their local market. In reality, when children do not have many literacy-focused experiences prior to their first day of school, there is an opportunity gap that can grow wider unless greater attention is given to classroom instruction. Without evidence-based focused interventions, we can miss the sensitive period for language and literacy development Dr. Montessori designed and then was later expanded upon by Muriel Dwyer (Dwyer, 1970). Research shows that what begins as an opportunity gap in early childhood, without intentional support, can soon become ever-widening learning gaps as students progress through elementary school, what Stanovich (1986) referred to as the Matthew Effect. For those students who fail to read with comprehension, especially as they enter 3rd grade when the curriculum shifts from "learning to read" to "reading to learn"—learning becomes more difficult, and they struggle to keep up with peers. Research points to the lifelong impact, as these students are less likely to complete high school, attend college, or become engaged citizens in their communities. This is the lens you must use to view the importance of your work. Children's future opportunities will depend on it.

End of Year (EOY) Decision Trees

As you near the end of the academic year, you'll schedule a final round of data collection using the same benchmark screener(s) used at the beginning and the middle of the school year. Figure 8.4 recommends that you administer assessments with all students. For those students who meet or exceed the literacy benchmarks, their learning has progressed over time and they will continue their work in the Montessori classroom demonstrating agency with the materials with continued guidance from their teacher. For those students who meet only some of the literacy benchmarks, the results should be reviewed to identify which areas of literacy will require additional support. Small-group and individual lessons will be planned to support this learning over the remaining weeks of school. And for those students who do not yet meet any grade-level benchmarks, a review of the data will highlight the areas of literacy that need support. For these students you'll want to focus on foundational skills. If children's receptive language needs support, additional lessons using three-part cards and reading nonfiction books that support topics being explored in the classroom will be of use. If students are struggling to read three- or four-letter phonetic words, additional lessons of encoding words with the Movable Alphabet may be warranted.

For all students, these data will also serve to inform two additional activities: authentic family engagement and planning next year's comprehensive assessment plan. For example, during the school year, teachers have had

Figure 8.4. End of Year (EOY) Decision Trees

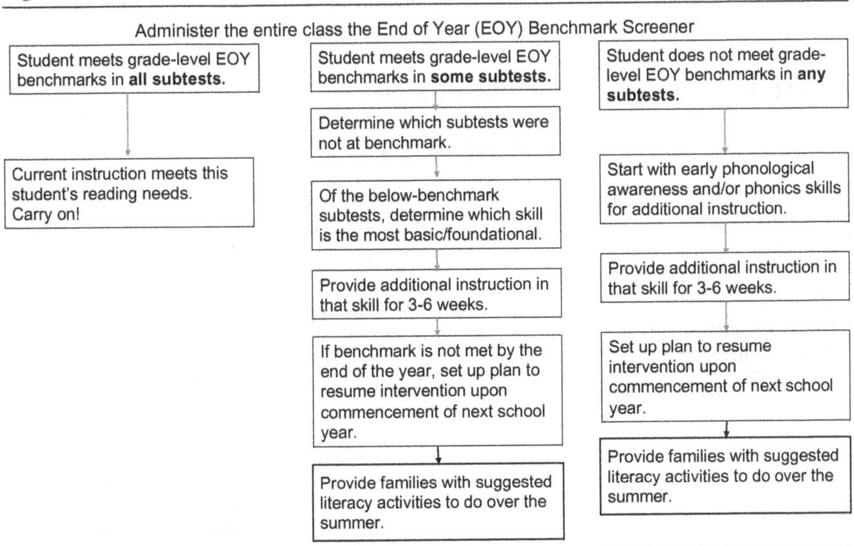

the opportunity to meet and discuss earlier assessment results with families. EOY data should be no different. In fact, this may be a wonderful time to meet with families and host a schoolwide "make & take" session at school or as a table set up during the end-of-year family picnic. Families can create literacy materials that respond to their child's learning and use them at home to avoid summer learning loss. This is a wonderful opportunity to also engage your community, perhaps by inviting local high school or college students studying to be teachers, who can serve as volunteers to support these activities. Family and community partnerships will be discussed in Chapter 12.

Also, scheduled meetings that engage teaching staff, literacy coaches, and school administrators should include a complete review of the data over the course of the school year. Reflection on EOY results can inform the following school year's assessment activities. What went well this year? Were there any identified areas of need regarding the data collection process, the opportunity to review student data with teaching staff, and the use of data to inform classroom instruction or individualized support for all students? What would you change for next year? Did the schedule for implementing assessments work, or would you revise certain dates due to holidays or academic breaks? Do you have all the materials and staff needed to successfully implement your comprehensive assessment plan next year?

This retrospective review of the data also provides insight at the classroom level (see Figure 8.5). If 80 percent or more of the students met EOY benchmarks, this represents a strong core Montessori curriculum (Tier 1). If, however, less than 80 percent of the students were able to meet these same benchmarks, this might be an opportunity to determine what might be

Figure 8.5. Reflection on EOY Benchmark Screener

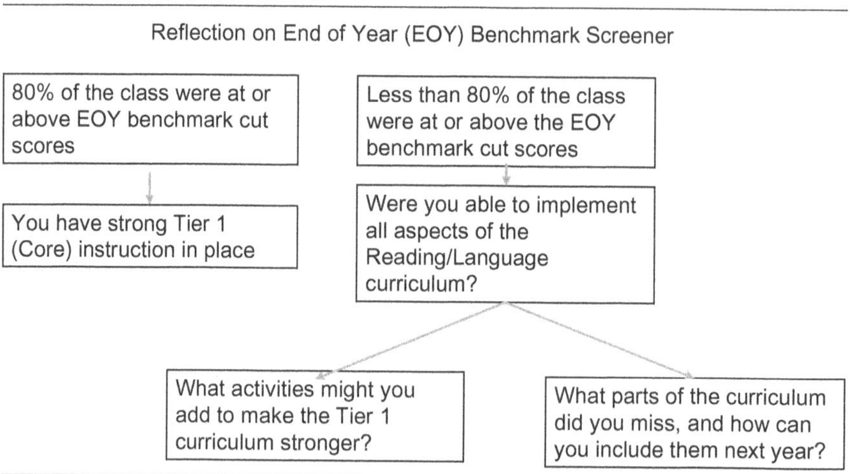

missing. Are the Language materials in the classroom complete or are additional materials needed to support learning across all areas of literacy? If the materials are present, would teachers benefit from professional development that includes links between Montessori materials and reading research? Maybe a refresher that covers the entire Language curriculum to encourage the use of not just some materials, but the full breadth of Montessori materials to meet the needs of students would be beneficial. Do student demographics represent a diverse school population? Then perhaps professional development and coaching that reflects working with dual-language learners could be a focus next school year. This is an important step where you can collectively brainstorm and revise practices that work best for your school's context.

The conclusion of the year provides time for reflection, short-term instructional changes, and planning for what may change or continue the following year. As the school year winds down, the Montessori teacher who provides instruction to a multigrade-level classroom has the advantage that they are not saying goodbye to their students for long. While the teacher can initiate one last concerted effort to address skills that may not yet be mastered or to introduce new learning, reflection that will lead to data-based decisions for the next year is also important at this time of the year.

CHAPTER 9

Lesson Application

In consideration of the previous chapter's case studies, it is important to examine the data collected and analyzed. The vocabulary assessment results from the early childhood classroom showed that all children would benefit from additional language instruction, with a particular emphasis on developing vocabulary in English for those children who spoke Spanish at home. Additionally, research supports language development as a key element of reading comprehension. If a student can decode a word but does not know the word's meaning, then comprehension is negatively impacted. Using these insights, it is deemed that some of the early childhood students would benefit from instruction with rich lessons from the language and cultural areas of the curriculum (science, social studies, geography, etc.).

While the lesson in Table 9.1 is intended for early elementary students, it illustrates how to provide students with strong background knowledge in science. A lesson like this can be adapted for learning about mammals, amphibians, or other animal classes (Figure 9.1).

Based on the data collected and analyzed for the elementary case study, it may be beneficial to include additional instructional activities that support orthographic mapping, the mapping of words and word parts on the brain through repeated exposures that enable automatic word recognition. The lesson on the ea phonogram (see Table 9.2) is an example of an activity designed to enhance a child's orthographic mapping skills. The three-part format of these cards (Figure 9.2) enables independent phonogram practice, even for beginning readers.

END-OF-SCHOOL-YEAR CONSIDERATIONS FOR LESSONS

As the school year draws to a close, it's easy for schools and educators to get caught up in end-of-the-year celebrations and activities. However, it's crucial to maintain a focus on teaching. With a limited number of school days available, the impact of summer learning loss, particularly on our most vulnerable students, cannot be overlooked. Research by Alexander and colleagues (2007) shows that the achievement gap between high- and low-SES students by the 9th grade is largely attributable to disparities in summer

Figure 9.1. Three-Part Cards

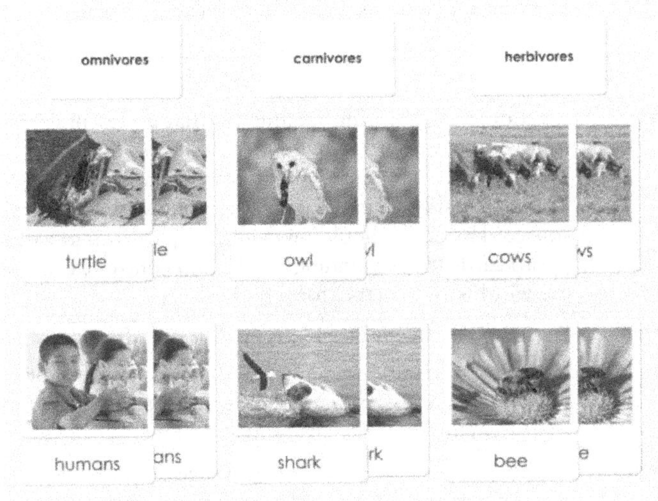

Photo Courtesy of Nienhuis Montessori

learning during the elementary years. With this in mind, we advocate for teachers to keep teaching as long as they possibly can.

The end of the school year often brings a wave of mixed emotions for all members of a school community. On the one hand, there's excitement about the new learning opportunities that lie ahead and the fresh challenges that a new academic year will bring. On the other hand, saying goodbye to one's current community of teachers and friends can be bittersweet. There's also a sense of trepidation as students, teachers, and parents alike say goodbye to familiar routines and brace themselves for the changes and unknowns that the new school year will inevitably introduce.

In this academic season, teachers who have spent months carefully planning and tailoring their curriculum sometimes find that their best-laid plans no longer align with the evolving needs of their students. The pressures that surround high-stakes testing further compound these challenges. Sometimes the focus on preparing for these exams can result in a significant loss of instructional time, forcing educators to shift away from their original plans. Additionally, end-of-year administrative requirements can detract from the time and energy that would otherwise be devoted to meaningful teaching and learning.

During the final months of the school year, educators are presented with a valuable opportunity to reflect on their practices and prepare for the year ahead. This period is not just about winding down; it's a crucial time to gather insights and recalibrate for future success.

Table 9.1. Lesson Using Three-Part Cards

Name of Activity	Carnivores, Herbivores, & Omnivores
Area	Science
Materials	A set of cards featuring six animals that represent each of the following groups: the five main vertebrate classes and invertebrates (a total of 18 animals). Each card displays a photo of the animal in its natural habitat along with its typical food source. The cards should be in a three-part format, consisting of photo cards, corresponding labels, and control cards that pair the word with the label for self-checking.
Aims	Direct: To learn about what type of food different animals eat. Indirect: To develop an understanding and appreciation of the complex relationships among different organisms within an ecosystem and the patterns of food chains.
Preparation	**Science lessons** that provide experience with learning about various animals (both vertebrates and invertebrates).
Age	6–9 years.
Presentation	1. Introduce the Concept: Begin by explaining the categories of carnivores, herbivores, and omnivores. Define carnivores as animals that eat meat, herbivores as animals that eat plants, and omnivores as animals that eat both meat and plants. 2. Set Up Header Labels: The teacher will demonstrate by placing header labels for each category: Carnivores, Herbivores, and Omnivores. 3. Model with Photo Cards: The teacher will choose three photo cards (one for each category) and place them under the corresponding headers, sounding out the words to emphasize each category. 4. Model with Label Cards: The teacher will select and place three label cards (one for each category) under the appropriate photo, sounding out the words for clarity. 5. Use Control Cards for Checking: The teacher will lay out the control cards for each match and compare them to verify the placements. 6. Student Activity: Direct students to categorize all 18 photo cards instead of just three. After completing the task, have each student write down the most surprising or interesting animal they discovered in each group.
Points of Consciousness	When the child appreciates the complex relationships among different organisms.

(*continued*)

Table 9.1. *(continued)*

Points of Interest	The different animals and the topic of what different animals eat.
Control of Error	Control cards, students' work, the teacher's observations
Variations	Incorporate different animals.
Extensions	Children can be supported with teacher directed research on the following questions: Why do some animals eat meat while others eat plants? How do different animals get their food? What are some adaptations that help animals get their food?

Figure 9.2 Phonogram Cards

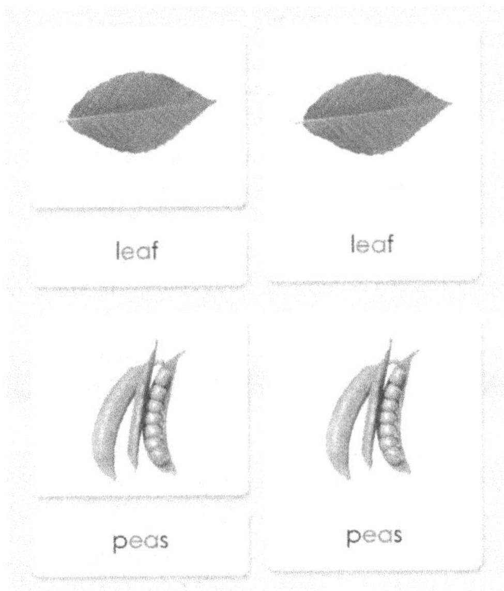

Photo courtesy of Maitri Learning

First and foremost, educators should take a step back and reflect on the data collected throughout the year. It's important to determine which strategies have been effective and can be built upon for the following year. Equally essential is identifying practices that have not yielded the desired results, which may need to be either eliminated or adjusted moving forward. In this

Table 9.2. Lesson With Focus on ea Phonogram

Name of Activity	ea phonogram cards.
Area	Language Arts.
Materials	A set of six to eight phonetic nouns containing the ea phonogram (e.g., *leaf* and *peas*). The ea phonogram is highlighted in red to emphasize the new sound and grapheme, while the remaining text is printed in black. Each noun is presented in a three-part format, including a photo card, a label card, and a control card (word and label combined). The images should feature familiar items to avoid introducing new vocabulary, ensuring that children can focus on reading without unnecessary challenges.
Aims	Direct: To read the ea word label, match it to the picture, and use the control cards to check their own work. Indirect: To form letter-sound connections that link the pronunciations, spellings, and meanings of words.
Preparation	Phonogram work with single letters.
Age	5–6 years.
Presentation	1. Introduce the Concept: Begin by explaining that the letters ea when paired together make the /ē/ sound. 2. Model with Photo Cards: The teacher will lay out all the picture cards pronouncing the name of each imaging, emphasizing the /ē/ sound. 3. Model With Label Cards: The teacher will place the label cards under the appropriate photo, sounding out the words for clarity. 4. Use Control Cards for Checking: The teacher will lay out the control cards for each match and compare them to verify the placements. 5. Student Activity: Direct students to conduct this activity independently. After completing the task, have each student write down the most surprising or interesting ea words.
Points of Consciousness	When the child forms letter-sound connections that link the pronunciations, spellings, and meanings of words.
Points of Interest	The different images and making the /ē/ sound.
Control of Error	Control cards, students work, the teacher's observations
Variations	Incorporate different images. Advance to new phonograms.
Extensions	Create an ea word list. Have the child read the list.

reflective process, it is crucial to ensure that all practices are unbiased and do not cause harm to any group of students.

The next essential step is to pause and reset. This involves identifying the current needs of students and focusing on the remaining weeks of instruction rather than dwelling on past shortcomings. Planning around mandated testing times is critical to maintaining a balanced approach to instruction. Educators should prioritize the most important elements of the curriculum, ensuring that time is devoted to providing targeted instruction that meets the needs of all learners. Moreover, collecting end-of-year (EOY) data at least 6–8 weeks before the official end of school allows for the data to inform another round of intervention, and to plan for summer support if needed.

In the final weeks of the school year, it is also important to prioritize the most meaningful rituals and routines. Reinforcing and re-creating community-centered routines helps to maintain a strong sense of connection among students. Creating special literacy-centered moments and celebrations can foster a love of reading and learning.

Finally, educators are encouraged to reflect on the power of literacy in the lives of their students. Standing up for students' rights to read and being a brave advocate for literacy are not just actions for the end of the school year—they are ongoing commitments that shape the educational experience and future success of every student.

As the school year comes to a close, it's important to view the remaining months not as a countdown to summer, but as a final opportunity to make a meaningful impact. The focus should always be on providing transformative instruction that meets students where they are and propels them forward. By staying committed to these principles, educators can ensure that every student finishes the year stronger, more confident, and better prepared for the challenges and opportunities that lie ahead. This is the time to power ahead with intentionality, using every remaining day to inspire, educate, and elevate students through the power of literacy.

So, how might end-of-the-year instruction look? Of course, lessons will remain consistent with the elements of explicit instruction and use sound assessment practices. But this time of year is the perfect time to engage students in reflective and forward-looking activities that not only wrap up the current year but also build excitement for the year ahead. One creative way to do this is by initiating a countdown to the first day of school in the fall. This activity can help students transition from the current year to the next, fostering a sense of anticipation and readiness for the new challenges and opportunities that await them. Another engaging activity involves using Venn diagrams to explore what might remain the same and what might change in the coming school year. This exercise encourages students to think critically about their experiences and expectations, helping them to mentally prepare for the adjustments they will encounter as they move forward in their educational journey.

Creating goodbye booklets is a wonderful way to help young students express their feelings about the end of the school year. Inspired by the style of *Goodnight Moon*, these booklets can serve as personal keepsakes where students can capture memories, say goodbye to their current grade, and express hopes for the future. This project can be both therapeutic and celebratory, giving students a creative outlet to process their emotions.

Additionally, writing top 10 lists for learning in various subject areas allows students to reflect on what they've learned and what has been most impactful for them. This exercise not only reinforces key concepts but also helps students to take pride in their academic achievements, making it a positive way to close out the year.

Involving parents and families in the end-of-year activities can also be highly beneficial. Providing them with summer lists for reading practice, library resources, and suggestions for building background knowledge over the summer months can ensure that learning continues beyond the classroom. These resources can help maintain the progress students have made and prepare them for a strong start in the fall. Encouraging parents to actively engage in their child's learning during the summer can make a significant difference in preventing learning loss and keeping the momentum going.

It is most important to maintain a sense of urgency regarding instruction. For students still demonstrating the need for reading support, consider the following elements that can be layered into Tier 1, core, Montessori instruction. Research has shown that teachers who model reading comprehension by making their thought process evident and verbally narrating what is happening in their minds is effective for all students, including those with learning disabilities (Vaughn et al., 2000). According to Vaughn and colleagues' meta-analysis, along with "thinking aloud," "frequent feedback to students on the quality of their work, elements missing from their work, and the strengths of their work" was particularly beneficial (2000, p. 103). Effectiveness was evident in all models of teaching. As an extension of "thinking aloud," direct instruction of how an individual can ask themselves questions while reading was vital to raising reading comprehension. Self-generated questions may be to check one's own comprehension (self-monitoring) or to engage more deeply with the text (self-questioning). Montessori instruction is built on the understanding that children learn best when they are actively engaged in their learning, and these strategies align with Montessori pedagogy. If you have had the added requirement of incorporating additional curriculum mandated by the district, self-monitoring and self-questioning should be layered into that instruction also. Ideally, this dialogue between teacher and student has occurred throughout the year. However, consider extra emphasis on these skills at this point in the year. Self-monitoring and self-questioning will serve students well over the summer and into their future educational endeavors. By incorporating these activities into the final weeks of school, educators can create a meaningful and memorable conclusion to the school year, while also setting the stage for continued growth and learning in the months ahead.

Part III

WRAPPING UP THE SCHOOL YEAR: PRIORITIZING, KEEPING ON, AND DEFINING NEXT STEPS

CHAPTER 10

Assessment

END-OF-YEAR SCREENERS

At the end of the year, a final screening test shows growth over time. Once again, this is a time to show that Montessori instruction is effective in student learning. Research tells us that strong Tier 1 instruction should result in 80% of the students being able to meet reading benchmarks set by these screening assessments. Fifteen percent of students should be able to reach the benchmark when given additional Tier 2 intervention support. Five percent may need Tier 3 interventions and support to master material. Using the same screener that was used as the BOY and MOY screening assessment, the entire class is administered this test one last time. (Screeners have three versions of the assessment to make this possible.) The window for this assessment usually falls in the last 6 weeks of instruction. When analyzing results, the teacher must look at the class as whole for trends that occur in the group at large and with individual students. For the class as a whole, the primary focus is whether or not 80% of the students are reaching the benchmark. If they are, this is evidence that the Tier 1 Core instruction is effective in teaching the key elements of literacy. If fewer than 80% of the class is meeting the benchmark, the teacher will need to disaggregate the data to determine which skills they may need to provide extra instruction in as part of their Tier 1, or core, instruction. As this is the end of the year, this information may inform instruction for the remainder of the current school year and planning forward for next year's instruction.

At the individual level, the teacher can use the beginning, middle, and end-of-year screeners to further develop a data story for each child. This is the quantitative piece that can add to observational data and help create the whole picture of a student's learning.

HIGH-STAKES TESTING

Public Montessori schools may be required to participate in statewide high-stakes testing, also known as an outcome measure. To speak plainly, this is frequently teachers' least favorite type of assessment. Keeping in mind that the best use of assessment is to help teachers know which students need extra support, the skills in which they need that support, and if instruction is helping the student learn the needed skill(s), high-stakes tests are not designed to do this as well as some other types of assessments. A high-stakes test is usually given at the end of the year to all students. It tests general knowledge and skills in comparison to a set of criteria. The criteria is often a set of standards. In the past, high-stakes tests have included the New England Common Assessment Program (NECAP), Partnership for Assessment of Readiness for College and Careers (PARCC), Smarter Balance, state tests, and the SAT/ACT. Often student scores are delayed, as official reports are distributed in the summer or following fall. Unfortunately, this often means the data are not used to guide that year's instruction. The test may offer some insight to the teacher if they look for trends in the data. For example, if all of the students in a class struggled to answer questions that were considered higher-level on Bloom's Taxonomy, maybe next year the teacher would try to emphasize this type of question. In general, high-stakes testing does not drive instruction in the specific manner that screening and progress monitoring assessment inform and guide individualized teaching.

One positive outcome of statewide assessments is that the data allow publicly funded Montessori schools to be compared to similar conventional public schools. As Montessori schools have become more accessible to families through charter and public schools, data from mandated ELA/reading assessments are building a growing body of evidence as to the effectiveness of the Montessori pedagogy. As an example, in a recent study conducted by members of the Arizona Montessori Charter School Association in collaboration with the National Center for Montessori in the Public Sector (Brown et al., 2024), a review of state reading outcomes of 3rd-grade students enrolled in publicly funded Montessori schools exceeded the state average. And when looking at longitudinal data over 4 years, Montessori 3rd-graders surpassed non-Montessori 3rd-graders on the Arizona ELA test by at least 20 percentage points (Brown et al., 2024). Similarly, in South Carolina, students enrolled in public Montessori schools met or exceeded state standards in math, ELA, science, and social studies (Culclasure et al., 2018). Since research points to a relationship between economic status and academic performance, it should be noted that students identified as living in low-income households who were enrolled in public Montessori schools outperformed their conventional school peers in reading and demonstrated steeper learning trajectories than their demographically similar non-Montessori peers. Even in Montessori early childhood settings, in a study, over 5,000 low-income Latinx pre-K students in Florida demonstrated greater school readiness after a single year of Montessori preschool when compared to peers who were enrolled in traditional preschool programs (Ansari & Winsler, 2020). Longitudinally, these same students who were enrolled in Montessori pre-K scored higher than their peers in 3rd-grade reading assessments.

These studies, and others like them, should serve as models. A review of their research protocols can serve as a road map to other Montessori schools and districts that wish to demonstrate student outcomes to families, policymakers, state departments of education personnel, and others. Some states have used these data to drive policy changes, such as having the Montessori curriculum added to their state's "approved curriculum" list. Though data can also serve as a point of tension in the Montessori community, it can equally serve as a much-needed source of evidence to the greater field of education, especially when we are working toward creating more equitable educational experiences for all students.

Using Formal Assessment in a Montessori Setting

Data to Drive and Refine Instruction- Throughout the school year, screening data can reveal the instructional needs of the whole class as well as ways to make individualized instruction more meaningful. As we have discussed previously, scheduling in education is a challenge for everyone; there is never enough time. Refining the individualization of instruction to reflect specific skills that need to be supported results in maximum effectiveness of time usage. The reflection flowchart at the beginning of this section (Figure 8.5) allows teachers to use the end-of-year screening data as they consider what worked for their students and how instruction can be enhanced in the future.

THE CLASS OBSERVATION TOOL

The Classroom Assessment Scoring System (CLASS) is a research-based observational tool that focuses on classroom procedures and interactions between teachers and their students. In particular, this observational tool captures three dimensions of teacher-child interactions that have been found to facilitate children's early learning and development, including their language and literacy knowledge (e.g., Burchinal et al., 2016; Hamre et al., 2014; Mashburn et al., 2008). These dimensions are (a) Instructional Support (i.e., concept development, quality of feedback, and language modeling); (b) Emotional Support (i.e., positive and negative climate, teacher sensitivity, and regard for student perspectives), and (c) Classroom Organization (i.e., behavior management, productivity, and instructional learning formats).

There is continuity in the use of domains, dimensions, and indicators in the second edition of the CLASS (Teachstone, 2022/2023), as "hundreds of studies have documented that the interactions described by CLASS predict positive learning and developmental outcomes for children across demographic and economic backgrounds" (p. 7). What has been revised in this edition includes

> more equitable and inclusive definitions of effectiveness, increased representation in its classroom examples, considerations for the equitable use of CLASS across diverse contexts in childcare settings, cultural communities, and language spoken, as well as supporting bias recognition to actively minimize it in CLASS observations. (Teachstone, 2022, 2023, p. 7)

When taken as a whole, this tool can provide administrators and educators with valid and reliable data about the ways in which teachers interact with their students, and when implemented across a school year, this tool can help document improvements in teachers' day-to-day practices. These observations last for 2 to 4 hours, and each cycle of observation and scoring takes 15–20 minutes. Each of the CLASS dimensions is rated on a 1 to 7 scale, with scores of 1 or 2 indicating low quality; 3, 4, or 5 indicating moderate quality; and 6 or 7 indicating high quality. Next is a brief overview of the three dimensions of the CLASS.

Instructional Support. The Instructional Support dimension of the CLASS focuses not on the content of curriculum or learning activities, but instead on the ways in which educators implement these activities and curricula to support children's early learning and development. According to the dimensions of the CLASS, effective teachers monitor their students' performance, facilitate their higher-order thinking skills, and offer quality feedback that builds on children's learning and understanding.

Emotional Support. The Emotional Support dimension of the CLASS captures teachers' effort to support children's socioemotional functioning through positive facilitation of teacher-child interactions and taps into teachers' enthusiasm, enjoyment, and emotional connections with children. In general, classrooms that score well on this dimension of the CLASS have teachers who are responsive to children's needs, acknowledge children's feelings, and support positive peer relationships.

Classroom Organization. The final dimension of the CLASS, Classroom Organization, captures teachers' behavior management, productivity, and facilitation of student engagement and is associated with various domains of early learning

THE CLASS IN MONTESSORI CLASSROOMS

An evaluation of early childhood programs in the state of Virginia used the first edition of CLASS to understand the quality of teacher-child interactions across various types of pre-K settings, including Montessori programs

(Office of Planning and Evaluation, 2016). Results revealed that the average scores for all pre-K programs were in the high range for Emotional Support and Classroom Organization, and the low to moderate range for Instructional Support. In this study, Montessori programs scored over a 3 on Instructional Support, which is promising, as this is higher than typically seen in other program evaluations.

Although teachers in Montessori and non-Montessori settings have been found to demonstrate similar quality teacher-child interactions (Office of Planning and Evaluation, 2010, 2016), the CLASS might underestimate some aspects of teacher-child interactions in Montessori classrooms. For example, in Montessori classrooms, children are required to use a great deal of self-regulation in everyday practice (e.g., rolling out mats, returning materials to their proper place on the shelf, waiting one's turn to use a material, etc.), which might not always be captured by observers. Because Montessori classrooms involve less teacher-directed instruction, the advisory committee for the second edition of the tool included a Montessorian, and observer notes specific to Montessori classrooms are noted in the revised User Manual (Teachstone, 2022, 2023, p. 30), with future training materials to hopefully be available for trained observers to become familiar with interactions typical within a Montessori classroom.

CHAPTER 11

Schedule/Logistics

MELDING A MONTESSORI CLASSROOM WITH OUTSIDE SCHEDULING REQUIREMENTS

Let's be honest: The school day is only so long, and there are only so many school days left as the school year comes to a close. Should outside requirements place additional instructional requirements on the Montessori teacher, there will have to be some creative thinking and, perhaps, some compromise. The end of the school year is perhaps the most difficult time to find instructional balance.

As mentioned earlier, with the winding down of the academic year, it's essential for educators to stay focused on teaching, despite the distractions of end-of-year celebrations, to combat summer learning loss, especially among vulnerable students. Implementing any new curriculum, adding in new assessments, working to collect a range of data, and addressing student needs using tiered instruction is a lot to undertake. Change comes in small steps. It is worth a second look at these systems, going deeper into what research has shown to be effective will benefit your students. The learning platform BRIDGE-RI provides free professional development in multiple areas of education. For more in-depth understanding and application of MTSS and tiered instruction, their modules are extremely valuable. In particular, embedded in their Tier 3 module is a data collection tool for selecting interventions and progress monitoring tools called the "Reading Intervention Map." With permission from BRIDGE-RI, we have included the Reading Intervention Map here, so you can see how you can take the learnings from this book to the next level. An editable version is available in the free module and can be accessed here: https://www.mtssri.org/mod/page/view.php?id=404.

First, we have included the directions (see Table 11.1) that will allow you and your colleagues to follow BRIDGE-RI's step-by-step process of documenting assessment measures and making classroom decisions based on those data. The map allows the teacher to record what is occurring at each tier of instruction.

Table 11.1. Mapping a Classroom's Tiered Instruction

Reading Intervention Map

Note that some aspects of this table are provided in color for clarity. A color version of the table is available as a PDF online under the Download tab at https://www.tcpress.com/effective-literacy-assessment-in-the-montessori-classroom-9780807786703. Color references in the text below refer to this.

Directions (delete these once you've completed your draft): Focus on one grade level to begin with and pilot before any scale-up.

1. Start with the top, shaded row (light blue) by inserting your valid and reliable assessment tool (i.e., your school's screening tool); data that indicates need/targets (may have more than one) in order from simplest skill to most complex (left to right); if you use a more global tool (e.g., STAR), this may require two rows—one for STAR and one for how you determine skills to target (e.g., intervention placement test).

2. In the next row, the orange, clearly state what the intervention target should be (e.g., if the student isn't meeting the benchmark in Phoneme Segmentation Fluency [PSF], then the intervention should target Phonological Awareness on up to the skills expected for the grade level) from the most foundational to the enrichment level (left to right).

3. Leave the white row blank for now, as that is where students' names, numbers, or initials will go later. There is also an accompanying spreadsheet template to gather the data points ahead of time in one place.

4. In the green, for Tier 1, insert your core/Tier 1 curriculum in each cell. In the columns to the right, where foundational skills gaps exist, be sure to include that these students require scaffolded instruction in Tier 1. Add here anything that is the responsibility of the Tier 1 teacher.

5. Move to the yellow next and fill in the interventions you have using the Evaluating an Intervention by the Taxonomy of Intervention Intensity notes you previously gathered above to inform which interventions target which need. If an intervention is multicomponent, you can merge columns on this map or put that same intervention name in multiple cells (as that intervention is addressing multiple needs comprehensively).

6. Then, go on to the red next to fill in the intensive interventions—again, informed by the Evaluating an Intervention by the Taxonomy of Intervention Intensity notes you previously gathered.

7. Next, in the darker blue, define the progress monitoring tool and measure (often the same one from the entrance decision rules) and the frequency of administration expectations. Refer to the manual and instructions specific to your school's valid and reliable tool.

Courtesy of the Rhode Island Department of Education

Grade Level: ________________

Date: ________________

*Intervention Mapping**

Goal: Make it clear for all teachers and staff how we will use data to inform intervention needs (entrance decision rules), what intervention we will deliver because we believe it addresses those needs, and how we will monitor progress.

Administer [insert name of universal screening]

Decision Rules (if more than one duplicate row)	**[Assessment indicator of need]**	**[Assessment indicator of need]**	**[Assessment indicator of need]**	**[Assessment indicator of need]**	**[Assessment indicator of need]**	**[Assessment indicator of need]**
Intervention Target ->	Intervention should address [indicate need]	Intervention should address [indicate need]	Intervention should address [indicate need]	Intervention should address [indicate need]	Intervention should address [indicate need]	Intervention should address [indicate need]
Students by last date decision rule ->	*[Insert names of students meeting decision rule]*	*[Insert names of students meeting decision rule]*	*[Insert names of students meeting decision rule]*	*[Insert names of students meeting decision rule]*	*[Insert names of students meeting decision rule]*	*[Insert names of students meeting decision rule]*
Tier 1 (instructional routines to support this skill)	[Indicate Tier 1 curriculum with scaffolding]	[Indicate Tier 1 curriculum]	[Indicate Tier 1 curriculum]	[Indicate Tier 1 curriculum]	[Indicate Tier 1 curriculum]	[Indicate Tier 1 curriculum]

Tier 2 (supplemental to Tier 1/core) intervention	[Tier 2 intervention -or- a double block of the intensive intervention]	[Tier 2 intervention]	[Tier 2 intervention]	[Tier 2 intervention]	[Tier 2 intervention/ enrichment]	[Tier 2 enrichment]
Tier 3 intensive intervention	[Intensive Intervention Program]	[Intensive Intervention Program]				
Progress monitoring protocols ->	Progress monitoring with [insert PM tool/ frequency]; set goal [insert goal]	Progress monitoring with [insert PM tool/ frequency]; set goal [insert goal]	Progress monitoring with [insert PM tool/ frequency]; set goal [insert goal]	Progress monitoring with [insert PM tool/ frequency]; set goal [insert goal]	Progress monitoring with [insert PM tool/ frequency]; set goal [insert goal]	Progress monitoring with [insert PM tool/ frequency]; set goal [insert goal]

Free resources for Tier 1 small group

* Adapted from Feinberg, N. (2021). *Reading Intervention Column Sort*. Unpublished.

CASE STUDY DISCUSSION AND ANALYSIS (EOY)

Case Study—Early Childhood

Scenario—For the final early childhood case study, we're returning to Khadija's classroom to track her students' progress across the academic year using the PALS Pre-K.

Khadija has recorded student growth with her ongoing classroom observations. Together with her reading coach, she was able to identify which students needed support and in which specific areas of literacy development, based on assessment results. Since January, she has continued to present individualized and small-group literacy activities that responded to assessment data. Together, they now looked across the three subtests of the PALS Pre-K to review name writing, uppercase letter recognition, and letter sound recognition, comparing outcomes between this EOY point in the school year with students' previous scores (see Table 11.3, EOY PALS Pre-K Assessment Data). They again reviewed the data using the same legend and were comfortable with the benchmarks they had set, as all of her 3-year-olds had now turned 4 years old by the start of the new calendar year.

Prompts:

- Begin with current **Name Writing scores** (EOY).
  - » How many students were assigned to Tier 1? __________
  - » How many students were assigned to Tier 2? __________
  - » How many students were assigned to Tier 3? __________
- What do you notice about these outcomes? Has Khadija's instruction been successful in supporting her students' name-writing skills?
- Now, in the same way, review the current **Uppercase Letter** scores (EOY).
  - » How many students were assigned to Tier 1? __________
  - » How many students were assigned to Tier 2? __________
  - » How many students were assigned to Tier 3? __________
- What do you notice about these outcomes? Has Khadija's instruction been successful in supporting her students' uppercase letter recognition skills?
- Which children will benefit from continued support in this area?
- And finally, review the current **Letter Sound** scores (EOY).
  - » How many students were assigned to Tier 1? __________
  - » How many students were assigned to Tier 2? __________
  - » How many students were assigned to Tier 3? __________
- What do you notice about these outcomes? Has Khadija's instruction been successful in supporting her students' letter sound recognition skills? Which children will benefit from continued support in this area?

Table 11.2. Tiered Instruction/RtI Legend

PALS Pre-K scores have been placed in one of three tiers to identify instructional needs

Tiers	Name Writing	Uppercase Letters	Letter Sounds
3	0–3	0–4	0–5
2	4–5	5–15	6–12
1	6–7	16–26	13–26

Table 11.3. Looking Across Three Points in Time: Beginning of Year (BOY) Screening, Middle of Year (MOY) Progress Monitoring, and End of Year (EOY) (3 Subtests of PALS Pre-K)

Name Writing (max score 7)				Uppercase Letter Recognition (max score 26)				Letter Sound Recognition (max score 26)			
Student	Score BOY	Score MOY	Score EOY	Student	Score BOY	Score MOY	Score EOY	Student	Score BOY	Score MOY	Score EOY
a	1	6	7	a	3	4	19	a	3	14	15
b	1	7	7	b	2	26	26	b	0	24	23
c	1	7	7	c	0	9	25	c	0	11	17
d	1	4	7	d	0	10	25	d	0	17	20
e	1	3	7	e	0	26	26	e	0	23	22
f	5	6	7	f	0	9	26	f	0	16	22
g	0	6	7	g	1	6	24	g	0	11	18
h	3	6	7	h	1	14	26	h	0	23	23
i	6	6	7	i	1	2	13	i	0	5	6
j	6	7	7	j	1	24	26	j	0	14	22
k	3	5	7	k	3	26	26	k	0	24	22
l	5	7	7	l	3	24	26	l	1	11	21
m	5	6	7	m	6	21	25	m	0	17	22
n	3	7	7	n	9	18	26	n	6	23	22
o	4	7	7	o	18	26	26	o	0	16	23
p	4	6	7	p	5	26	26	p	0	11	23
q	4	7	7	q	23	25	26	q	13	23	25
r	4	7	7	r	11	15	26	r	1	5	15

If end-of-year scores are collected within 6 weeks of school's end, there is still ample time to encourage students' learning before the end of the academic year. With this in mind, there is one student in Khadija's classroom who has demonstrated some growth this school year but has not progressed to the same degree as her peers. Isolate the data line for student "i"—draw your finger from the BOY to the EOY scores. This student has quickly mastered the ability to write her name. And there is ample growth in her uppercase letter recognition. But we can see there is still opportunity for growth in her ability to recognize letter sounds. Khadija and the reading coach have collaborated throughout the school year to identify through additional diagnostics if this student might benefit from receiving more targeted interventions. They have agreed that, because there has been growth and because the student will continue in Khadija's classroom for her final year in the Montessori 3–6 classroom, they would maintain the current instruction schedule. For student "i," this includes ongoing lessons using the Montessori language materials (Tier 1 instruction), as well as small-group and individual lessons offered by both Khadija and the reading coach. Khadija will also develop some home materials that the student can use over the summer break to avoid "summer slide," the learning loss that some children experience by the time they return to school in the fall. Khadija and the reading coach will revisit this decision at the start of the next school year when they review their new pre-assessment data together.

Case Study—Elementary

It is the beginning of May, 6 weeks before school closes for the summer. The 4th-grade Montessori teacher gives the end-of-year Acadience screening assessment to her entire class, following the parameters of the public school district in which her class is embedded.

Table 11.4 displays the assessment results of the 20 4th-grade students in the class. The chart below shows the students' composite scores. The composite score is an overarching score that combines the individual's scores on each subtest.

Consider the distribution of students at or above benchmark, slightly below benchmark, and significantly below benchmark. National norms used for MTSS state that with a strong Tier 1 (Core) program, 80% of students should be at benchmark, 15% slightly below, and 5% significantly below.

What conclusions can be drawn about Tier 1 instruction in each of these classrooms (Figures 11.4 and 11.5)?

How might these data affect the teacher's decisions as she plans for next year?

What do these assessment data tell the teacher?

What decisions might the teacher make at this point of the year based on this dataset?

Table 11.4. Elementary Case Study 4th-Grade EOY Data

Mrs. A's 4th Grade End-of-Year Acadience Screener Result		
Student Name	Composite Score	Ranking at benchmark 391 or higher ○ 331–390 slightly below benchmark ◍ 0–330 significantly below benchmark ●
Student A	390	◍
Student B	410	○
Student C	224	●
Student D	395	○
Student E	399	○
Student F	391	○
Student G	395	○
Student H	395	○
Student I	401	○
Student J	391	○
Student K	346	◍
Student L	397	○
Student M	388	◍
Student N	399	○
Student O	402	○
Student P	410	○
Student Q	396	○
Student R	392	○
Student S	403	○
Student T	392	○

Table 11.5. Elementary Case Study 5th-Grade EOY Data

Mrs. B's 5th Grade End-of-Year Acadience Screener Result		
Student Name	Composite Score	Ranking at benchmark 415 or higher ○ 341–41 slightly below benchmark ○ 0–340 significantly below benchmark ●
Student 1	330	●
Student 2	416	○
Student 3	339	●
Student 4	350	○
Student 5	400	○
Student 6	422	○
Student 7	419	○
Student 8	444	○
Student 9	294	●
Student 10	415	○
Student 11	403	○
Student 12	490	○
Student 13	301	●
Student 14	340	●
Student 15	425	○
Student 16	380	○
Student 17	456	○
Student 18	418	○
Student 19	413	○
Student 20	420	○

Now look at the EOY Acadience screener data from the 5th-grade Montessori classroom (Table 11.5).

What do these assessment data tell the teacher?

What decisions might the teacher make at this point of the year based on this dataset?

CHAPTER 12

Closing

WORKING WITH FAMILIES, THE COMMUNITY, AND SCHOOL PERSONNEL TO SUPPORT LITERACY

Ripple et al. (2024) noted that "Montessori practitioners sometimes struggle to create genuine opportunities for families to engage meaningfully with their child's development and co-construct curriculum, possibly due to the specificity and complexity of the Montessori curriculum" (p. 36). Though many of the Montessori didactic materials can be found in classrooms, there is the opportunity to build on cultural lessons by including activities that reflect the children's identity, home, and community and that are also designed to meet their individual learning needs (Ripple et al., 2024). As families hold expertise in these areas, co-developing materials that build on children's interests and strengths can serve as prime opportunities to nurture authentic and effective family partnerships. As an example, families could inform Grace and Courtesy lessons in Early Childhood classrooms. The American Montessori Society (n.d.) defines Grace and Courtesy lessons as the formal instruction of "social skills (students) will use throughout their lives, for example, saying 'please' and 'thank you,' interrupting conversations politely, requesting rather than demanding assistance, and greeting guests warmly." Prior to the beginning of the year, teachers can reach out to families "to ask what they want their children to be able to know and do. Part of the work required when increasing opportunities for access means intentionally using a strengths-based lens rather than a deficit mindset when working with students" (D'Cruz & Slade, 2024, p. 54). These opportunities weave Montessori principles with culturally sustaining pedagogy, inviting "educators to not only acknowledge students' identities and experiences but to also actively uplift and sustain their cultures" (p. 54).

As the Montessori teacher, or any other teacher, considers how the science of reading, assessment protocols, and/or other requirements are to be implemented in the classroom, it would be wise to consider the roles and responsibilities that school-based volunteers, literacy leaders and interventionists, and other school personnel can play in the implementation process. For example, in one school, volunteer "grandparents" were trained to administer weekly progress monitoring tests. Although progress monitoring tests are usually only 1 minute in length, meaning that they do not take much time from students' routines for this process, this creative solution addressed three relevant needs: The teacher was provided with real-time data, the teacher's schedule now had more time to devote to instruction and meeting the needs of their students, and there was also an authentic family partnership activity to address this responsibility. Other schools have literacy teachers whose sole job is to provide interventions. In still other cases, librarians, art teachers, or other teachers who may have a free block of time are pulled into classrooms to provide support. Time is a valuable commodity in any classroom, and we must all be better at developing creative solutions that engage the constellation of human resources in the school community to support both teachers and the students they serve.

According to teachers, an essential element in successful data use included communication with families regarding students' progress (Kearns et al., 2021). This was also found by the Flamboyan Foundation's research (2021), which points to positive outcomes when teachers engage families in authentic opportunities to support children's learning:

- Students are more likely to stay in school and more likely to graduate from high school.
- There is increased student achievement.
- Absenteeism is reduced.
- Student motivation, attention, and persistence toward learning are improved.
- Student conduct issues are mitigated, special education referrals are minimized, and students' self-confidence and social skills are improved.

Though family engagement is an important element of a healthy school environment, not all opportunities will influence student outcomes equally. For example, school performances and celebrations may serve as gateways to creating two-way transactional communication with families. By welcoming families into the school and providing something for them, such as a relaxed and positive potluck dinner, trust is built between the teachers and caregivers. Stronger examples of family engagement that will leverage student learning and development include home visits and academic partnering between school and home, where teachers model and explain learning support strategies that can be replicated in the child's home. Families can demonstrate the elements of literacy valued in their homes. For example, cooking together and reading recipes, oral storytelling, and reading books in their first language may be important parts of students' daily lives.

Communication with families may include the ability to answer questions through text messaging using education apps—for example, ClassDojo. This tool has the capacity to instantaneously translate questions written

Figure 12.1. Community and Family Connection Continuum of Impact

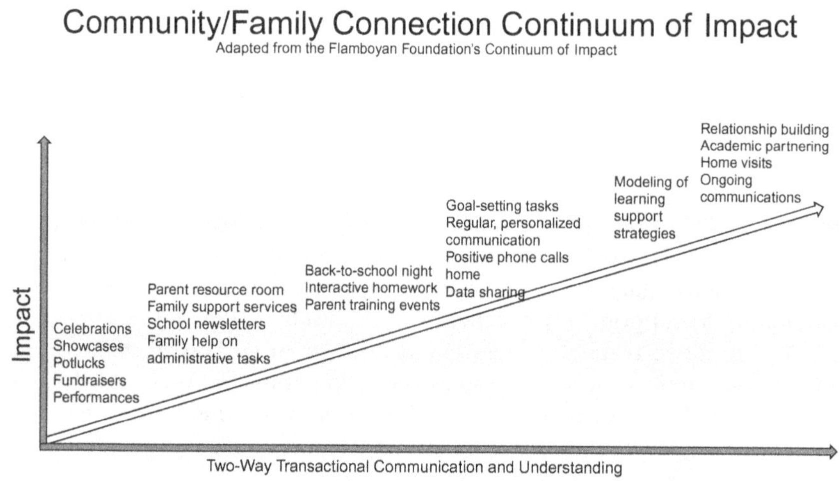

in Spanish by a parent and received in English by a monolingual English-speaking teacher, as well as translate responses sent in English by the teacher but received by the parent in their home language. New technology has the capacity to break down language barriers that can often create unequal experiences for families. Figure 12.1 illustrates the community/family connection continuum of impact.

Many barriers and biases must be addressed to nurture reciprocal family partnerships. Nawal Qarooni, in her book *Nourishing Caregiver Collaborations* (2023), states that "we are conditioned to believe that caregivers who excelled in formal education are the ones who will support their children the most. This harmful narrative simply isn't true" (p. 10). Qarooni (2023) asks us to interrogate our beliefs about what constitutes a family and the assumptions we bring to our work about how families should look and sound. And there needs to be a shift away from a false narrative that learning only happens at school.

The National Association for Family, School and Community Engagement (NAFSCE) released the *Family Engagement Core Competencies: A Body of Knowledge, Skills, and Dispositions for Family-Facing Professionals* in 2022. The document focuses on eight competencies encouraging schools to

1. respect, honor, and value families,
2. embrace equity throughout family engagement,
3. build trusting reciprocal relationships with families,
4. foster community partnerships for learning and family well-being,
5. co-construct learning opportunities with families,

6. link family and community engagement to learning and development,
7. take part in lifelong learning, and
8. advocate for systems change.

These competencies guide "families, teachers, principals, afterschool programs, and others, working together to support each child in distinct ways. (Because) when these partnerships are strong, children succeed, family well-being improves, and schools and communities grow more equitable and just" (NAFSCE, 2022, p. 1). The American Montessori Society's 2023 School Accreditation Standards require that schools provide families with documentation, support, and enrichment opportunities on topics such as the "Montessori philosophy and curriculum; family and parenting issues; child development; anti-bias, anti-racist education; justice, equity, diversity, inclusion education; and health and safety issues" (Standards 9.3 and 9.10).

For those who teach younger children, guidance is provided by the National Association for the Education of Young Children (NAEYC, 2019) Family Engagement and Competencies for Early Childhood Educators (Standard 2). This standard, titled Family-Teacher Partnerships & Community Connections, asks educators to know, understand, and value the diversity of families; to collaborate as partners with families in young children's development and learning through respectful, reciprocal relationships and engagement; and to use community resources to support children's learning and development and to support families and build partnerships among early learning settings, schools, and community organizations and agencies. And the National Head Start Association released a brief (Wasser Gish et al., 2024) focused on their Whole Child–Whole Family approach to working with families that included

- customizing supports to meet the individual needs of children and families;
- offering comprehensive supports across all domains of development;
- that supports would be co-designed between educators and families;
- that these supports would be coordinated across all environments where the child lives, learns, and plays to align efforts; and
- the supports would be continuous, iterative across the child's early childhood years of development.

Just as a comprehensive plan was designed to schedule assessments across the school year (see Figure 4.2), a similar plan can be developed outlining a variety of family engagement opportunities to support all children's learning (see Table 12.1). We have designed a guiding document to help educators and administrators intentionally plan for authentic and responsive

Table 12.1. Family Engagement Planning Guide

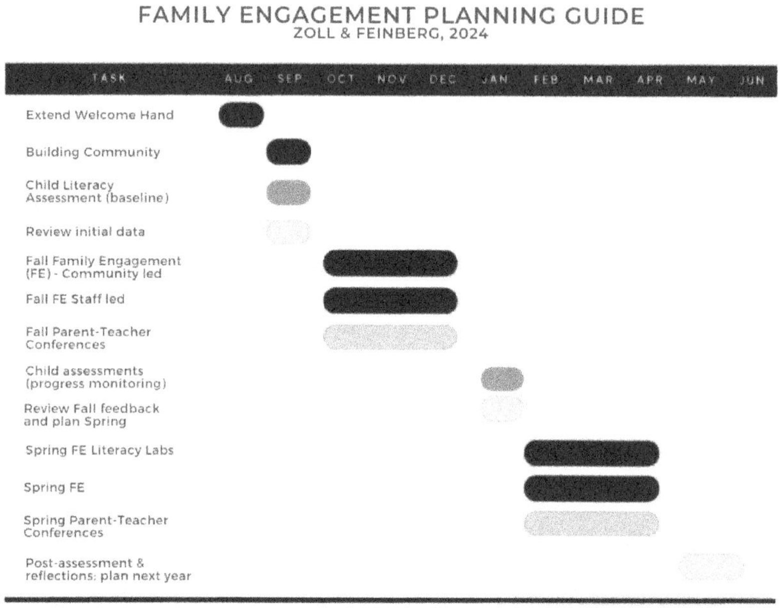

family partnerships with families. The Planning Guide is designed to also help coordinate efforts to gather information about children's language and literacy development that will then inform evidence-based professional development and home-school connections (see Appendix C, available as a PDF online under the Download tab at https://www.tcpress.com/effective-literacy-assessment-in-the-montessori-classroom-9780807786703).

SCHOOL PERSONNEL TO SUPPORT LITERACY: INSTRUCTIONAL AND LITERACY COACHES

In Chapter 8, we reviewed the EOY Decision Tree and discussed opportunities to build professional development opportunities for teaching staff informed by assessment results across all classrooms. For example, if most students recognize letter sounds (a subtest of the PALS Pre-K), then a refresher on using Sandpaper Letters would most likely not be useful to teachers leading early childhood classrooms. Rather, if students are unable to read three- or four-letter phonetic words or struggle to read words that contain uncommon letter patterns (-dge, -tion, -eigh), this would be an opportunity to revisit encoding activities to build students' recognition of letter patterns and their sounds to help build fluency.

For schools that have the support of literacy coaches, they can serve as a conduit between assessment schedules, data results, instructional planning, work with families, professional development, and other program resources. As you develop your comprehensive assessment plan, you'll want to collaboratively align the work of the literacy coach with the components of the plan. Literacy coaches can serve as additional educators who might lead small-group and individual lessons with those children identified by the data as needing additional support. Just as teachers track lessons offered to students, literacy coaches may want to consider creating personal literacy plans (PLPs) for each student. An example of a PLP, recognized by the U.S. Department of Education's Doing What Works initiative, has been included in Appendix D (available as a PDF online under the Download tab at https://www.tcpress.com/effective-literacy-assessment-in-the-montessori-classroom-9780807786703). The document your school selects to use, either as a hard copy or through the use of a digital app, would contain information about the lessons offered to students and note if the student mastered the literacy goal or would benefit from additional practice with the material. The PLP is a living document, as it contains relevant notes that reflect students' current learning happening between formal assessments. Whether there are parents who volunteer to read with students—or an assistant or lead teacher who provides new or follow-up lessons—everyone who works with the child in the classroom will note the activity in the document. These materials are useful reference materials to review with families during conferences to note all the lessons the student has been working on in class.

Whether observing, demonstrating, reflecting, or providing feedback, literacy coaches fill an important role in Montessori schools. They are alchemists serving as a bridge between teachers' understanding of assessment data and the transformation of this information into classroom practice. Literacy coaches allow for the continuation of the morning work period by offering to lead individual or small-group instruction to identified students who would benefit from additional support, thereby protecting the teacher's and students' learning time. As stated earlier, many of the suggestions noted in this book will not change the opportunities for children to experience agency in their learning. To have freedom to select materials that are of interest to them; to extend their thinking through research, reading, and writing; to work collaboratively with their peers—all of this remains the same viable Montessori practice. Rather, the work between the classroom teacher and the literacy coach will take place outside the classroom and will be focused on planning, reflection, and shared teaching of small-group interventions. These planning periods will then inform the lessons and materials shared with the students. In this approach we have another triangle layered upon the teacher, the Montessori materials, and the classroom environment. In addition, there is the literacy coach, the classroom teacher, and the literacy data to create an effective and powerful approach to meeting the needs of all students.

CONCLUSION

Montessori education has made its mark across the globe. What started with the vision and strength of one woman, Montessori schools have situated themselves across cultures, across geography, and now, with growing frequency, within the cradle of public schools. While Montessori practices are being implemented within non-Montessori contexts, this provides opportunities for educators to explore what works in different education settings. What evidence-based assessment and instructional practices might be explored in the interest of meeting the needs of all learners? In an effort to have a fully literate populace, we must reimagine our work in schools and deeply consider the use of data-gathering and analysis and the influence of these results on classroom practice. There must be a collective reckoning to ensure that not just some students but all students are proficient readers with the skills needed to realize their academic potential and future service in their communities.

Lucy Recio, in their keynote address at the Montessori Public Policy Initiative conference (September 2024), invited Montessorians to become "imagination activists." You are invited to hear their words as a clarion call for all educators, school administrators, and policymakers to work collectively to create rich, engaging, and intentionally designed learning experiences to ensure all children's human and academic success. Rather than the reading war metaphor of a pendulum shifting from one instructional extreme to another, how might we instead work proactively to design an education system that leads with equity and the best of what research can offer about student learning and teachers' guidance and instruction to ensure that all students flourish as readers, writers, deep thinkers, and citizens ready to engage in both the local and global community? This is the very heart of the vision proposed by Dr. Montessori.

> Rather than working with guilt and despair, Imagination Activists work by inspiring others, giving people permission to dream, and expand their sense of what is possible. They highlight the options not on the table, and envision a future that engenders their deepest qualities and values. They raise collective ambition to help make the "impossible" seem possible. Imagination activists start with where they are and reclaim our imaginations—rewilding them with visions and possibilities. They create gaps in-between business as usual to exercise the more beautiful world our hearts and imaginations know is possible.

> Imagination Activists bring together their rewilded imaginations with others and allow this to ferment into collective action. They are what Anasuya Sengupta calls pragmatic revolutionaries, driven by the knowledge and faith that another world is possible, but willing to engage with reality and meet the world fearlessly as it is today. In this way their work is rooted deeply in collective values. In creating the conditions for a new praxis to open that allows us to ask: "what if the world were different?" If we want to create a different possibility, a different way of living, we need to allow ourselves to imagine differently, together. We need to hold onto the ways, seen and unseen, that we are connected, how together, we can sustain our passions, our love for this work, and our care for one another at the center of our activism. (Recio, 2024)

This book has been an attempt to provide a comprehensive guide to integrating Montessori Language instruction with Structured Literacy practices, and to support teachers and administrators in developing effective, research-based systems that address the needs of all learners without disrupting or supplanting the Montessori curriculum. As Montessori pedagogy increasingly intersects with public school standards and reading legislation, it's crucial to link these approaches in a way that upholds the Montessori philosophy while implementing structured literacy practices that enhance student outcomes.

We urge educators, administrators, and policymakers to consider the impact of these integrated practices and to take action to ensure that every child receives the literacy support they need to flourish. By embracing the tools and frameworks outlined in this book, we can close opportunity gaps, foster strong readers, and empower the next generation to be active, informed, and thoughtful citizens.

References

Acadience Reading Pre-K: PELI. (2020). https://acadiencelearning.org/acadience-reading/prek-peli/

Alexander, K. L., Entwisle, D. R., & Olson, L. S. (2007). Lasting consequences of the summer learning gap. *American Sociological Review*, *72*(2), 167–180.

American Institutes for Research. (n.d.). *Example diagnostic tools*. Diagnostic Assessment Tools: Implementation Tools | NCII. National Center on Intensive Intervention. https://intensiveintervention.org/tools-charts/example-diagnostic-tools

American Montessori Society. (2023). *AMS school accreditation standards and criteria*. AMS Office of School Accreditation, American Montessori Society.

American Montessori Society (n.d.-a). *The Montessori uninterrupted work period*. American Montessori Society. https://amshq.org/Educators/Membership/Member-Resources/The-Montessori-Uninterrupted-Work-Period#:~:text=At%20the%20Elementary%20level%2C%20a,task%20or%20research%20project%20together

American Montessori Society (n.d.-b). *Montessori Terminology*. American Montessori Society. https://amshq.org/About-Montessori/What-Is-Montessori/Terminology

Anderson, R. C., & Pearson, P. D. (1984). A schema-theoretic view of basic processes in reading comprehension. In P. D. Pearsons, R. Barr, M. L. Kamil, & P. Mosenthal (Eds.), *Handbook of reading research* (pp. 255–291). Longman.

Ansari, A., & Winsler, A. (2020). The long-term benefits of Montessori pre-K for Latinx children from low-income families. *Applied Developmental Science*, *26*(2), 252–266.

Archer, A. L., & Hughes, C. A. (2011). *Explicit instruction: Effective and efficient teaching*. Guilford Press.

Association Montessori Internationale. (n.d.). *Glossary of Montessori terms*. https://montessori-ami.org/resource-library/facts/glossary-montessori-terms

Bennett, R. E. (2011). Formative assessment: A critical review. *Assessment in Education: Principles, Policy & Practice*, *18*(1), 5–25.

Berninger, V. W., Vaughan, K., Abbott, R. D., Begay, K., Coleman, K. B., Curtin, G., . . . & Graham, S. (2002). Teaching spelling and composition alone and together: Implications for the simple view of writing. *Journal of Educational Psychology*, *94*(2), 291.

Black, P., & William, D. (1998). Assessment and classroom learning. *Assessment in Education: Principles, Policy & Practice*, *5*(1), 7–74.

Brown, K., Powell, K., & Woodford, L. (2024). *Montessori: Evidence based reading curricula*. National Center for Montessori in the Public Sector. https://azcharters

.org/2024/04/24/montessori-evidence-based-reading-curricula-a-review-of-data/

Brown, M. W., & Hurd, C. (1947). *Goodnight moon*. Harper & Row.

Burchinal, M., Zaslow, M., & Tarullo, L. (2016). Quality thresholds, features, and dosage in early care and education: Secondary data analyses of child outcomes. *Monographs of the Society for Research in Child Development, 81*(2), 75–87.

Cabell, S. Q., & Hwang, H. (2023). Leveraging content-rich English language arts instruction in the early grades to improve children's language comprehension. In S. Q. Cabell, S. Neuman, & N. P. Terry (Eds.), *The handbook on the science of early literacy* (pp. 175–185). Guilford Press.

Carta, J. J., & Greenwood, C. R. (2023). Multi-tiered systems of support: An approach for reducing disparities in school readiness and increasing equity in early literacy and learning opportunities for young children. In S. Q. Cabell, S. Neuman, & N. P. Terry (Eds.), *The handbook on the science of early literacy* (pp. 347–358). Guilford Press.

Chappuis, S., Stiggins, R., & Chappuis, J. (2011). *Student assessment for learning: Doing it right, using it well*. Assessment Training Institute.

Colorado Department of Education. (2023). *Continuum of high impact strategies*. https://www.cde.state.co.us/familyengagement/highimpactstrategies

Common, E. A., Bross, L. A., Oakes, W. P., Cantwell, E. D., Lane, K. L., & Germer, K. A. (2019). Systematic review of high probability requests in K-12 settings: Examining the evidence base. *Behavioral Disorders, 45*(1), 3–21.

Culclasure, B., Fleming, D. J., Riga, G., & Sprogis, A. (2018). *An evaluation of Montessori education in South Carolina's public schools*. The Riley Institute at Furman University.

D'Cruz, G., & Slade, E. (2024). Access and full implementation: Challenges and opportunities in public Montessori. In H. Gerker & C. Jones (Eds.), *Montessori in contemporary culture* (pp. 48–68). American Montessori Society.

Debs, M. (2019). *Diverse families, desirable schools: Public Montessori in the era of school choice*. Harvard University Press.

Duffy, M., & Duffy, D. (2016). *Children of the universe: Cosmic education in the Montessori elementary classroom*. Parent Child Press.

Dunn, L. M., & Dunn, D. M. (2007). *Peabody Picture Vocabulary Test, 4th edition (PPVT-4)*. American Guidance Service.

Dunn, L. M., Lugo, D. E., Padilla, E. R., & Dunn, L. M. (1986). *TVIP: Test de vocabulario en imagenes Peabody: Hispanic-American adaptation*. Pearson.

Dwyer, M. (1970). *A key to reading and writing for English*. Nienhuis Montessori.

Epstein, P. (2012). *An observer's notebook: Learning from children with the Observation C.O.R.E., 2nd edition*. Montessori Foundation.

Erbeli, F., Rice, M., Xu, Y., Bishop, M. E., & Goodrich, J. M. (2024). A meta-analysis on the optimal cumulative dosage of early phonemic awareness instruction. *Scientific Studies of Reading, 28*(4), 345–370.

ESSA. (2015). *Every Student Succeeds Act*. U.S. Congress Reauthorization of the Elementary and Secondary Education Act of 1965. https://www.congress.gov/114/plaws/publ95/PLAW-114publ95.pdf

Farrell, L., Davidson, M., Hunter, M., & Osenga, T. (2020, January 10). *The simple view of reading*. The Center for Literacy & Learning. https://www.cdl.org/the-simple-view-of-reading/

Flamboyan Foundation. (2021). *Family engagement matters*. Flamboyan Foundation. https://assess.flamboyanfoundation.org/wp-content/uploads/2022/08/2021-Family-Engagement-Matters.pdf

Flamboyan Foundation. (2022). *Academic partnering: Creating meaningful experiences with families*. Flamboyan Foundation. https://assess.flamboyanfoundation.org/wp-content/uploads/2022/08/Academic-Partnering-Creating-Meaningful-Experiences-with-Families.pdf

Fletcher, J. M., & Vaughn, S. (2009). Response to intervention: Preventing and remediating academic difficulties. *Child Development Perspectives, 3*(1), 30–37.

Florida Center for Reading Research. (n.d.). *Response to Intervention overview*. https://fcrr.org/reading-success/intervention

Gersten, R., Compton, D., Connor, C. M., Dimino, J., Santoro, L., Linan-Thompson, S., & Tilly, W. D. (2008). *Assisting students struggling with reading: Response to intervention (RtI) and multi-tier intervention for reading in the primary grades: A practice guide. (NCEE 2009–4045)*. National Center for Education Evaluation and Regional Assistance, Institute of Education Sciences, U.S. Department of Education. https://ies.ed.gov/ncee/wwc/Docs/PracticeGuide/rti_reading_pg_021809.pdf

Gough, P. B., & Tunmer, W. E. (1986). Decoding, reading, and reading disability. *Remedial and Special Education*, 7, 6–10. https://doi.org/10.1177/074193258600700104

Greenwood, C. R., Bradfield, T., Kaminski, R., Linas, M., Carta, J. J., & Nylander, D. (2011). The response to intervention (RtI) approach in early childhood. *Focus on Exceptional Children*, *43*(9), 1–22.

Halle, T., Zaslow, M., Wessel, J., Moodie, S., & Darling-Churchill, K. (2011). *Understanding and choosing assessments and developmental screeners for young children: Profiles of selected measures*. Office of Planning, Research, and Evaluation, Administration for Children and Families, U.S. Department of Health and Human Services.

Hamre, B., Hatfield, B., Pianta, R., & Jamil, F. (2014). Evidence for general and domain specific elements of teacher–child interactions: Associations with preschool children's development. *Child Development*, *85*, 1257–1274.

Harlen, W., & James, M. (1997). Assessment and learning: Differences and relationships between formative and summative assessment. *Assessment in Education: Principles, Policy & Practice*, *4*(3), 365–379.

Herman, J. M. (2023). Mandate or myth? The uninterrupted 3-hour work cycle. *Montessori Life,* Spring, 46–49.

Herman, J. M., & Saylor, L. (2024). Research and observation: Pedagogical essentials for building a better world. In H. Gerker & C. Jones (Eds.), *Montessori in contemporary culture* (pp. 15–31). American Montessori Society.

Himmele, P., & Himmele, W. (2017). *Total participation techniques: Making every student an active learner*. ASCD.

Hochman, J., Wexler, N., & Lemov, D. (2017). *The writing revolution: A guide to advancing thinking through writing in all subjects and grades.* Jossey-Bass.

Hwang, H. J., McMaster, K. L., & Panayiota, K. (2023). A longitudinal investigation of directional relations between domain knowledge and reading in the elementary years. *Reading Research Quarterly, 58*(1), 59–77. http://doi.org/10.1002/rrq.481

Institute of Medicine (IOM) & National Research Council (NRC). (2015). *Transforming the workforce for children birth through 8: A unifying foundation.* National Academies Press.

Invernizzi, M., Sullivan, A., Meier, J., & Swank, L. (2004). *PALS Pre-K Teachers Manual.* University of Virginia.

Kearns, D. M., Feinberg, N. J., & Anderson, L. J. (2021). Implementation of data-based decision-making: Linking research from the Special Series to Practice. *Journal of Learning Disabilities, 54*(5), 365–372. https://doi.org/10.1177/00222194211032403

Knowledge Matters Campaign. (2022/2024). *Statements from the Knowledge Matters Campaign Scientific Advisory Committee.* https://knowledgematterscampaign.org/statement-from-the-knowledge-matters-campaign-scientific-advisory-committee/

Kober, N., & Stark Rentner, D. (2020). *History and evolution of public education in the US.* Center on Education Policy. George Washington University. https://files.eric.ed.gov/fulltext/ED606970.pdf

Malcolm, U. (2022). *Evidence-based assessment in the science of reading. LD@School.* Learning Disabilities Association of Ontario. www.ldatschool.ca/evidence-based-assessment-reading/

Mallett, J. D., & Schroeder, J. L. (2015). Academic achievement outcomes: A comparison of Montessori and non-Montessori public elementary school students. *Journal of Elementary Education, 25*(1), 39–53.

Mapp, K. L., & Kuttner, P. J. (2013). *Partners in education: A dual capacity-building framework for family-school partnerships.* SEDL. www.dualcapacity.org/

Mashburn, A. J., Pianta, R. C., Hamre, B. K., Downer, J. T., Barbarin, O. A., Bryant, D., . . . & Howes, C. (2008). Measures of classroom quality in prekindergarten and children's development of academic, language, and social skills. *Child Development, 79*, 732–749.

Massachusetts DESE. (2015). *What is MTSS?* www.youtube.com/watch?v=18Wj_5ctHKo

Mathes, P. (2016, June 23). *Curing dyslexia: What is possible?* Hoot Education. https://youtu.be/eDhP7Sh57Q8?si=KLC7EW94XAuM2ny5

McAndrews, S. L. (2020). *Literacy assessment and metacognitive strategies: A resource to inform instruction, prek-12.* The Guilford Press.

McDowell, M. (June 18, 2024). *Keeping the focus on what's important.* Edutopia. www.edutopia.org/article/keeping-focus-basics-schools?utm_content=linkpos1&utm_campaign=weekly-2024-06-19&utm_medium=email&utm_source=edu-newsletter

Montessori, M. (1913/2013). *The 1913 Rome lectures: First international training course.* In Feez, S. Quade, L., Montessori, C, & Verheul, J. (Eds.). The Montessori Series, 18. Montessori-Pierson Publishing Company.

Morgan Herman, J. (Spring 2023). Mandate or myth: The uninterrupted 3-hour work cycle. *Montessori Life, 34*(4), 46–49. American Montessori Society.

National Assessment of Educational Progress (NAEP). (2023). *NAEP Long-term trend assessment results—Reading and mathematics.* www.nationsreportcard.gov/highlights/ltt/2023/

National Association for Family, School and Community Engagement. (2022). *Family engagement core competencies: A body of knowledge, skills, and dispositions for family-facing professionals.* NAFSCE. https://nafsce.org/page/CoreCompetencies

National Association for the Education of Young Children. (2019). *Family engagement standards in professional standards and competencies for early childhood educators.* www.naeyc.org/sites/default/files/globally-shared/downloads/PDFs/resources/position-statements/standards_and_competencies_ps.pdf

National Association for the Education of Young Children (NAEYC) & National Association of Early Childhood Specialists in State Department of Education (NAECS/SDE). (2003). *Joint position statement on early childhood curriculum, assessment, and program evaluation building an effective, accountable system in programs for children birth through age 8.* NAEYC.

National Center for Intensive Intervention. (n.d.-a). *Phonological awareness literacy screening (PALS)—PALS for kindergarten.* NCII. https://charts.intensiveintervention.org/screening/tool/?id=88889f2c3498bf22

National Center for Intensive Intervention. (n.d.-b). *Using effective methods to elicit frequent responses.* In methods to elicit responses: Training modules | NCII. https://intensiveintervention.org/explicit-instruction-frequent-responses

National Center for Montessori in the Public Sector (NCMPS). (n.d.) *About the* Montessori *Census.* www.montessoricensus.org/about-the-montessori-census/

National Institute of Child Health and Human Development. (2000). *Teaching children to read: An evidence-based assessment of the scientific research literature on reading and its implications for reading instruction* (Report of the National Reading Panel. NIH Publication No. 00-4769). U.S. Government Printing Office.

National Research Council. (2008). *Early childhood assessment: Why, what, and how.* National Academies Press.

Neuman, S. B., Quintero, E., & Reist, K. (2023). *Reading reform across America: A survey of state legislation.* The Albert Shanker Institute. www.shankerinstitute.org/sites/default/files/2023-07/ReadingReform%20ShankerInstitute%20Full-Report%20072723.pdf

Oesting, T. (2022). *To plan or not to plan: Thoughts on student work plans.* Classroomechanics blog. www.classroomechanics.com/plan-student-work/

Office of Planning and Evaluation. (2010). *Pre-kindergarten program evaluation report.* http://apslegacymateriell.com/cms/lib2/VA01000586/Centricity/Domain/141/PREK%20FINAL%2005%2028%2010%20w%20APP.pdf

Office of Planning and Evaluation. (2016). *Early childhood program evaluation report.* www.apsva.us/wp-content/uploads/2015/05/Early-Childhood-Evaluation-Report-FINAL.pdf

O'Shaughnessy, M. (2016). The observation scientist. *NAMTA Journal, 41*(3), 57–99.

Pearson, P. D., & Gallagher, M. (October 1983). The instruction of reading comprehension. *Contemporary Educational Psychology, 8*(3). University of Illinois,

National Institute of Education. https://www.researchgate.net/publication/49176503_The_Instruction_of_Reading_Comprehension

Pianta, R. C., Hamre, B. K., Hayes, N., Mintz, S., & LaParostart, K. M. (2012). *Classroom Assessment Scoring System—Secondary (CLASS-S)*. University of Virginia.

Pianta, R. C., La Paro, K. M., & Hamre, B. K. (2008). *Classroom Assessment Scoring System (CLASS)*. Paul H. Brookes Publishing Company.

Pickering, J. S. (2021). *Montessori strategies for children with learning differences: The MACAR model*. Parent Child Press.

Puranik, C. S., & Lonigan, C. J. (2012). Name-writing proficiency, not length of name, is associated with preschool children's emergent literacy skills. *Early Childhood Research Quarterly*, *27*(2), 284–294. www.ncbi.nlm.nih.gov/pmc/articles/PMC3328802/pdf/nihms329784.pdf

Qarooni, N. (2023). *Nourishing caregiver collaborations: Elevating home experiences and classroom practices for collective care*. Routledge.

RAND Reading Study Group. (2002). *Reading for understanding: Toward an R&D program in reading comprehension*. RAND.

Reading League. (2023). *Curriculum evaluation guidelines*. www.thereadingleague.org/wp-content/uploads/2023/03/The-Reading-League-Curriculum-Evaluation-Guidelines-2023.pdf

Reading League Compass. (n.d.). *Policymakers and state education agencies*. www.thereadingleague.org/compass/policymakers-and-state-education-agencies/

Reading Rockets. (2024a). *Instructional routines, gouping, and the ELA block*. www.readingrockets.org/classroom/instructional-routines-grouping-and-ela-block

Reading Rockets. (2024b). *K-5 small-group literacy instruction: Sample schedule and activities*. www.readingrockets.org/classroom/instructional-routines-and-grouping/k-5-small-group

Reading Rockets. (2024c). *K-5 whole-group literacy instruction: Sample schedule and activities*. www.readingrockets.org/classroom/instructional-routines-and-grouping/k-5-whole-group

Recio, L. (2024). Montessori Public Policy Initiative (MPPI) keynote address, September 28, 2024. Leesburg, VA.

Reimer, M. (n.d.). *Montessori terms—Points of interest*. Melissa Reimer's EPortfolio. https://blogs.ubc.ca/melissareimer/montessori-terms/

Rhode Island Department of Education (RIDE). (n.d.). *Comprehensive Assessment System: Rhode Island criteria and guidance*. R.I. Department of Elementary and Secondary Education.

Ripple, T., Jones, A., & Christensen, O. (2024). Innovation and adaptation in the Montessori prepared environment. In H. Gerker & C. Jones (Eds.), *Montessori in contemporary culture* (pp. 32–47). American Montessori Society.

Scarborough, H. S. (2001). Connecting early language and literacy to later reading (dis)abilities: Evidence, theory, and practice. In S. Neuman & D. Dickinson (Eds.), *Handbook for research in early literacy* (pp. 97–110). Guilford Press.

Schroeder, J. (2004). *Ripples of innovation: Charter schooling in Minnesota, the nation's first charter school state*. Progressive Policy Institute. https://files.eric.ed.gov/fulltext/ED491210.pdf

Schwartz, S. (2024). Which states have passed 'science of reading' laws? What's in them? *Education Week*. www.edweek.org/teaching-learning/which-states-have-passed-science-of-reading-laws-whats-in-them/2022/07

Seidenberg, M. S. (2018). *Language at the speed of sight: How we read, why so many can't, and what can be done about it*. Basic Books.

Shonkoff, J. (2024). *Eye on early childhood blog*. https://eyeonearlychildhood.org/2024/06/18/jack-shonkoff-joins-the-930-call-and-shares-his-next-early-childhood-quest/

Snow, K. (2011). *Developing kindergarten readiness and other large-scale assessment systems: Necessary considerations in the assessment of young children*. National Association for the Education of Young Children.

Stanovich, K. E. (1986). Matthew effects in reading: Some consequences of individual differences in the acquisition of literacy. *Reading Research Quarterly*, 22, 360–407.

Sweller, J. (2011). Cognitive load theory. *Psychology of Learning and Motivation*, *55*, 37–76.

Teachstone. (2022, 2023). *Reference manual: Classroom Assessment Scoring System, CLASS. Pre-K-3rd Grade, 2nd edition*. https://info.teachstone.com/class-2nd-edition-pre-k-3rd-reference-manual

Timeline of Maria Montessori's Life. (n.d.). https://montessori-ami.org/resource-library/facts/timeline-maria-montessoris-life

Vanderbilt University. (2024a). *What strategies can educators implement to prevent or address challenging behaviors?* IRIS Center. https://iris.peabody.vanderbilt.edu/module/bi2-elem/cresource/q1/p05/

Vanderbilt University. (2024b). *What strategies can educators implement to prevent or address challenging behaviors?* IRIS Center. https://iris.peabody.vanderbilt.edu/module/bi2-sec/cresource/q1/p06/

Vaughn, S., Gersten, R., & Chard, D. J. (2000). The underlying message in LD intervention research: Findings from research syntheses. *Exceptional Children*, 67(1), 99–114. https://doi.org/10.1177/001440290006700107

Voyager Sopris. (n.d.) https://www.voyagersopris.com/blog/edview360/The-Deep-Reading-Brain-and-the-Good-Life

Wasser Gish, J., Chazan-Cohen, R., & Warren, T. (2024). *Strengthening whole family comprehensive supports in early childhood: Implications for Head Start and Early Head Start*. National Head Start Association.

Wien, C., Guyevskey, V., & Berdoussis, N. (2011). Learning to document in Reggio-inspired education. *Early Childhood Research & Practice, 13*(2). https://files.eric.ed.gov/fulltext/EJ956381.pdf

Willingham, D. T. (2021). *Why don't students like school? A cognitive scientist answers questions about how the mind works and what it means for the classroom* (2nd edition). Jossey-Bass.

Wolf, M. (2017). *What is deep reading and why does it matter?* EdView 360 blog series, Voyager Sopris. https://www.voyagersopris.com/blog/edview360/The-Deep-Reading-Brain-and-the-Good-Life

Wolf, M. (2018). *Reader, come home: The reading brain in a digital world*. Harper Collins Publishers.

Woodford, L. (2024). One voice *can* start a movement in Arizona. *Montessori Public*, Spring, *8*(2). National Center for Montessori in the Public Sector. www

.montessoripublic.org/wp-content/uploads/2024/04/MP_Articles_V8-2_Woodford.pdf

Yenawine, P. (2013). *Visual thinking strategies for preschool: Using art to enhance literacy and social Skills.* Harvard Education Press.

Zoll, S. (n.d.). *Personal literacy plans.* U.S. Department of Education & the Doing What Works at WestEd Project. https://dwwlibrary.wested.org/resources/397

Zoll, S. (2012). *From "at risk" to "at promise": An evaluation of an Early Reading First project* (Published doctoral dissertation). Retrieved from ProQuest. (3522948).

Zoll, S. (2017). The Montessori experiment in Rhode Island (1913–1940): Tracing theory to implementation over 25 years. *Journal of Montessori Research 3*(2), 39–54.

Zoll, S., Ansari, A., & Saylor, L. (2023). Assessment in Montessori education. In A. K. Murray, E.-M. Tebano Ahlquist, M. McKenna, & M. Debs (Eds.), *The Bloomsbury handbook of Montessori education* (219–229). Bloomsbury.

Zoll, S., Feinberg, N., & Saylor, L. (2023). *Powerful literacy in the Montessori classroom: Aligning reading research and practice.* Teachers College Press.

Zoll, S., & Rosenquest, B. (2011). Sustainable practices in mentoring: Tools to support child outcomes and a mentoring protocol in early language and literacy. *NHSA Dialog, 24*, 1–16.

Glossary

GLOSSARY OF ASSESSMENT TERMS

Acadience: A free popular screener whose subtests can also be used for progress monitoring.

BOY: Beginning of year.

Comprehensive assessment system: A cycle of assessments that includes screening and progress monitoring measures.

Diagnostic assessments: Given to selected students to get specific information regarding strengths and weaknesses.

DIBELS: Dynamic Indicators of Basic Early Literacy Skills, a free popular screener whose subtests can also be used for progress monitoring.

EOY: End of year.

ESSA: Every Student Succeeds Act (2015).

FAPE: Free and Appropriate Public Education.

Formative assessment: An evaluation that gathers information used to inform instruction.

Intervention: Additional instruction put in place to support specific skill areas.

IRIS Center: IDEA (Individuals with Disabilities Education Act) and Research for Inclusive Settings.

MOY: Middle of year.

MTSS: Multi-tiered system of support. A tiered approach to addressing students' needs by considering the whole child and both academic and socioemotional facets of learning.

Outcome assessment: Measures effectiveness on a broad scale; it is often high-stakes.

PALS assessment: The Phonological Awareness Literacy Screening or PALS Pre-K (Invernizzi et al., 2004). An assessment of foundational literacy skills.

PAST assessment: Phonological Awareness Screening Test. Free diagnostic assessment for grades K through adult that measures phonological awareness skills. Available online.

PELI: Preschool Early Literacy Indicators. An assessment of oral language and pre-reading skills for ages 3–5.

Phoneme: The smallest unit of speech sound.

Phonemic awareness: The ability to manipulate, delete, and add sounds in words.

Phonics: The ability to decode printed words.

Phonological awareness: The ability to listen to and recognize individual sounds, word parts, and words.

PPVT: Peabody Picture Vocabulary Test. A diagnostic assessment that measures receptive vocabulary at the pre-K to adult levels.

Progress monitoring assessment: A short assessment that is administered weekly, every other week, or monthly to determine if an intervention is effective.

QPS: Quick Phonics Screener. A diagnostic that tests various phonics (decoding) skills.

RtI: Response to intervention, a tiered approach to addressing students' academic needs.

Screener: An assessment given at the beginning, middle, and end of year to everyone in the class to determine if students are at or below grade level in reading or math.

Simple View of Reading: Created by Tunmer and Gough (1986), this framework states that decoding and language comprehension are equally important in their contribution toward reading comprehension. Decoding x Language Comprehension = Reading Comprehension.

Standards: Standards explicitly state the information, knowledge, and/or skills that should be learned in each subject at each grade level.

Summative assessment: An evaluation of skill mastery following instruction.

Tier 1: Core instruction. This is the instruction all students receive and are guaranteed in a public school as a right (all students have the right to a Free and Appropriate Public Education—FAPE).

Tier 2: Small-group instruction added to core instruction that addresses specific student needs and is usually provided by the classroom teacher.

Tier 3: Intensive intervention added to core instruction that addresses specific student needs. Usually provided in a small group or individually by a specialist.

GLOSSARY OF PUBLIC SCHOOL ACTIVITIES/INTERVENTIONS

Choral readings: When students read a text aloud together.

Decodable texts: Short connected readings that focus on specific phonics skills. Decodable texts provide students the opportunity to practice phonics rules in an actual reading.

Echo readings: When the teacher (or fluent reader) reads a segment of text and the student(s) repeats the same text out loud in an attempt to match the expert's pace and expression.

Heggerty: A commonly used phonological awareness intervention that includes practice with phoneme deletion, addition, and substitution.

Repeated readings: When a student reads the same short text again and again to gain fluency. With each successive reading, pace and flow should improve.

Timed readings: When a student reads a short text out loud multiple times and records how long it takes them to do so each time. Pace should improve with each reading. Accuracy (reading the correct words) must be retained as pace increases.

UFLI (University of Florida Literacy Institute): A free online intervention that focuses on phonics. Includes decodable texts.

Vanderbilt PALS: A reading intervention for grades K and 1 that focuses on phonological awareness and phonics. Available at https://frg.vkcsites.org/what-is-pals/pals_reading_manuals/ Example lesson: https://youtu.be/4gqRTUAuAQQ?si=Pnd_a39ACog8mMPt

GLOSSARY OF MONTESSORI ACTIVITIES

CVC word cards: As students master letter sounds and demonstrate growing capacity encoding (making) words, they will move on to a series of word cards that contain consonant-vowel-consonant (CVC) words to read (decode).

Decodable books: Short books that focus on specific phonics skills. Decodable books provide students with the opportunity to practice phonics rules in an actual reading.

Grammar activities: A series of Montessori activities that support students' understanding of the parts of speech: nouns, verbs, conjunctions, adjectives, etc.

I Spy Game: A tray containing 3–5 small objects used to extend children's understanding of initial, medial, and ending letter sounds.

Movable Alphabet: Consists of a box with 26 compartments and blue and red wooden letters. Each compartment contains multiples of a given letter of the alphabet. The material supports students' understanding of the phoneme-grapheme connection (letter sounds and their matching letter shape) and the wooden letters are used to encode or "make" words and sentences.

Phonetic object box: A box containing 10–12 small phonetic objects (cat, mug, lid, etc.) that children can match to corresponding written labels.

Phonogram cards: Highlight sound/spelling combinations. As an example, the phonogram eigh- makes the sound /ā/. The card contains up to 10 words that include eigh-: sleigh, eight, weigh, etc . . .

Sandpaper letters: Lowercase letters formed from fine-grit sandpaper and mounted to wooden tablets. Sandpaper letters offer children guidance in letter formation.

Index

Please note that page numbers followed by the letter *f* in this index indicate a figure; those followed by the letter *t* indicate a table.

Acadience Reading subtests, 55, 59, 62, 126, 189
AIMSweb (Achievement Improvement Monitoring System), 119
Alexander, K. L., 146
Alphabet knowledge, 51, 54, 69*t*
American Institutes for Research, 61
American Montessori Society (AMS), 22, 23–24, 25, 33, 134
  accreditation reports, 72
  assessment surveys, 119
  School Accreditation Standards, 61, 175
  Teacher Research Panel, 28
Amplify CKLA (Core Knowledge Language Arts), 33
Anderson, R. C., 120
Ansari, A., 25, 158
Anthropological Chart tool, 26
Archer, Anita, 42, 130, 133
Arizona Charter School Association, 34
Arizona Department of Education (ADE), 34
Arizona Montessori Charter School Association, 158
Assessment, 46–64, 105
  assessment cycle, 47
  comprehensive systems, 18, 47–50, 49*f*, 189
  data analysis, 106
  diagnostic tests, 49–50, 50*t*, 58–61, 113, 189
  Dr. Montessori's practices, 25–27
  early childhood screening assessment, 50–52
  elementary screening assessment, 55–58
  formative, 11, 17, 189
  high-stakes testing, 157–159
  in Montessori classrooms, 23–25, 62–63
  Montessori three-period lesson decision tree, 106–108, 107–108*f*, 109*f*
  observational data, 116–120
  outcome assessment, 49–50, 50*t*, 189
  overview, 46–47
  progress monitoring, 49–50, 50*t*, 109–113, 111*f*, 114*f*
  qualitative considerations, 115, 117*f*
  quantitative changes, 114–115
  screening assessments, 49–50, 50*t*
  summative, 17–18
  See also Beginning of Year (BOY) assessment; End-of-Year (EOY) assessment; Middle of Year (MOY) assessment
Authors' methodology: book structure, 5–8

Background knowledge, 11, 29, 121–123
Beginning of Year (BOY) assessment, 37, 48
  PALS assessment in early childhood case study, 75, 76*t*
  screening process, 57*t*–58*t*

Bennett, R. E., 17, 58
Berninger, V. W., 96
Biographical Charts, 26, 116
Black, P., 17, 58
Bluffview Montessori School, Minnesota, 1
Bordeaux, K., 61
BRIDGE-RI (learning platform), 162
Brown, Katie, 25, 34, 158
Burchinal, M., 159

Cabell, S. Q., 120, 120, 123
Carta, J. J., 19–20
Casa dei Bambini (Children's House), 72
Case studies
  early childhood, 73–82
  early childhood End-of-Year (EOY) assessment, 166–168
  early childhood Middle-of-Year (MOY) assessment, 135–140
  elementary level End-of-Year (EOY) assessment, 169*t*–170*t*, 168–171
  elementary Middle-of-Year (MOY) assessment, 139–140
Chappuis, S., 118
Charter schools, 1
  Laurel Heights Elementary School case study, 73–82
Choral readings, 132, 191
City Academy High School, Minnesota, 1
ClassDojo, 173–174
Classroom Assessment Scoring System (CLASS), 120, 159–161
Coaches, instructional and literacy, 176–178
Cognitive load theory, 39
Colorado Department of Education, 40, 41
Common, E. A., 41
Common Core State Standards (CCSS), 18, 128
Comprehension: in PELI assessment framework, 54
Comprehensive assessment systems, 18, 189
Correct Letter Sounds subtest, 59, 60*t*
Cosmic curriculum, 123
Culclasure, B., 25, 158
Curriculum evaluation guidelines, 99–101, 104*t*
CVC word cards, 13, 81, 82, 191

Data-Based Decision Making, 129
Data-Based Individualization, 128–129
Data collection, 46–48. *See also* Assessment
D'Cruz, G., 172
Debs, M., 1
Decoding, 96
  decodable texts, 191
  See also Encoding, role of
Diagnostic assessments, 49–50, 50***t***, 58–61, 113, 189. *See also* Assessment
Diary of Individual Psychology (notebook tool), 116
DIBELS. *See* Dynamic Indicators of Basic Early Literacy Skills (DIBELS)
Doing What Works initiative, 177
Duffy, D., 123
Duffy, M., 123
Dunn, D. M., 120, 124
Dunn, L. M., 120, 124
Dwyer, Muriel, 142
Dynamic Indicators of Basic Early Literacy Skills (DIBELS), 55, 59, 62, 110, 119, 126, 189

Early childhood
  End-of-Year case study, 166–168, 167*t*
  Middle-of-Year case study, 135–140
  screening assessments, 50–52
Echo readings, 133, 141, 191
Education apps, 173–174
ELA instruction, 67–68
  in Montessori classrooms, 70–73, 120–124
  in public schools, 68–70

Elementary grades
  End-of-Year assessments, 169*t*–170*t*, 168–171
  Middle-of-Year case study, 139–140
  screening assessments, 55–58
Elkonin boxes, 90, 92, 95*f*
Encoding, role of, 95–99
End-of-Year (EOY) assessment, 48
  data collection, 151
  decision trees, 143*f*, 143–145, 144*f*
  early childhood case study, 166–168, 167*t*
  elementary level case study, 169*t*–170*t*, 168–171
  screening, 157
Engagement
  families, 172–176, 174*f*, 174*f*
  students, 117, 132, 132*t*–133*t*, 160
  See also Interactions
Epstein, P., 25
Erbeli, F., 53
Error control, 42, 101, 149
Every Student Succeeds Act (ESSA), 128
Explicit Instruction (Archer & Hughes), 42
Explicit Instruction models, 42, 44–45, 130–135, 134*f*

Family engagement, 172–176, 174*f*, 176*f*
Farrell, L., 10
Fidelity of implementation, 2, 23, 68, 115
First Sound Fluency (FSF), 59, 60*t*
Flamboyan Foundation, 40, 41, 173
Fletcher, J. M., 11
Florida Center for Reading Research, 19
Formative assessments, 11, 17, 189
Free and Appropriate Public Education (FAPE), 128

Geographic Landforms Nomenclature, *122*
Georgia Department of Education, 56
Gersten, R., 68
Goodbye booklets, 152
Gough, P. B., 10, 121, 190
Grace and Courtesy lessons, 172
Gradual Release of Responsibility, 42
Grammar
  grammar activities, 191
  in student writing contexts, 102*t*
  symbol definitions, 103*f*
Great Stories, 123
Greenwood, C. R., 19–20

Halle, T., 24
Hamre, B., 159
Harlen, W., 17, 58
Heggerty Phonemic Awareness Curriculum, 33, 80, 191
Herman, Jana Morgan, 17, 22
High-quality instructional materials (HQIM), 67
High-stakes testing, 157–159
Himelee, P., 130
Himelee, W., 130
Hochman, J., 97
Hochman Method, 97
Hughes, Charles, 42, 133
Hwang, H., 120, 122, 123

IDEA (Individuals with Disabilities Education Act), 130
I Do, We Do, You Do model, 42, 92, 117*f*, 130
Initial sounds, 52
Institute of Medicine (IOM), 19, 24
  IOM/NCR report, 19
Instructional coaches, 176–178
Interactions
  parent, 40–41
  student, 39–40
  See also Engagement
Intervention, 189. *See also* Response to intervention (Rtl)
Invernizzi, M., 51, 120, 189
iReady, 126
IRIS Center, Vanderbilt University, 130, 189
I Spy Game, 12, 80, 81, 91, 191

James, M., 17, 58

Kearns, D. M., 129, 173
Khalsa, Nirvair, 34
Khalsa Montessori School, 34
Knowledge Matters Campaign, 121
Kober, N., 4
Kuttner, P. J., 40

Language instruction. *See* ELA instruction
Laurel Heights Elementary School case study, 73–82
Legislation regarding reading instruction, 2–3
Lesson application, 39–45, 89–104, 146–153
  encoding, role of, 95–99
  explicit instruction, 42, 44–45
  lesson implementation, 41–42
  lesson plan format, 42, 43–44
  parent interactions, 40–41
  rituals and routines, 39
  student interactions, 39–40
Lesson plan format, 42, 43–44
LETRS phonics surveys, 61
Letter Naming Fluency/Letter Sound Fluency (LNF/LSF), 60*t*
Letter sounds, 51–52
Literacy
  and early childhood education, 5
  as human right, 4
  literacy coaches, 176–178
  in Montessori classrooms, 28–35
Lonigan, C. J., 78

Maitri Learning, 92, 95
Malcolm, U., 11
Mallett, J. D., 25
MAP (Measures of Academic Progress), 119
Mapp, K. L., 40
Mashburn, A. J., 159
Massachusetts Department of Education, 129
Massachusetts DESE, 128
Matthew Effect, 142
MAZE subtest, 59, 60*t*
McAndrews, S. L., 59
McDowell, M., 46
Metal Insets, 79*f*
Middle of Year (MOY) assessment, 48
  case studies, 135–141
  decision tree, 86*f*
  flowchart, 87*f*
Montessori, Maria, 1, 71–72
  assessment practices, 25–27
  on observational data, 116, 117
Montessori classrooms
  CLASS assessment system, 160–161
  ELA instruction, 70–73
  interventions, layering, 130
  language instruction in, 120–124
  Peabody Picture Vocabulary Test (PPVT), 124–125
  schedules, 65, 67–68
  work plans, 65–66
  See also Case studies
Montessori education
  background and statistics, 1
  family engagement, 172–176, 174*f*, 176*f*
  history of assessment, 23–25
  impact of, 178–179
  literacy instruction, 28–35
Montessori Public Policy Initiative (MPPI), 34
Movable Alphabet, 89–90, 90*f*, 93*t*, 94*f*, 192
Multi-tiered systems of support (MTSS), 19–23, 127–129, 189
  Reading Intervention Map, 163*t*–165*t*

Name Writing, 51, 78
National Assessment of Educational Progress (NAEP), 68
National Association for Family, School and Community Engagement (NAFSCE), 40, 174, 175
National Association for the Education of Young Children (NAEYC), 18, 24, 175
National Association of Early Childhood Specialists (NAECS), 18

National Center for Montessori in the Public Sector (NCMPS), 1, 34
National Center on Intensive Intervention (NCII), 61, 110, 112, 130
  NCII Screening Assessment Tools Chart, 56
National Head Start Association, 175
National Reading Panel, 59, 66
National Research Council (NRC), 18–19, 24, 109
  IOM/NCR report, 19
Neuman, S. B., 120
New England Common Assessment Program (NECAP), 158
NICHHD, 59, 66
No Child Left Behind, 126
Nonsense Word Fluency (NWF), 59, 60*t*
Nourishing Caregiver Collaborations (Qarooni), 174
Nursery rhymes, 52

Observational data, 63
Observation apps, 46
Oesting, T., 66
Office of Planning and Evaluation, 161
Opportunity gaps, 4, 78, 142
Oral Reading Fluency (ORF), 59, 60*t*
Orton-Gillingham Structured Literacy, 33
O'Shaughnessy, M., 25
Outcome assessment, 49–50, 50*t*, 189

Parent interactions, 40–41
Partnership for Assessment of Readiness for College and Careers (PARCC), 158
Parts of Books (Maitri Learning), 95, 95*f*, 99, 102*t*
Peabody Picture Vocabulary Test (PPVT), 63, 73–74, 120, 124–125, 135–136, 138*t*, 190
  BOY/MOY, 139–140
Pearson, P. D., 120
Personal literacy plans (PLPs), 177
Phonemic Segmentation Fluency (PSF), 59, 60*t*
Phonetic object box, 12, 57, 80, 81, 86, 93, 192
Phonics, 190
Phonogram Cards, 149*f*, 150***t***, 192
Phonological awareness, 190
  PELI assessment framework, 54, 190
  phonemes, 190
Phonological Awareness Literacy Screening (PALS), 73–74, 76***t***, 189
  (PALS Pre-K), 51–55, 119–120, 135–136
Phonological Awareness Screening Test (PAST), 59, 61, 190
Pianta, R. C., 120
Pickering, J. C., 17
Poverty and socioeconomic stratification, 71–72, 146
Powell, Kelly, 34
Powerful Literacy in the Montessori Classroom (Zoll et al.), 2, 10–11, 63
Preschool Early Literacy Indicators (PELI), 53–55
Print awareness, 52
Progress monitoring tools, 49–50, 50*t*, 190
Puranik, C. S., 78

Qarooni, Nawal, 174
Quick Phonics Screener (QPS), 61, 190

RAND Reading Study Group, 120
Reading Intervention Map (BRIDGE-RI), 162, 163*t*–165*t*
Reading League, 67, 99
  Compass, 2
Reading Rockets, 68
Reading Rope (Scarborough), 10–11, 20, 33, 121
Reading screeners, 62–63
Recio, Lucy, 178–179
Recordkeeping documents, 26
Reggio Emilia approaches, 24
Repeated readings, 141, 191
Response to intervention (RtI), 19–20, 127–128, 190

Rhode Island Department of Education (RIDE), 18, 106
Rhyme awareness, 52
Ripple, T., 172
Rituals and routines, 39
Rosenquest, B., 125

Sandpaper Letters, 53, 74, 78, *79*, 82, *89f*, *91t–92t*, 135, 176, 192
Saylor, Laura, 17
Scaffolding, 19. *See also* Tiered instruction
Scarborough, Hollis, 10–11, 33, 121
Scheduling, 65, 162–171
  Montessori scheduling and outside requirements, 67–68, 126, 162–165
  traditional schedules, 66–67
Schroeder, J. L., 1, 25
Schwartz, S., 2
Science of Reading, 10, 120
  matrix, *12t–16t*
  Structured Literacy, 42
Screening assessments, 49–50, *50t*, 190
  early childhood, 50–52
  elementary, 55–58
Seidenberg, M. S., 48
Shonkoff, J., 70
Simple View of Reading model, 10, 121
Simple View of Writing model, 96–97, *97f*, 190
Slade, E., 172
Smarter Balance tests, 158
Snow, K., 24
Socioeconomic stratification, 71–72, 146
Standards, 18–19, 190
Stanford Achievement Test, 119
Stanovich, K. E., 142
Stark Rentner, D., 4
STAR Reading assessment, 56
Structured Literacy, 42
  overview, 10–11
  terminology, 11–23
Student engagement, 117, 132, *132t–133t*, 160
Student interactions, 39–40
Summative assessments, 17–18, 190
Sweller, J., 39

Teachstone, 159–160, 161
think-pair-share, 17
Three-Part Cards (Maitri Learning), *96f*, *147f*, *148t–149t*
Three-Period Lessons, 90, 92, 95
  decision tree, 106–108, *107–108f*, *108f*
  and Explicit Instruction, 133–135, *133f*
Tiered instruction, 19–23, 75–77, *77t*
  identifying tiers, 78, 190
  Tier 1 instruction, 67–68
  tiered interventions, 113
Timed readings, 141, 191
Timeline of Maria Montessori's Life, 27
Total Participation Techniques (Himelee & Himelee), 130
Tunmer, W. E., 10, 121, 190

University of Florida Literacy Institute (UFLI), 33, 191

Vanderbilt Letter-Sound Fluency, 110
Vanderbilt PALS, 80–81, 191
Vanderbilt University, 41
  Research for Inclusive Settings, 130
Vaughn, S., 11, 152
Visual Thinking Strategies, 17
Vocabulary/oral language
  PELI assessment framework, 54

Wasser Gish, J., 175
"Whole child" instruction, 128
Whole Child–Whole Family approach, 175
Whole Words Read subtest, 59, *60t*

Why Don't Students Like School? (Willingham), 121
Wien, C., 24
William, D., 17, 58
Willingham, Daniel, 40, 121
Winsler, A., 26, 158
Wolf, Maryanne, 121
Woodford, Leslie, 25, 34
Word awareness, 52
Work plans, 65–66
Writing instruction
  grammar in student writing contexts, 102*t*
  Simple View of Writing, 96–97, 97*f*
  writing activities, 100*t*–101*t*

Yenawine, P., 17

Zoll, Susan, 1, 10, 125, 134

About the Authors

Natasha Feinberg is an associate professor at Rhode Island College in the Elementary Education Department. She instructs preservice teachers in the areas of reading and writing as well as directing the Master's of Education in Reading program. Prior to her work in higher education, Dr. Feinberg had 17 years of experience as a reading specialist/literacy coach in the Rhode Island public school system, where she was involved in all three tiers of instruction. She has a YouTube channel, @AxelsonAcademy, that provides examples of reading and writing instruction, professional development, and literacy recommendations in the hope that she can reach beyond the walls of the classroom to support teachers in all settings and places. Dr. Feinberg coauthored *Powerful Literacy in the Montessori Classroom: Aligning Reading Research and Practice* (Teachers College Press, 2023). In her free time, she loves to garden and shares her knowledge of flowers through her YouTube channel The Garden Mouse. She lives in Rhode Island with her husband and two super-fluffy ragdoll cats, Pumpkin and Pickle.

Susan Zoll's research speaks to the need for increased access to high-quality early language and literacy opportunities for all children. She works alongside teachers to transform literacy data into effective classroom instruction and to engage families as partners in students' learning. Dr. Zoll, PhD, serves on the AMS Research Committee and the AMS Innovation Fellowship Think Tank. She holds an AMS-Early Childhood credential, having served as a Montessori educator, teacher trainer (Language), Head of School, and Associate Professor in Early Childhood Education. Dr. Zoll has coauthored three books published by Teachers College Press: *Powerful Literacy in the Montessori Classroom: Aligning Reading Research and Practice* (2023); this volume; and *The Montessori Journey* (2026). You can find Dr. Zoll's writing on Substack, Logos, and Praxis, as well as on her website, www.dr-susan-zoll.com

Laura Saylor, Dean of the School of Education at Mount St. Joseph University, holds a PhD in Educational Studies from the University of Cincinnati and an MEd from Xavier University. With over 30 years of experience, including teaching and leading a Montessori school, Dr. Saylor frequently presents at national conferences. Her research focuses on the intersection of cognitive science and Montessori education. She is the coauthor of *Powerful Literacy in the Montessori Classroom: Aligning Reading Research and Practice* (Teachers College Press, 2023) and has contributed a chapter to *Montessori in Contemporary Culture* (BookBaby, 2024) titled "Research and Observation: Pedagogical Essentials for Building a Better World."